The Long Walk

Indian Plantation Labour in Sri Lanka in the Nineteenth Century

The Long Walk

Indian Plantation Labour in Sri Lanka in the Nineteenth Century

I.H. vanden Driesen
Department of Organisational & Labour Studies
University of Western Australia
Perth, Western Australia

PRESTIGE

Published by
Prestige Books
3/28, East Patel Nagar
New Delhi 110 008

ISBN: 81-7551-047-1

1997

Rs. 500
Prestige Books
International

Photo Typesetting by
Pivot Computers
Delhi 110 006
Ph. 98110-35585

Printed at
Chaman Offset Printers
New Delhi 110 002

Contents

To Cynthia, Nedra, Manik, Maya and Rohan

Preface

It is almost an axiom now that the Preface to an academic work should include the author's justification for writing it. In this instance, the reasons are simple enough. I have long been interested in the origins of Indian communities abroad, and that interest has recently been sharpened by the many misfortunes which have attended those communities in their adopted homes. To this must be added the attention which Australians—and particularly those in the West—have begun to turn upon South Asian affairs. My presence in Perth, the hub of much of this new enthusiasm, prompted me to indulge in my personal academic predilections, secure in the knowledge that encouragement and assistance would not be lacking. My confidence was not misplaced. My colleagues in the Department of Economics, and particularly its Chairman, Professor R.T. Appleyard, gave me all the support I could wish for, and I would like publicly to thank them for their goodwill. I must also acknowledge the financial assistance provided by the Departmental Research Committee to cover the several costs associated with the preparation of the manuscript, the effort which Jane Bowerman and Geoff Ward put into the production of the two maps, and the zeal and good humour with which Enid Grattan-Guinness and Mary Scott turned an untidy draft into a finished typescript.

University of Western Australia **I.H. VANDEN DRIESEN**

Foreword

This study of early Indian labour migration to Sri Lanka first appeared in 1982 as a research paper of the Centre for South and South-East Asian Studies of the University of Western Australia.

Then titled "Indian Plantation Labour in Sri Lanka: aspects of the history of immigration in the 19th Century," it was well received by scholars in the field and achieved a wide though numerically limited circulation. Thereafter, from time to time it was suggested that the study should be brought out as a book and made accessible to a wider audience, but other research concerns on my part prevented this being done. In recent years the growing Australian pre-occupation with India re-kindled my interest in Indian labour history and prompted me to expand and prepare my earlier effort for publication. I am grateful to Dr. Beverley Hooper, of the School of Asian Studies at the University for permitting publication of this book and to Jan Burrows and Jenny Young who laboured long and hard in preparing it for the printer.

University of Western Australia **I.H. VANDEN DRIESEN**
Perth
1997

Chapter 1

Introduction

The Rise of the Plantations and the Genesis of Indian Labour Immigration to Sri Lanka*

The Economic Background

The emergence of the plantation system and the commencement of a steady migration of Indian workers to Sri Lanka are two of the most important features of that country's economic history in the first half of the nineteenth century. The one cast the economy of the Island into a commercial mould and impressed upon it a form which it bears to this day; the other led to the growth of a community of "strangers" destined in the nineteenth century to create a social problem which dwarfed all others,[1] and in the twentieth century to become a political bone of contention between their former motherland and the country of their adoption.

The third decade of British rule had almost run its course before the term "plantation agriculture" became meaningful in Sri Lanka. For this particular deployment of the factors of production to take root and flourish, a necessary pre-requisite was an attitude to economic activity which early Governors either did not possess or else found difficult to translate into practice. Some were content to confine themselves to the mere collection of revenue, others admitted the possibility of a prosperous commercial agriculture, yet did little that was positive to encourage its growth, and the one man who thought the plantation assured of a brilliant development in the hands of private enterprise, found himself thwarted by forces over which he had no control.[2]

This last was Sir Edward Barnes, Governor from 1820 to 1822 and 1824 to 1831. From his first arrival in the Colony, Barnes sought by both official and personal influence to demonstrate the advantages that might be gained from attention to the growth of coffee, cotton and pep-

* Where official correspondence and books prior to 1948 have referred to Sri Lanka as Ceylon, the latter has been allowed to stand unchanged.

per; particularly coffee which could, he thought, be produced profitably and in large quantities. Itinerant middlemen had for some years collected a few hundred-weight of that crop from trees that grew along the roadsides and around the peasants' homes in the hill country, and its flavour was said to be "superior in quality to the coffee of Java, and . . . near to that of Arabia."[3] All that was needed was a favourable economic climate, and its creation became the goal towards which the Governor worked throughout his term of office. In 1820 he abolished the export duty of 5% hitherto charged on home-grown coffee,[4] four years later he exempted coffee land from the payment of the land-tax of one-tenth the produce,[5] in 1829 he repealed the duties charged on the import of agricultural and manufacturing implements, and freed all those employed in coffee growing or in any related manufacture from performing the annual compulsory public service required from all Sri Lankan inhabitants.[6] But these measures did not produce the results Barnes had hoped for. One obstacle which the Governor lacked the power to remove still stood between him and success. This was the West India interest whose influence was such that they had secured for themselves a privileged rate of customs duty on the import of coffee from their slave-worked plantations. As things then stood, West Indian coffee paid an import duty of 6d. the pound, while East Indian coffee, under which the Sri Lankan product was classified was called upon to pay a further 3d.[7] The additional duty of 50% was sufficient to make the difference between the failure and success of plantation coffee culture in Sri Lanka. Barnes appealed strenuously against it, but with no success.[8] The Lords of the Committee of Trade in the Privy Council were not disposed to make the smallest of concessions, dismissing the request with the observation that "the present state of West India concerns were such" that they were not prepared to recommend any alteration in the duty on coffee.[9]

The perpetuation of the discriminatory tariff effectively nullified what had already been done to encourage the growth of a virile plantation agriculture. Until it was removed, coffee in Sri Lanka could be nothing more than a minor crop; haphazardly grown, unscientifically collected, and productive of little profit.

Though Barnes was not destined to see Sri Lanka emerge a prosperous planting colony, it was not long before his aims were realised. Barely four years after his term of office had ended, several events occurring in quick succession swept aside the barriers to plantation development and held out to the Island the promise of an opulent future. The first of these had to do with the fiscal charges on Sri Lankan and West Indian coffee. By 1835, the West India interest had so declined in influence that it was no longer powerful enough to ensure the continuance of a favourable differential tariff. In that year duties on both categories were equalised and the Sri Lankan product entered England on the payment of 6d. per pound.

Of almost equal importance was the steep rise in the demand for coffee, apparent not only in Britain but over the greater part of Western Europe; especially Belgium and France. In Britain alone the per capita consumption of coffee, which in 1801 stood at 1 oz. per annum moved up in 1841 to 1lb. 5½oz.[10] An increasing proportion of this rising world demand came to be diverted by chance in Sri Lanka's direction. The abolition of slavery in 1834 in Jamaica. Dominica and Guiana—Sri Lanka's most formidable rivals—destroyed the very basis on which the coffee industry had rested in those countries. The output of West Indian coffee began to fall off at a time when the market for the commodity was fast expanding. An upward surge in prices and a search for other centres of supply was the inevitable outcome. With it the door was thrown open to the establishment of plantation coffee in Sri Lanka.

The expanding market, dwindling competition and rising prices engendered an immediate interest in large-scale coffee-culture. A stream of investors from abroad poured into the Island and by 1840 the tide had reached proportions large enough for contemporaries to bestow upon it the title of "coffee mania."[11]

Imports of Coffee into the United Kingdom[12]

Year	West Indies (lb)	Sri Lanka (lb)
1827	29,419,598	1,792,448
1837	15,577,888	7,756,848
1847	5,259,449	19,475,904

Coffe Prices[13]

Year	Per Bushel s.d.
1834	15.3
1835	15.3
1836	22.6
1837	22.3
1838	30.8
1839	25.0
1840	32.2
1841	36.0
1842	45.0

It was in the demand for land that the activities of the new planting community found its first expression. The soil and climate best suited to their needs lay in the hilly central regions of the colony, and with crown land going cheap at 5s. the acre,[14] a large acreage changed hands in a comparatively short space of time.

Land Sales[15]

Year	Acres	Year	Acres
1835	434	1839	9,570
1836	3,920	1840	42,582
1837	3,662	1841	78,686
1838	10,401	1842	48,535
		1843	59,800
		Total	257,589 Acres

Coincident with the demand for land was the need for labour. Thousands of workers were required to clear the forests, prepare the estates for planting, tend the seedlings, and gather in the crop. That such a work-force could be mustered locally was the expectation of the early plantation owners, but it soon became apparent that for a variety of reasons adequate supplies of indigenous labour were not to be had and that a "labour problem" had to be overcome if the planting enterprise was to succeed.

The Genesis of Indian Immigrant Labour

It was in the very nature of things that a traditional economy could not of itself loosen the tie which bound the agriculturist to the soil in order to oblige the coffee planters with the supply of labour they so sorely needed. The traditional system of service labour had been abolished in 1833.[16] But the expected "free market" had not immediately taken its place. The legal change was merely imposed from above and was neither the outcome nor the reflection of any stresses within the economy. A small number of the local population, it is true, were prepared to undertake the clearing of forest[17]—a necessary first step in the establishment of a plantation—but the overwhelming bulk of the peasantry continued to cultivate their little holdings and turned a deaf ear to the offer of wages. "This was an unanticipated reaction, for the British officials assumed that the Sinhalese would offer their services for money wages in order to better themselves. But this was an assumption based on experience of human behaviour in an individualistic society. In traditional Ceylon the basic structure of the social fabric and the constitution of its ethos were such, that there was no inducement for individuals to exert themselves in accumulating wealth."[18] With wants severely limited by the narrowness of their economic horizons, the peasantry in general set little value on the mere possession of money. "For what should they do with more than food and raiment.[19]

That this attitude had a firm socio-economic base does not appear to have occurred to those who first encountered it. They had yet to learn that receptiveness to the notion of "wage labour" presupposes the possession of abstract conceptions which are largely non-existent in a traditional structure. At a loss to account for this strange phenomenon some hastily concluded that the Sinhalese were innately prone to idleness, "the only luxury on which a native of India sets any value."[20] "There is not an inhabitant of this Island," observed Governor Maitland, "that would not sit down and starve the year out under the shade of two or three coconut trees, the whole of his property and the whole of his subsistence, rather than increase his income by his manual labour.[21]

Others, however, were somewhat closer to the mark, being discerning enough to identify several characteristics of the existing socio-economic system which strengthened the antipathy to working for wages. The first of these had to do with caste. It was early discovered that a high proportion of the potential working-class were for social reasons averse to hiring themselves out as labourers. The Chief Officer of an administrative district in the planting area once declared that he would prefer to hire labour for Government work "if the Kandyans would receive it without injury to their feelings." But though the Government had let it be understood that payment would be made "to this suggestion the natives would not listen."[22]

A second consideration which obstructed the efforts of would be employers was the wide-spread possession of land. "They have as a general rule, their own paddy fields, their own cows, bullocks, their own fruit gardens; and the tending and managing of these occupy all their attention. Their wants are few and easily supplied, and . . . they really have no inducement to work on the coffee plantations."[23] There was thus little "landlessness" among the people. True, these holdings were small, yet they sufficed to provide their owners with a considerable degree of economic independence since "the merest strip of irrigated land yielded enough rice to raise the tiller above the necessity of toiling for hire under a master."[24] Conditions in Sri Lanka were very different to those in the rural areas of England from which most of the new investing class had come. There, the second Enclosure movement had given rise to a rural proletariat obliged to accept badly paid employment as an alternative to ending in the workhouse. "In England the study of Statesmen is to find employment for the poor, while in Ceylon the difficulty is to find poor to employ."[25] Since the bulk of the population had not yet been reduced to such straits as to be forced to sell their labour in order to keep the wolf from the door, an exasperated British planter could well complain in a letter home, of an "unhealthy state of independence" enjoyed by the peasants.[26] "You would really be surprised to know the extraordinary state of independence in which these people live. I can assure you . . . that almost two-thirds of the population snap their fingers at the English (so little dependent are they upon them)."[27]

Quite apart from the desire for independence it is relevant also that the mechanics of rice-cultivation—the main occupation of the peasantry—required that a considerable portion of the year be spent in the fields. The Sinhalese, even if so disposed, would have been unable to undertake the sort of sustained labour which work on the plantation involved. The likelihood of their taking employment any distance away from their villages was altogether remote, and was a further obstacle to the fluidity of labour acknowledged by Government officials, one of whom, having drawn attention to "the objection that the people have to quitting their districts" observed that no money would "tempt them to remain long from their own country and their homes."[28]

The emergence of that cash nexus which was a pre-requisite to the break up of the old economy had clearly to await the further development of the plantation system, and the planter was consequently obliged to look elsewhere for his labour. It was his good fortune that cheap labour, in large quantities, was available in the great neighbouring country of India, where in many areas, objections to working for wages had long since broken down. There is a considerable literature and some controversy on the timing and impact of this phenomenon, i.e., whether it occurred prior to or after the advent of British rule, and whether all sectors of the economy were equally affected.[29] What is relevant for our purposes is that by the time the plantation era opened in Sri Lanka in the thirties of the nineteenth century a significant portion of the rural population in South India was employed as agricultural wage-labour. Some were peasants who for a variety of reasons had lost their holdings, others were cultivators of plots which yielded sub-marginal incomes, and others again belonged to agricultural castes long accustomed to working for hire.[30] These several categories were converted into a labour pool on which the planter could draw by the offer of a wage-rate that was between two and three times higher than that ruling in South India.[31] It was evident to both the landless and the under-privileged that the accumulated earnings of a short stay on the plantations could be used to purchase property, settle debts, and bring about a general improvement in their economic well-being. As a result, short-term migration to the coffee estates began in 1839, bringing to the industry the labour supply it was unable to find locally.

Over the remainder of the coffee period a gradually rising population and a deterioration of the handicrafts ensured that migrant labour continued to make the journey to Sri Lanka.[32] The magnitude of this flow was at times influenced by other variables, of which the state of the harvests and the availability of public employment nearer home were the most important. Bad harvests and famines were frequent during the course of the century, and when they occurred, many who would not otherwise have moved, seized upon emigration as a solution to the simple problem of staying alive.[33] Government-sponsored irrigation schemes and railway construction in South India after the mid 1850s, worked in the opposite direction, absorbing many who might otherwise have sought employment abroad.[34] The gluts and shortages occasioned by these forces did not, however, lead Sri Lanka to adopt the indentured system operated by other plantation colonies interested in the Indian labour market. The distance between the two countries was thought to be too small to merit the introduction of indentures, and throughout the coffee era migration was free and governed by the state of the market. This is unique in the history of Indian labour migration and sets it apart from its experience elsewhere. To this special characteristic must be added yet another. The journey from Indian village to Sri Lankan plantation was mostly performed on foot. The long walk took its toll, heavier initially than at the end of the centry but always serious enough to occasion concern.

From the standpoint of Sri Lanka's economic history, the influx of immigrant labour was an important and significant event. Its coming made possible the economic revolution which plantation development engendered, and in this way did fundamental changes in one country contribute to similar changes in another. Moreover, with its arrival, there appeared for the first time a landless working-class proper; a class tied to its employers by the cash nexus alone, dependent on the sale of labour-power for its sustenance. Not only was this class relationship something original, it had certain other novel characteristics as well. Since the new bearing of labour to capital did not initially touch any consequential proportion of the indigenous population, the young working-class was composed entirely of immigrants and opposed to a class of employers as alien as itself. Settlement too, took place in particular districts, i.e. those in which estates were situated, and immigrants lived there in the separate concentrated groups which the provision of "line" accommodation forced upon them. There occurred as it were, a wholesale transference of a little bit of India, with its customs, religious beliefs and other social relationships.

The earliest immigrants came with the very definite intention of returning home after a period of time, but with the passing years many decided to make Sri Lanka their permanent habitat and as a result the Indian Tamil community was well established at the end of the coffee era. Over a million strong today they comprise the second largest racial unit in the Island, and employed largely on the plantations yet continue to play the role for which they were first intended.

NOTES

1. K.M. de Silva, *Social Policy and Missionary Organisations in Ceylon, 1840-1855*, p. 270.
2. See I.H. vanden Driesen, "Coffee Cultivation in Ceylon," Part I, *The Ceylon Historical Journal*, July 1953, pp. 33-61.
3. *Asiatic Journal*, Vol. XII, p. 444, Memoir of M. Burnand.
4. C.O.54. 77. 8th April 1820. Regulation 6 of 1820.
5. C.O.54. 113. 25th August 1831, Barnes to Gooderich.
6. C.O.54. 105. 4th November 1829. Regulation 4 of 1829. Until 1832 all inhabitants of the Island were obliged to work without payment on the roads and bridges in the districts in which they lived. This was the compulsory service known as Rajakariya.
7. C.O.54. 105. 15th July 1829. Barnes to Murray (Encl); Tennent, *op. cit.* p. 230; L.A. Mills, *Ceylon under British Rule*, p. 226.
8. C.O.54. 105. 15th July 1829. Barnes to Murray (Encl).
9. C.O.54. 95. 2nd August 1826—Barnes to Bathurst; C.O.54. 105 15th July 1829—Barnes to Murray; C.O.54. 106. 23rd January 1829—Lack to Hay; C.O.54. 106. 19th March 1829—Lack to Hay; C.O.54. 107. 2nd September 1830—Barnes to Hay; C.O.54. 109. 8th February 1830—Lack to Twiss; C.0.54. 109. 21st December 1830—Lack to Howick; C.O.54. 113. 27th July 1831—Barnes to Gooderich; C.O.54. 114. 10th December 1831—Horton to Gooderich; C.O.55. 72. 1st February 1829—Murray to Barnes; C.O.55. 72. 21st February 1829—Hay to Barnes; C.O.55. 72. 1st January 1831—Gooderich to Barnes.
10. Tennent, *op. cit.*, Vol. II, pp. 228-229.
11. C.O.54. 130. 2nd November 1833—Horton to Gooderich; C.O.54. 171. 16th July 1839—Mackenzie to Normanby; C.O.54. 179. 9th April 1840—Mackenzie to Russell; C.O.54. 189. 9th August 1841—Campbell to Russell; C.O.54. 190. 22nd November 1841—Campbell to Russell;

C.O.54. 199. 18th November 1842—Campbell to Stanley; C.O.54. 203. 23rd March 1843—Campbell to Stanley (encl.). On the financing of early plantation agriculture, see I.H. vanden Driesen, "Some Aspects of the financing of commercial enterprize in 19th century Ceylon," *University of Ceylon Review*, July-October 1960.

12. Tennent, *op. cit.* pp. 228-29. J.T. Danson, *Economical and Statistical Studies*, pp. 205-6.
13. *Blue Books*, 1835-42. Prices listed are the *highest* paid in Sri Lanka.
14. In June 1844 the upset price was raised to 20s. the acre. C.0.55. 85. 27th April 1844—Stanley to Campbell.
15. C.O.57. 28, and *Blue Books*.
16. G.C. Mendis, *The Colebrook-Cameron Papers*, Vol. 1, pp. XXIII-XXX; C.R. de Silva, *Ceylon under the British Occupation 1796-1833*, Vol. II, pp. 385-413.
17. J.E. Tennent, *Ceylon*, Vol. II, p. 235.
18. R. Pieris, "Society and Ideology in Ceylon during a Time of Troubles 1795-1850," *University of Ceylon Review*, IX (July 1951) p. 177.
19. R. Knox, quoted by Pieris, *op. cit.*
20. C.O.416. 2 A.I.
21. C.O.54. 20. 28th February 1806—Maitland to Camden; see also C.R. de Silva *op. cit.*, p. 345, and pp. 404-5.
22. C.O.416. 2. Questions 28-30, *Agent of the Seven Korales*.
23. W. Boyd, "Ceylon and its Pioneers," in *The Ceylon Literary Register*, no.32, Vol. II, 24th February 1888, p. 249.
24. C.O.54, 235. 21st April 1847—Tennent to Grey.
25. J. Steuart, *Notes on Ceylon*, p. 73.
26. R. Pieris, *University of Ceylon Review*, Part 3, Vol. X, No.1,—pp. 80-81. J.E. Tennent makes a similar observation in *Ceylon*, Vol. II, p. 233.
27. *Extracts of Letters from Ceylon* (Anon), n. 72.
28. C.O.416. 20. G.25. Eden to Board of Commissioners, 28th December 1829, p. 73; C.0.54. 235. 21st April 1847—Tennent to Grey.
29. The main lines of this debate are well summarized in "The Indian Economy in the 19th Century—A Symposium" by Morris D. Morris, Toru Matsui, Bipin Chandra and T. Raychaudhuri.
30. For an exhaustive study of this question see Dharma Kumar, "Land and Caste in South India"; see also "The Emergence of an Industrial Labour Force in India" by Morris D. Morris.
31. C.0.54. 235. 21st April 1847—Tennent to Grey; M. Roberts, "Indian Estate Labour in Ceylon during the Coffee Period (1830- 1880)," *The Indian Economic and Social History Review*, Vol. III, no.1 (March 1966), p. 3; an excellent summary of the factors responsible for Indian emigration overseas can be found in "Indians in Malaya" by Kernial Singh Sandhu, Chapter II.
32. D. Kumar, *op. cit.*, pp. 128-43 and 186-93.
33. *Ibid.*, pp. 128-43; in this volume see pp. 50 and 114.
34. See pp. 50, 78 and 114 below.

Chapter 2

The First Phase: Unassisted Immigration—1839-1851

The First Arrivals

Indian immigration to Sri Lanka began in earnest in 1839.[1] By that date the news that comparatively well-paid employment was available in the Colony appears to have spread rapidly through the poverty-stricken villages of South India and immigrants began to come over on their own initiative. Such records as there are do not permit statistical analyses of the areas of origin of this migrant flow. In fact, one is warned against any such undertaking by administrators in India who point out that in the nineteenth century "the official figures of emigration overseas . . . do not exhibit the districts to which those who leave the country belong but the port from which they embark."[2] Yet, though a head-count by origin is impossible, the evidence available is plentiful enough to permit a description of the chief centres of supply. The overwhelming majority of the immigrants came from the Madras Presidency, and within it mainly from the districts of Madura, Tinnevelly, Ramnad, Trichinopoly, Salem, South Arcot, Chingleput, Tanjore, Mysore, Malabar and Travancore.[3] The first wave of immigrants came largely from Malabar and as a result all Indian labourers came to be officially designated "Malabars."[4] The term continued to be so used throughout our period, even though immigration from Malabar appears to have become inconsequential before the end of the coffee era.[5]

Categorization by caste is similarly a task which defies numerical analysis. There are records which suggest that a high proportion of the immigrants came from the lower castes such as Paraiyan, Pallan and Shanan.[6] But on the whole, as Dharma Kumar warns "the evidence regarding . . . caste . . . is too uncertain a basis for trying to estimate how many of these belonged to each category."[7]

In these early years the immigrants normally came over in groups of from 25 to 100 persons. One of their number was elected "Headman" or "Kangany," a position which gave him a considerable influence over his fellows. It was he who conducted their journey, negotiated their engagements, and later superintended their labour, in return for which he usually received from each of his subordinates a trifling portion of their pay.[8] Given the importance of the role delegated to him it is likely that the Kangany was a man of some standing in his village and that his election was perfunctionary rather than democratic.

In order to reach the planting districts, some of these labour gangs travelled by sea to Colombo and other parts of the western coast, from whence they made their way inland. The greater portion, however, either crossed over by boats from Ramnad to Talaimannar, a short sail of four to five hours or else made what was almost a land journey over Adam's Bridge—a string of islets lying between Talaimannar and the Indian coast. From Talaimannar they moved south along the western seaboard to Arippu, where some turned off and travelled east to Mihintale and then south to the coffee centres of Matale and Dumbara. The remainder continued through Arippu to Puttlam, then struck inland through Kurunegalla to the coffee-growing areas.[9] By either route the total distance was a fraction over 150 miles, and was always accomplished on foot.

Though this new immigrant labour had the advantage of being cheap—wages averaged 15s. to 18s. per month[10]—it possessed certain features which often had adverse effects upon employers. One was the floating nature of the immigrant population. Most stayed for periods of between five and twelve months, then returned home with their savings, coming back or being succeeded by others in the following year. An undertaking like coffee culture, so utterly dependent on foreign labour, was thus liable to be embarrassed at the most crucial moments by fluctuations in supply. A good harvest at home could, for example, either delay the arrival or greatly reduce the number of annual entries. Again, remuneration had always to be made in the silver currency of India, but the value of Indian coin tended to fluctuate on the exchanges, and it was frequently difficult for employers to arrive at that correct assessment of their wage bills which the ordered running of a plantation demanded.[11]

The Economic Background

Despite the influx of immigrants after 1839, the next three decades, with the exception of a year or two, were characterized by acute shortages in labour supply. The annual rate of entry, moreover, showed violent fluctuations which were seldom a reflection of the state of the market. These deficiencies were most seriously felt in the early years of plantation development. The acreage under coffee, which had expanded rapidly under the stimulus of rising world prices in the late 1830s continued to grow even when quotations declined some years later, since the industry was still yielding considerable profits. The need for estate labour consequently remained high and though a spectacular growth in immigration occurred after 1842, supplies consistently remained short of effective demand.

Coffee Prices[12]—Plantation		Acreage under Coffee[13]	
	s.		acres
1838	- 80 per cwt.	1838	- 10,395½
1839	- 102	1839	- 13,441¾
1840	- 99	1840	- 12,780⅗
1841	- 61	1841	- 13,678
1842	- 78	1842	- 14,769
1843	- 55	1843	- 31,769
1844	- 56	1844	- 44,221
1845	- 46	1845	- 43,734¾

IMMIGRATION RETURNS[14]

Arrivals

Year	Men	Women	Children	Total
1839*	2,432	188	99	2,719
1840	3,326	307	181	3,814
1841	4,523	363	164	5,050
1842	9,025	279	166	9,470
1843	35,195	957	448	36,600
1844	74,840	1,181	724	76,745
1845	72,526	698	177	73,401

Departures

Year	Men	Women	Children	Total
1839*	1,956	161	85	2,202
1840	3,464	256	153	3,873
1841	4,243	274	117	4,634
1842	10,691	345	228	11,264
1843	15,868	914	436	17,218
1844	38,337	825	535	39,697
1845	24,623	145	36	24,804

* After April of that year.

Between 1848 and 1849 the coffee industry experienced its first depression when a drastic fall in prices drove thousands of acres out of cultivation and enabled only the best estates to stay in business.[15] Immigration, however, showed a remarkable falling off long before any contraction in the acreage under coffee occurred. The decline, in fact, began in 1846, at a time when the industry was yet a prosperous and expanding one and the demand for labour was as high as it had been before.

There is a sizeable body of evidence to show that the diminution in immigration after 1845 was brought about mainly by the deplorable social and economic disabilities which labour had to endure while employed in Sri Lanka, and when travelling between India and the plantation. The onset of the depression three years later hastened the decline somewhat, but its effects, together with those created by political unrest in the Kandyan provinces in 1848 should not be overestimated. The Governor, Lord Torrington, himself expressed such an opinion when he observed that the fall in immigration was the result "not of a fear of the Kandyans, but of causes arising from bad treatment at the hands of plantation owners."[16]

Coffee Prices[17]
Plantation Coffee

	s.
1845	- 46 per cwt.
1846	- 46
1847	- 43
1848	- 32
1849	- 32.

Acreage under Coffee

	acres
1845	- 43,734¾
1846	- 56,869½
1847	- 56,832½
1848	- 51,505⅜
1849	- 43,338½

Immigration Returns[19]

Arrivals

Year	Men	Women	Children	Total
1845	72,526	698	177	73,401
1846	41,862	330	125	42,317
1847	44,085	1,638	417	46,140
1848	29,936	1,685	551	32,172
1849	27,732	1,430	268	29,190

Departures

Year	Men	Women	Children	Total
1845	26,623	145	36	24,804
1846	13,833	48	23	3,873
1847	5,897	79	33	4,634
1848	22,680	557	152	11,264
1849	10,479	335	84	17,218

The Social and Economic Condition of the Plantation Worker

To the immigrants of the 1840s the prospect of not returning to India with the fruits of their labour was an ever-present fear. Of the many thousands who sought their fortunes in Sri Lanka a distressingly high proportion did not live to see their homes again. Over the period 1839-1849, arrivals in the Island totalled 357,618, while departures amounted to 157,910; leaving a deficit of 199,708 to be accounted for. This is not to say that nearly 200,000 plantation workers found graves in Sri Lanka in little more than a decade, i.e. that mortality was 55.8%. There is reason to believe that a good number of those who left annually were not enumerated in normal fashion at the point of exit. Mr Halliley, the Customs Officer, declared that "although the correct number of arrivals could always be ascertained, . . . it was impossible to do the same with departures. Competition among the Dhoney Tindals, who cleared out in ballast, enabled them to pick up passengers all along the coast of Mannar, and . . . 25% got away from the Island by this means, that could not be accounted for."[20] Making allowances for those who departed in this manner, and also for the very small number, said to be about 5% who settled in the Island, a contemporary journalist, A.M. Ferguson, put the immigrant death-rate at about 25%.[21]

It is significant that neither the Government nor the planters were inclined seriously to challenge this estimate, yet, it is apparent that the latter rests on far too many assumptions, for the annual rates of settlement and of unenumerated departures are little better than well informed guesses. In the circumstances it is perhaps more correct to replace an approximate percentile death-rate with the more general statement that immigrant mortality appears to have been excessively high in the early years of the coffee era.[22]

Attempts to explain why mortality was high were early made by both the planting body and the Colonial Administration. The planters contended that one did not need to look further than the poor physical condition of the immigrants and the difficult circumstances which surrounded their march to the coffee districts. Their case, as it was first put in 1846, ran briefly as follows. In order to reach the coffee-growing areas, immigrants had, after crossing the Gulf of Mannar, to travel a distance of some 150 miles on foot. A fair section of the routes over which they moved ran through comparatively unhealthy and uninhabited country, with little or no shelter on the way and occasionally without water for long intervals. These hardships combined with extreme poverty proved fatal to many, and large numbers died by the roadside. Of those who survived, a great proportion arrived at their places of employment so emaciated by disease, that they were quite unable to work and in many cases died for want of shelter and food. The remainder, accustomed to the dry climate of Southern India, found the humidity of the hill-country an additional hazard. They succumbed readily to a host of diseases and several were soon unfit to earn a living, hence they ended by becoming "the victims of beggary, disease and want."[23]

It seems to follow from this analysis that conditions on the estates had little to do with the death-rate. Poverty, the climate, and the failure of the Colonial Administration to provide adequate facilities on the line of march, emerge as the accountable factors. The charge against the Administration appears to be substantiated by the findings of a Commission appointed by the Chamber of Commerce in December 1846 to investigate the state of the roads in Sri Lanka. The Commissioner in his description of the Puttlam-Kurunegalla highway wrote that he "saw many dead coolies lying unburied along the side of the road," and that there were "but two sheds on this line of road, fit for the accommodation of the great number of coolies daily passing and repassing to and from their country."[24]

These remarks, however, do not in any way irrefutably prove the planters' case, for they give no indication of the direction in which the immigrants were travelling at the time of their death. The planters were seeking to absolve themselves of all responsibility for the high rate of mortality by contending that immigrants generally died on the march from India and not on the return trip, and that such deaths as there were on the estates were the result either of an unfavourable climate or of the debilitating effects of the long journey from the coast. But this argument is a difficult one to accept. There is a wealth of evidence to suggest firstly, that more deaths occurred amongst out-going labourers than incoming ones; secondly, that a proportion of the mortality on the estates was not the outcome of either climatic factors or diseases contracted on the march; and thirdly, that at least part of the responsibility for the high immigrant death-rate can be laid squarely at the door of the planting community.

Chief protagonist of the view that mortality on the inward journey was negligible was Sir James Emerson Tennent, Colonial Secretary from 1845-1849 and Lieutenant-Governor from 19th April to 29th May 1847.[25] In support of his opinion Tennent was able to cite an impressive quantity of evidence, gathered in the main through a questionnaire sent out at the end of 1846 by Governor Sir Colin Campbell to certain of the Magistrates and Police Officers stationed in the planting areas and along the roads to the coast. Of the replies received, the three most important were sent in by Mr J.S. Colepepper, the Superintendent of Police, Kandy, Mr A. Walker, Police Magistrate, Kandy, and Mr W. Morris, Assistant Government Agent, Kurunegalla. Colepepper, who like Walker was able to inspect the immigrants after they had reached the very centre of the planting districts, observed that "the coolies were generally poor when they arrived, but in a healthy and working condition." Walker expressed a similar opinion: "Most of the gangs arrive in a healthy condition."[26] Morris' evidence is of even greater value, since the road from the coast to the interior ran for 46 miles through the district he administered. In the course of a detailed reply, he declared, "The Malabar coolies arriving in the central provinces by the Puttlam road, are cleanly and healthy in appearance. They are seldom if ever found sick on the road, nor admitted into hospital at Kurunegalla. When returning to their country they are invariably dirty, their clothes old and usually in rags . . . the slovenly, ragged appearance of the returning coolies is in strong contrast to the cleanly and healthy looking new-comers, and whilst on the march, the latter are close and compact, the former straggling; the strong and healthy in the van and the weak and sickly in the rear, a gang of 100 sometimes extending a distance of several miles. The sick at first attempt to keep up with their companions, but gradually drop off."[27]

In the face of evidence of this sort, furnished by responsible officers of the Administration, it is difficult to accept the planters' claim that immigrant mortality was mainly incurred on the march up to the central province. It seems more reasonable to assume that the greater part of the dead who cluttered the roads to the coast were the pitiful litter left behind by worn-out, diseased gangs on their homeward journey. That the planters should have argued so strenuously to the contrary makes one suspect that they were attempting to divert attention from themselves. Perhaps conditions on the estates were incredibly bad? Tennent for one believed that they were. He scathingly commented that the "treatment meted out to immigrant labour by their employers . . . was not in every instance or in every particular, such as humanity or even policy would have required in order to encourage and secure a continuance of their resort to Ceylon. . . . Sufficient care has not been exhibited to ensure their comforts on the estates, to erect healthy and suitable dwellings for their shelter, or to provide rice and other necessaries for their support when located at a distance from bazaars. When attacked by disease they are sometimes driven off to die, instead of being tended by medical advisers or conveyed to hospitals of the Government; their wages instead of being punctually paid are frequently allowed to be months in arrears or even altogether withheld, and their importunities or irritation silenced by blows or personal restraint.[28]

General criticisms of this nature, together with the more particularized account provided by the Government questionnaire enable one to reconstruct the details of immigrant life on the plantations.[29] It becomes evident for a start that the accommodation provided was far from satisfactory. Labour was unhealthily housed in dwellings commonly described as "cooly lines." One building of about a hundred yards in length was divided up into a number of tiny rooms and into each went as many as six to eight persons.[30] The essentials of sanitation, privacy and protection from disease do not appear to have received much consideration. How to incur the minimum of expenditure on the quartering of his work force was apparently the employer's sole concern.

Poor accommodation was probably the least of the disabilities which immigrant labour had to endure. There is evidence to show that many suffered assault at the hands of their employers and that on a number of estates instruments of torture such as stocks and whipping posts were set up and frequently resorted to, though their use was expressly forbidden by law. Colepepper, for example, alludes to an occasion when a planter had quite openly admitted that he had hung up a labourer by his hands and then "whipped the skin off him" with such deadly effect, that his luckless victim had been unable to work for three weeks.[31]

On many estates it became normal procedure for payment to be stopped if rain, fog etc., held up work for any length of time. And worse still, employees were frequently turned away after long months of labour with less than the total sum of wages due, or with no wages at all. Both practices were of course illegal; the latter for obvious reasons, the former since immigrants were hired by the month and not by the amount of work performed. In circumstances such as these the aggrieved worker had two courses open to him. He could either seek redress in a court of law or desert the estate. The first expedient was not made use of as often as it might have been since a great number were altogether ignorant of the legal code. A proportion of those who were not, were frightened off by the experience of certain of their fellows who had dared to take the step, as plaintiffs were sometimes severely beaten by their late employers after they had left the precincts of the courthouse. Colepepper in particular refers to many such attempts to scare labourers away from legal action. In one of the cases cited, a man who had the temerity to ask for his wages found himself taken to court on a trumped-up charge and imprisoned for eight days. After his release he had returned to his estate and persisted in asking for payment. He was then cruelly flogged by his employer and finally arrived at the Police Station bleeding from nose and mouth and with open wounds all over his body.[32]

With the search for justice so fraught with danger, desertion might have appeared a more feasible alternative. Yet, this was the sort of antidote which if it helped minimise one evil merely gave rise to another, for planters began intentionally to keep wages in arrears as the most effective means of preventing workers from abandoning the estate.

Another avenue of protest open to the disgruntled immigrant was that of staying on the estate and refusing to work. Those who tried the experiment discovered that it served only to call forth violent outbursts from their employers which occasionally culminated in the perpetration of shocking atrocities. On one such occasion a labourer unpaid for months had threatened to stop work, but this did not induce his employer, one Mr Harrington, to make good the amount owed; he had whipped the man to death instead.[33]

The medical aid available to the Indian immigrant was less impressive in reality than it was on paper. The facilities provided by the Administration were of three different types. Firstly, there were "peons and petty officers" stationed along the road from the coast to the coffee districts, whose duty it was to patrol the line of march and convey the sick and the dead to Government hospitals and rest-houses. The number so employed could not have been large since the total expenditure on their wages over the four years for which detailed statistics are to be had (1843-46) amounted to no more than £425.0.2d. If we assume that peons were paid £1 per month (i.e. only 2s. above the highest rate received by estate-labour) and petty officers £2 per month, then £425 spread over four years would barely suffice to support two officers and five peons. Thus, the routes to the plantations, each of them 150 miles in length, could not have been served by more than one officer and three peons apiece.

Secondly, rest-houses and sheds were constructed at convenient points along the line of march, and at certain of these medical care was made available to the ailing immigrant. Of the number, size and condition of these structures little is known, but such evidence as there is suggests that they were small and badly maintained. Between 1843 and 1846, the expenditure on "building and repairing Hospitals, Resthouses and Sheds" along the roads to the coast amounted to £313.15.3d. and the wage bill for "persons taking care of and attending on sick coolies in the Hospitals and Resthouses" to £344.8.9d. That these sums were grossly inadequate becomes apparent when it is pointed out that over the same years, a total of at least 277,354 immigrants, i.e. 206,655 arrivals and 70,699 departures, performed the march from the coast to the coffee districts and back.[34] It is hardly surprising that the Commission appointed by the Chamber of Commerce to report on the state of the Puttlam-Kurunegalla highway, should have remarked that there were "but two sheds on this line of road fit for the accommodation of the great number of coolies daily passing and repassing to and from their country."[35]

Thirdly, hospital facilities of two descriptions were extended to the Indian labourer. There were "epidemic" hospitals set up to deal with smallpox and cholera, to which access was open to both immigrants and local inhabitants. In addition there were ordinary "general" hospitals of which some were set aside for the "exclusive use of Malabars," and others shared with the indigenous population.[36] Of the epidemic hospitals little need be said. Smallpox was a regular scourge in the 1840s and cholera not an infrequent one. Much life-saving could not have taken place in the institutions established for their relief, since positive cures were then unknown, and it is unlikely that very many of those admitted ever emerged alive. There were six smallpox hospitals in all—one in each province—and expenditure upon them varied with the intensity of the epidemic in each area. The total disbursement between 1843 and 1846 was relatively heavy—£5,266.11.6d.—and provides us with some indication of the frequency of the disease. The cholera hospitals appear to have been more make-shift in nature and were probably temporary structures set up whenever an outbreak was reported. That they could not have been otherwise is demonstrated by the fact that there was no annual expenditure in each of the several provinces for the maintenance of a permanent establishment.[37] In the final analysis one would not be far wrong in describing the epidemic hospitals as "isolation centres" devised mainly to segregate the afflicted and to prevent the further contamination of the immigrant work-force and the indigenous population.

The "general" hospitals had a more vital role to play as it was their function to preserve the life of the immigrant. About the institutions established for the "exclusive use of Malabars" very little information is to be had. They appear to have been four in number, and sited at Gampola, Kurunegalla, Puttlam and Matale. The only proofs we have of their existence, are a few passing references in the replies to Campbell's circular, and some general headings relating to hospital expenditure in a set of accounts sent in with Tennent's despatch of 21st April, 1847.[38] The latter does not clearly indicate the exact location of these hospitals, but makes it evident that they could not have been little more than glorified shacks, as "the expense of subsisting sick and destitute coolies in the hospitals and cost of medicines and other articles supplied to them" for the years 1843-46 amounted to under £550, while the cost of their construction and maintenance (which in addition included the costs of putting up and repairing rest-houses and sheds) totalled £313.15.3d. over the same period.[39]

Of the "general" hospitals shared equally by immigrant and local inhabitants there were two. One was in Colombo and hence seldom used by the plantation worker. The other, sited in Kandy, was run by the local Friend-in-Need Society and financed partly by the Government and partly by Europeans resident in and about the town. A high proportion of the inmates were drawn from the surrounding estates and this institution was the only "general" hospital of any standing available to the Indian immigrant. What we know of it does not redound to its credit. Exclusive of walls and verandahs, the hospital measured 56⅙ft. by 17¾ft. and its general condition, as the planters themselves declared "was only one remove from total neglect."[40] That this was the inevitable result of a chronic shortage of finances becomes apparent when we consider the total budget on which the institution was obliged to manage during our period.[41]

	Government Contribution	**Total**		**Government Contribution**	**Total**
	£ s.d.	£ s.d.		£ s. d.	£ s. d.
1837 -	0.0.0.	73. 4.7.	1844 -	40.0.0.	311. 2.10½
1838 -	15.0.0.	158. 4.7½.	1845 -	82.0.0.	455.18.4.
1839 -	25.0.0.	139. 0.7½.	1846 -	319.0.0.	700.11.9.
1840 -	40.0.0.	184. 1.3.	1847 -	85.0.0.	445. 8.4½
1841 -	40.0.0.	155.14.3.	1848 -	79.1.6.	341. 4.8.
1842 -	40.0.0.	195. 2.6.	1849 -	228.0.0.	311. 2.0
1843 -	40.0.0.	389.13.11½			

Restricted facilities are the usual concomitant of limited funds, and there is ample reason to believe that the Kandy hospital was no exception to this general rule. Such returns as are available on admissions and deaths cover only three months of the year 1846 but even these show a frightful mortality. Out of a total of 401 persons admitted to hospital, death claimed as many as 259—giving a case-rate of 64.5%.[42]

Month	**Admissions**	**Deaths**
June	152	84
July	145	100
August	104	75

The returns of the Gampola Hospital, specially set aside for immigrants, is the only other institution for which figures are available, and make scarcely less dismal reading. Out of a total of 164 admissions, deaths amounted to 85, i.e., a case-rate of 51.82%.[43]

There are hardly any references in the hospital reports to the nature of the diseases responsible for these staggering case-rates. The Gampola return makes no mention of the cause of death, while the Kandy report merely says that the greatest mortality was caused by fever and dysentery. Beyond this and a Government official's observation that large numbers died annually from dropsy—a disease "brought on by exposure and neglect,"[44] no further evidence has yet been brought to light.

The three major "killers" mentioned, i.e. fever, dysentery and dropsy, are at best generic terms and can hardly be considered satisfactory indicators of the cause of death, but one can with the use of modern medical knowledge, hazard a guess at the specific ailments probably included in these general categories. There can for instance be little doubt that typhus accounted for a proportion of those who died of fever. Tennent in 1847 remarked that the incidence of febrile disease was high where labour was used "to open ground which had lain fallow for long," and in the same year the Assistant Agent of Kurunegalla, Mr W. Morris, wrote that it had been observed "that coolies on freshly opened land suffer greatly from fever, which disappears after the ground has been some time exposed to the sun's rays."[45] Both statements are in conformity with what we now know about the epidemiology of scrub typhus, and their validity is affirmed by the well-known authority Sir Philip Manson Bahr, who in his standard work "Tropical Diseases" declares, "The risk of contracting scrub typhus is great in the fringe of forest clearings . . . where the mite vectors are most common. Thus . . . plantations overgrown by weeds, cleared jungle and abandoned vegetable gardens are dangerous."[46] Malaria must also have been responsible for numerous deaths, as the routes from the coast ran past scores of abandoned irrigation tanks in areas known even then to be malarial.[47] However, since the disease took time to develop, immigrants infected on the march would not have shown signs of the fever until after they had reached the plantations. Here some succumbed, while those who survived became reservoirs of infection tainting the health of fellow labourers who had come through the journey unscathed. That the doctors of that era should sometimes have erred in their diagnosis is by no means remarkable. Ignorant of the role of the mosquito as a vector, they believed that the disease was propagated by the evil odours given out by swamps and marshes. Hence the plantations of the hill country were to them the most unlikely places in which to look for endemic malaria.

Though the dysenteries by which the immigrant was afflicted were in all probability both bacillary and amoebic in nature, medical knowledge in the 1840s had not advanced sufficiently to identify them specifically. It is unlikely that the latter could have been productive of any great mortality. Amoebic dysentery is generally gradual and insidious in its onset, prolonged in character, and when fatal, only so after the elapse of many months. The bacillary type on the other hand, is acute in genesis, of short duration, and, if untreated, fatal in the course of a few short days. This second variety, therefore, must necessarily have been chief executioner in Sri Lanka, for the floating nature of the immigrant population was such that those who contracted amoebic dysentery would not normally have entered the last stages of the disease until after they had returned to their homes in India. Of bacillary dysentery, Manson Bahr has this to say, "Bacillary dysentery is especially apt to attack those who are in an enfeebled state owing to starvation, unsuitable dietary, physical exhaustion, or exposure, or whose health has been undermined and resistance lowered by some chronic infection such as tuberculosis, scurvy or enteric.[48] Several of these prerequisites were to be found on the plantations. Most immigrants lived on a poor diet in an effort to save part of their meagre wages; many were for the same reason insufficiently clothed; and a proportion were probably subject to at least one of the chronic infections referred to. That dropsy is a symptom and not a disease in itself does not appear to have been well understood in the first half of the nineteenth century. Fundamentally it is an excess of water contained in any of the tissues or in the spaces surrounding them. Of the many ailments which produce this condition, two at least could well have been wide-spread amongst the estate population and responsible for the mortality reported, i.e. malaria and malnutrition. The likely incidence of the former has already been noticed and as victims of the disease sometimes develop a general dropsical condition there is every chance that their deaths were mistakenly classified under that head.

That malnutrition was common amongst the immigrant population is suggested by those replies to Campbell's questionnaire in which mention is made of the immigrants' practice of saving on expenditure by eating as little as possible of the cheapest available diet.[49] Such qualitative and quantitative insufficiency of food can produce in time a state of extreme anaemia, accompanied more often than not by acute dropsy. In this condition a patient would be receptive to a host of infections, e.g. pneumonia, blood poisoning, etc., any one of which could easily prove fatal. Yet, in an age of limited medical knowledge the real cause of death might well have been missed and the mortality attributed to dropsy, and this in all probability is what happened during the period under review.

Though typhus, malaria, etc., took their toll, there can be little doubt that malnutrition was the real villain of the piece. A well-fed labour-force would obviously have been better able to resist the ailments to which the rigours of plantation work exposed them.[50] An adequate diet, however, was a luxury the immigrant could ill afford. Wages in Sri Lanka at 15s. to 18s. the month were higher than any available in India, but there is no denying that in the absolute sense payments were wretchedly low. Having resorted to the Island with the avowed purpose of accumulating a surplus which he could take back with him, the immigrant had no choice but to forego the consumption of wholesome yet relatively expensive foodstuffs if he wished to put anything by. Much of the initial susceptibility to illness was thus largely due to economic causes which may not have had such dire results if estate labour had enjoyed the luxury of a higher wage-rate.

If malnutrition was responsible for the immigrants' proneness to disease, there were other factors which increased the likelihood of a fatal result. Chief of these was the unwillingness many patients showed to entering Government hospitals. This reticence was due in part to the suspicion most immigrants then had of the efficacy of Western medical treatment; misgivings which in Sri Lanka were heightened by the large percentage of deaths amongst those who had sought such relief. The hospital in consequence came to be regarded, not as a curative institution but as a place to which people were sent to die. "Leave me to die in peace where I am" were words said to be commonly heard on the lips of ailing labourers in the estate lines.[52]

More important than the fear of western physic was a consideration of a purely economic nature—the desire to avoid the loss of wages which absence from the plantation entailed. Sick-pay in the 1840s was a thing unheard of, and the immigrant who was in Sri Lanka for what he could earn, and more importantly, for what he could take away as savings, stayed on at work for as long as he was able, hoping that his master's ministrations (if available) or else the herbs and charms of his more knowledgeable fellow-workers would lead to a speedy cure.[53] These evils might well have been considerably mitigated if medical facilities of even a rudimentary nature had been provided on the estates. The authority of the Superintendent would have gone far toward breaking down the prejudice against western medicine, and at least a proportion of the labour-force might have been prevented from falling seriously ill. But such steps were seldom taken. The evidence before us shows that though some planters occasionally turned their hands to a little amateur doctoring, and a few others made arrangements with medical men whereby the latter prescribed medicines and attended on the labourers, the general practice was to ignore the sick. Those who died were buried without inquest or inquiry and the seriously ill often driven out on a charge of idleness, to die by the roadside and be buried by the Police. This last practice appears to have been widespread and one official was moved to write that "judging from the number brought into the hospital at Gampola, and the great many that are found dead in various parts of the country, I feel inclined to believe that they are, in the pathetic words of one of the patients in the hospital, driven away when sick from the estate 'like dogs.' If the sick coolies were properly attended to, such an incredible number of sick and emaciated Malabars could not be seen roving about the place. I therefore attribute the deaths on the high-roads, by the paths and at this hospital, as well as the great number of helpless beings daily lingering out a life of wretchedness and starvation, to a want of due care and attention on the part of the planters."[54]

Not an entirely just criticism of the planters, this comment. True, they might have provided a modicum of medical relief and desisted from the cruel practice of driving out the sick, but weight should surely be given to the variety of reasons other than neglect which contributed to the rate of immigrant mortality. Moreover, to attribute deaths *in* the hospitals solely to the negligence of estate owners is to be hopelessly prejudiced. The prime reason for the unprecedented mortality in the hospitals was that patients were often past saving when admitted. A number no doubt were the victims of some estate manager's inhumanity, but a great many must have reached the condition they were in by starving themselves, by working when unwell, and by refusing the medical aid extended to them. Few, if any, came voluntarily. The Police Magistrate of Matale once observed that the sick who received attention in the hospital in his district were "generally picked up in an exhausted state, either on the road, or in the bazaars, sometimes by their countrymen but generally by the Police; they then are well attended to, there being here a medical sub-assistant who is very attentive to them, but from the miserable state in which they come into his hands, more than half of those who go into hospitals never leave it again alive. As soon as the patient thinks he is able to walk, he secretly leaves the hospital. Sometimes he is brought back having been found exhausted on the road, but more frequently found dead, a mile or so from the hospital."[55]

With the hospitals so few in number, with conditions within them so far from satisfactory, with a proportion of the patients being admitted in a moribund condition, and with others leaving at the first sign of improvement, it becomes evident that responsibility for the mortality in the government medical institutions cannot fairly be laid at any single door. The neglectful parsimony of the Administration, the indifference of the planter, the ignorant conservatism of the Indian and above all the grinding poverty which characterized every facet of the immigrant labour system must each be alloted a due portion of the blame.

Accounts of the high death rate, the whippings and assault, the non-payment of wages and the host of other disabilities to be met with in Sri Lanka spread rapidly through the South Indian villages in the mid 1840s. The effect on labour supplies was disastrous. Between the peak year of 1844 and the end of 1846 immigration fell from 76,745 to 42,317—a decline of almost 45%,[56] and this at a time when with fresh land still coming into cultivation—nearly 25,000 acres between 1844 and 1846—the demand for labour stood higher than ever before. The shortage grew so severe that the understaffed estate became the general rule.[57] The Police Magistrate of Matale, for example, reported in 1846 that while the 40 estates in his district required at least 8,000 hands to be efficiently worked, the total force then in employment amounted to no more than 3,900.[58]

The non-payment of wages appears to have done more towards achieving this result than any of the other abuses to which the labourer was subject. This was only to be expected, since it destroyed the immigrant's sole motive for resorting to the Island. There was little point in his running the risks attendant on employment in Sri Lanka if the only compensating factor was eventually to be withheld. That the practice was widespread is certain. The Governor, the Colonial Secretary, and several other officials besides, all agreed that the acute scarcity of labour experienced after 1845 was primarily due to "the disheartening effects upon the coolies of being kept many months in arrears of the wages due to them."[59] Small wonder then, that the Police Magistrate of Kandy, in reply to a query put by the Governor on the treatment meted out to Indian labour, should have been moved to reply that "this class of the population is in a much worse condition in the Central Province than the negro slave was described to be in the West Indies in former days, as to their wants, their treatment from their employers, the mode of enforcing discipline and labour, and the remuneration received"[60] or that the Police Magistrate of Gampola, another large planting district, should have met the same question with the comment that "conditions in Ceylon were as nearly intolerable as Egyptian bondage or West Indian slavery."[61]

An examination of the problems of wage default and physical ill-treatment brings one immediately to the economics of the labour question as viewed through the eyes of the planter. In an age when the principle of general limited liability was as yet unknown, the greater part of Sri Lanka's coffee plantations were owned, not by companies or big capitalists, but by small independent proprietors most of whom were acutely short of capital. With a heavy proportion of their funds borrowed from banks and other financial institutions, all that they possessed (and much that they did not) went into estates on the success of which depended their very existence.[62] Sufficient had to be earned to pay off the bank, to meet the costs of running the plantation and to provide themselves with the necessities of life. Men thus economically situated were not inclined to be over-sensitive of the feelings of others. They worked their labour hard and at the same time sought to expend as small a proportion of their limited capital as possible on such facilities as accommodation, medical attention etc.

This disinclination to concern themselves with labour welfare was strengthened by the attitude which most planters then took towards coffee growing. Their approach to the industry was essentially of a short-term nature. It was generally held that vast profits could be made within the space of a few years, a view encouraged by the lucrative prices being offered at the time, after which the enriched planter could return home to a life of ease and comfort. In the circumstances it is not surprising that many should have considered the provision of amenities on the estates a rather pointless burden on their limited stores of capital.

There is every likelihood that the short-term approach to coffee also had much to do with the non-payment of wages. Default was common even when the industry was prosperous and may well have been due to the planter's belief that he could make his fortune and leave the Colony before his estate acquired a bad reputation and labour became difficult to obtain.[63] Admittedly, a proportion of those who did not share this optimistic conviction were also guilty of keeping wages in arrears. But the practice fits in well with what we know about the general shortage of capital, and can be viewed as an ingenious method of raising a forced interest-free loan from amongst the labouring population.

In times of depression of course, wage default became particularly widespread. Desperate planters, aware that failure to pay the banks would lead to the seizure of their plantations and that any reduction of expenditure on the preparation of the coffee bean could lead to a further decline in price, tended to regard the withholding of wages until other debts had been met as the line of action likely to have the least unfavourable immediate result. They must have realised that in time the practice would recoil upon their estates, but there was little else they could do. Those who were proprietors were often faced with bankruptcy, and those who were employees were frequently unpaid themselves. "In many instances Superintendents . . . pleaded that they themselves were unpaid, and were quite unable to pay their labourers."[64]

The physical ill-treatment of the estate worker was probably a misguided attempt at raising labour productivity and in that sense can be considered an effect of capital shortage and the short-run approach. We must be wary, however, of reducing to completely economic terms a pattern of behaviour for which other explanations can also be offered. For instance, the Police Magistrate of one of the hill country stations observed that some superintendents were either ex-servicemen or lads fresh from school. Power was something they had not had before, hence its possession was an experience quite beyond their control. A proportion of the ex-servicemen "had in their previous calling not been considered fit to be corporals, now freed of the tyranny under which they had lived, they tyrannize others as a form of retaliation."[65] Tennent appears to have shared this view and once remarked that of those placed in charge of labour many were "ex-soldiers, lads from school and . . . persons without education or any other recommendation than the accident of European birth."[66]

Besides, one should not discount the influence which early environment must have had upon the average coffee planter. In the England from which he hailed, long hours, low wages and brutal treatment were the normal lot of the working class. Accustomed to harshness at home, he instinctively adopted similar methods in Sri Lanka. True, ill-usage was often carried to great lengths upon the estates, but that would not have embarrassed the consciences of many; for though the slave trade was legally dead, its shadow still lay heavily over much of the western world, and the average planter, firmly believing that the dark races were immeasurably inferior to those of lighter hue was seldom prepared to credit them with feelings deserving of any great consideration.[67] Of the absentee owners many had no inkling of the brutalities to which their employees were subjected. Yet, it is said that even those who eventually became aware of what was going on, generally turned a blind eye on their subordinates "since good overseers were too valuable to lose."[68]

What of discipline on the estates? Perhaps the immigrant needed an iron hand to make him labour satisfactorily—or for that matter to make him work at all? Such evidence as we have completely rules out this contingency. The Indian worker we are told, was obedient and inoffensive, with a "disposition and habit . . . to suffer in silence."[69]

It must be emphasized, however, that all planters and superintendents were not disposed to maltreat labour as a matter of course. Both Tennent and Colepepper refer to a "minority" who treated their men with consideration but were too few to make their voices heard in protest.[70] Far from winning the respect of their fellows this rare fraternity quickly earned their dislike and on one occasion at least came to be attacked in print by a more callous compatriot who held them up to scorn as "pseudo-philanthropists . . . . champions of coolies, caffres, and of every savage under the sun the eager betrayers of their own countrymen."[71]

Policy and Legislation

There were two distinct aspects to official immigration policy during the first phase of the coffee era. One had to do with the Government's attitude towards the problem of labour supply, and for the most part bore on the controversial question of whether or not it was the function of the state to participate actively in the process of recruiting labour for the plantations. The other concerned itself with the immigrant *after* he had arrived in the Island and covered what might be described as his physical and legal welfare.

Though the first aspect of Government policy was slow in evolving, the second was notable for the promptitude with which it appeared. The plantation system was barely two years old and the flow from India had scarcely begun before coffee growers made "many earnest representations" to Governor Sir Robert Wilmot Horton, pleading the necessity for a legal enactment which would facilitate the hiring of estate labour.[72]

Horton's reponse was both favourable and immediate. In October 1837, he submitted for the sanction of the Colonial Office an Ordinance "for the better regulation of servants, labourers and journeymen artifices under contracts for hire and service." Despite the somewhat general titling of the bill there can be little doubt that is was primarily intended to cover estate labour. The provisions of the Act show a heavy weightage in that direction, and Horton himself admitted that it had been framed to meet the needs of "numerous speculators in the cultivation of coffee."[73] A first essay in the field of labour relations, the Ordinance was understandably of a "highly experimental" nature. The Governor claimed to have taken great pains to guard against the introduction of any clauses which would bear heavily on labour, and apparently was rather elated that despite this, employers were favourably inclined towards the bill.[74] A mere glance through the proposed Act, however, suffices to show that employers had every reason to be so disposed. The provisions legalizing the hiring of labour were innocuous enough. It was laid down (a) that every contract, except for workers by the day, or by the job, was to be taken in law to be a contract for one month, terminable on a week's notice from either side; (b) that a written contract was valid for the period of one year, provided it was signed by both parties, and provided also that the labourer was present in the Island at the time of signing; (c) that in the case of those not resident, the validity of the contract was to cover a period of three years; and (d) that wages were to be paid by the month.

On the other hand the penal side of the bill was of a very different complexion. Here it was a matter of one rule for the man and no rules at all for the master. The Ordinance decreed (a) that any labourer who refused to work, willfully disobeyed orders, neglected his duty, was insolent or committed some other form of misconduct was punishable . . . by forfeiture of all wages then due, if not exceeding the wages of one month," and liable in addition to imprisonment, with or without hard labour; (b) that if for any reason other than illness, a labourer was absent from work, or responsible through carelessness for breakages and other damage, an abatement of his wages could be ordered by the court on the employer's testimony alone; (c) that those guilty of fraud and those who tried by violence, threats, intimidation, etc., to prevent others from accepting employment, could be tried and imprisoned with or without hard labour according to the discretion of the court.[75]

This was all there was to the Ordinance of 1837. It does not appear to have occurred to those responsible for it that a scale of punishments applicable to employers guilty of similar breaches of the law should also have been included. The worker was merely delivered up to an employer whose rights were safe-guarded by the imposition of penalties on broken agreements and neglect of duty, whose evidence alone was sufficient to bring about a term of imprisonment, and against whom it was difficult to protest because of the clause forbidding intimidation. It is hardly surprising that Horton should have declared that the Ordinance was "generally satisfactory to the cultivators of coffee."[76]

The proposals of 1837 received short shrift at the hands of the Colonial Office. The Secretary of State, Lord Glenelg, was quick to observe that the law failed "in the essential condition of reciprocity; the offences of employers against their servants not being made punishable." In a sharp reply to Horton condemning both the severity of the penalties and the lack of a reciprocal scale of punishments, he flatly refused to recommend confirmation of the Ordinance unless it was put into a more acceptable form.[77] With this exchange ended the first attempt at labour legislation in the coffee era. Horton, his term almost at an end, made no effort to re-submit the Act in a modified shape, and the new Governor, Mr Stewart Mackenzie was evidently not disposed to pursue what had become a controversial question immediately upon his assumption of the administration. Instead, he preferred to concern himself with the improvement of facilities along the land route from India. In 1840, four rest sheds were constructed at Government expense on the Puttlam-Kandy road.[78] This was a modest exercise, but one of some historical significance since it inaugurated the Government's entry into the field of immigrant labour welfare, an area which in later years was to become a veritable battleground.

Mackenzie, however, could not remain inactive for long. With every passing year the acreage under coffee—and hence the number of planters faced with insecurity of labour supplies—was increasing rapidly. Moreover, the Public Works Department had also become a considerable employer of Indian labour and by the end of 1840 had found it necessary to raise its customary wage rate of 15s. per month to 18s., in order to secure new recruits in the planting districts.[79] The immigrant, with two sources of employment open to him, now began to play one against the other, deserting public employer for private and vice versa as either of these alternatives appeared the more advantageous. Neither the Government, with its annual revenue deficit,[80] nor the planting community, with its chronic shortage of capital, could afford to tolerate this practice for long. Their mutual need for a device which would enable them to hold on to their respective labour forces found expression in a fresh demand for legislation and resulted in the drafting at the end of the year of Ordinance 16 of 1840.

The new bill was basically similar to that submitted earlier by Governor Horton, although it reflected the urgency of the times by proposing that breaches of covenant should not await redress by a slow-moving court action, but should be presented criminally and hence promptly.[81] The provisions of the Act were to be binding only on those who were willing to enter into such an agreement, but considering the prevailing circumstances, the condition was a meaningless one as most employers could be expected to make some form of "agreement" a precondition of employment.

In an explanatory dispatch accompanying the Ordinance, Mackenzie predicted that the proposed bill would benefit not only the employers but the work force as well, since the former would be compelled to provide good wages, accommodation, diet, etc., if they were to attract labourers into renewing their yearly agreements.[82]

The Colonial Office was not impressed. Secretary of State, Lord John Russell, noticed the close similarity between the new Ordinance and that proposed in 1837; particularly their common failure in providing "for the punishment of various offences committed by a servant without any corresponding provisions for the offences that may be committed by the employers." He accordingly refused to advise confirmation till a more equitable law was submitted or until some sound explanation of the course adopted in the bill was supplied.[83]

It was fortunate for the immigrant that Whitehall was thus alert, for by 1841 a considerable portion of the official hierachy in Sri Lanka had become part-time coffee planters. Those who sat in the Governor's Executive Council were in effect killing two birds with a single stone. They could claim that the Ordinance was vital to the Government and at the same time rest assured that it would serve their private interests. Whether the Home authorities were aware of this is conjectural, but it is clear that they intended to use their influence to hold the balance between master and man. An attitude not a little influenced perhaps, by the activities of anti-slavery bodies in Britain, whose very existence "had a salutary effect similar to that of vigilance committees, neither delinquency nor official supineness being likely to pass unnoticed."

With the coffee mania now in full stride and with capital desperately in search of labour, neither the Administration nor the planting community in Sri Lanka could afford any further delay in the framing of a labour Ordinance. Sir Colin Campbell, who had followed Mackenzie as Governor in April 1841, hastily brought the rejected bill into line with Colonial Office demands through the insertion of a clause making employers who failed to honour agreements, e.g. by failing to pay wages etc., liable to a fine of £10, or in default, of a period of imprisonment not exceeding three months. Submitted in the form of a fresh Ordinance—Ordinance 5 of 1841, the new bill was duly confirmed and came into force that year as the first labour law of the coffee era, if not in the Island's entire history.[84]

The new law had hardly entered the statute book before a fresh problem emerged to threaten the interests of the planter. By early 1842 the needs of the rapidly growing acreage under coffee could no longer be adequately met by the flow of immigration, and "labour shortage" became the new theme of the planting fraternity's lament. The question was one of the first to occupy the attention of the Ceylon Agricultural Society, set up in 1842, but a special sub-committee appointed by that body to investigate the possibilities of importing labour directly from India could hold out little hope for the proposal and declared that the best course the Society could take was to persuade its members to afford immigrants "inducements and facilities to come over on their own responsibility" since contracts entered into with labourers in India would not be binding in Sri Lanka.[85]

The sub-committee's conclusions, which in effect placed the onus of securing a regular supply of labour upon the individual planter, were not readily accepted by the Society's membership. The latter inclined to the view that if inducements and facilities were needed to attract the prospective immigrant, it was the duty of the Government to provide them. The outcome of this stand was a request for official aid, the first of a series destined to provoke acute controversy in the years ahead.

The planters' demands did not amount to much. All that they asked for was the provision of elementary welfare facilities, mainly in the shape of rest-houses and wells, along the line of march from the coast to the central districts.[86] But their appeal fell upon deaf ears. The official reply was that the state of the revenue would not allow the added expenditure, and that in any case, it was the responsibility of the planting body to mitigate the evils from which the immigrant suffered.[87] In the light of past events this was not a consistent stand for the Government to take. The Agricultural Society was merely demanding the continuation of a policy begun by Campbell's predecessor, Mr Stewart Mackenzie, who in 1840 had set up four rest-houses along the road from Kandy to Puttlam.[88] The revenue deficit of 1843 was good enough reason for refusing the request, but to claim in addition that it was the planter's business to undertake what the Government had previously done, was nothing if not contradictory.

Even more mystifying was the course adopted by Campbell soon after his refusal of aid. By 1843, revenue stood again above expenditure, a happy trend that continued until 1846, and the Governor proceeded immediately to improve conditions upon the road to the coast. Hospitals were set up at Kandy and Puttlam with medical sub-assistants in charge, rest-houses were constructed at convenient points, and peons and Government officers stationed on the road to offer assistance to immigrant labour.[89] The sums expended on these facilities were not large. Over the period 1843-1845 the total disbursement for constructing, equipping and staffing hospitals and rest-sheds on the immigrant routes was only £1,204; yet, it is undeniable that Campbell provided more than was originally asked for.

The most likely explanation of this contrary behaviour is that the Agricultural Society's demands were put before the Government had had time to evolve a policy towards what was essentially a novel problem. In the circumstances, it was sensible to buy time with a refusal, but with the rate of immigration mounting rapidly a policy had to be formulated without delay, and it is apparent that the Government early decided that wells, rest-houses and medical relief were welfare measures of a sort even temporary residents had a right to expect.

When put into force the new policy failed to evoke the merest of comments. It went practically unnoticed since the planting community no longer had reason to fear a scarcity of labour and had for the time being lost interest in the state of the Northern roads. By mid 1843, the knowledge that comparatively well paid employment was available in the Island had spread to the remotest villages of South India, and an increasing stream of immigrants had begun to come over of their own volition. Though not for long. The planter's dream of quick profits with its consequent withholding of wages and maltreatment of labour speedily convinced the immigrant that there was little point in risking the privations of the journey to Sri Lanka for a monetary consideration he all too frequently did not receive. Before the end of 1845 it became apparent that the flow from India was fast subsiding. The acreage under plantation coffee had risen by nearly a third between 1843 and 1844, but the absolute inflow of immigrant labour had declined slightly over the same period, thus reducing the ratio between the available work-force and the area under cultivation from three persons per acre to two. The trend continued in the following year and by the end of 1846 the total fall in immigration amounted to 45%.[90]

On September 9th, 1846, a public meeting was convened in Kandy to consider the labour crisis. There "reluctant to ascribe it to any cause dependent upon themselves or incident to the management of their own estates," the planters declared that the Government was in fact responsible for the fall in labour supplies. It was held that the failure of the authorities to provide adequate medical relief and other welfare measures had led to so high an immigrant death-rate that prospective immigrants were being discouraged from making the journey to Sri Lanka.[91]

As it was thought that an approach to the Colonial Government would not be productive of any results, the meeting decided to appeal directly to Lord Grey, the Secretary of State for the Colonies. A memorial in which the planters repeated their argument that high mortality had caused the decline in immigration was accordingly drawn up and submitted to the Governor for transmission to Whitehall. The route from the coast to the coffee districts, they said, passed through such desolate territory that a proportion of the immigrants succumbed on the march; part of the remainder arrived in so attenuated a condition that they were unable to work and "in many cases died for want of shelter and food." Yet others, unaccustomed to the humid climate of Sri Lanka, fell too ill to work and hence became the "victims of beggary, disease and want." For all this the Government was held chiefly responsible on the grounds that it had neglected the roads and provided hospital accommodation that was "only one step removed from total neglect." The solution to the labour problem the memorialists believed, lay in reducing the rate of mortality, and that this might be achieved they proposed (a) that the local Government "be made to pay an allowance towards providing hospital attendance at the principal labour stations and along the roads"; and (b) that "cooly Protectors be appointed in the principal towns under the control of an interested Board, in connection with Government and at the expense of the latter, to see that labourers were protected from maltreatment at the ferries and elsewhere; that wells on the road were kept clean and open, and that sheltering places were preserved."[92]

After the memorial had been dispatched to London the planters concentrated their attention on the local Legislative Council. Through the three unofficial members who represented their interests in that body, they attempted to introduce an Ordinance "For the Protection and Encouragement of Indian Labourers resorting for employment to Ceylon." The Ordinance proposed that a board of five trustees, made up of two persons annually nominated by the Government and three persons similarly chosen by the Legislative Council, be vested with the power to regulate a scheme whereby (a) rest-houses and hospitals were to be constructed along the roads travelled upon by immigrants, and (b) sums of money were to be made available to meet the cost of transporting Indian labour to Sri Lanka.[93] The first demand of course, had been put before, but the second was more far-reaching than any previously made and was particularly significant since it called on the Government to associate itself directly with the actual flow of immigrant labour.

To pay for these facilities it was suggested that a new tax be introduced, based either on the number of acres in cultivation or on the number of Indians employed on each estate.[94] This willingness of planters to defray the expenses of the scheme is of the utmost importance. It clearly demonstrates that they were asking not for state *assistance* but for state *participation* in the control of the immigration process.

Though the projected bill was immediately ruled out by the Governor on the perfectly legal grounds that unofficial members were not permitted to initiate legislative action,[95] its effectiveness was not altogether nullified. For while the Governor alone was constitutionally allowed to introduce Ordinances and subjects for debate, all other members could enter in the minutes their reasons for wishing to propose a bill or debate a question. A full and exact copy of these minutes was regularly sent in to the Colonial Office and the planters had therefore done enough to indicate to Whitehall that important interests were at stake, and that the labour problem was not one that could be long ignored.

In the light of these events, the Colonial Government had to do more than merely rule the planters out of order. Whitehall had to be assured that the charges listed in the memorial were without substance, and above all, a clear and unequivocal line had to be laid down on the Government's attitude towards immigration. As a first step towards these ends, the Colonial Secretary, Sir James Emerson Tennent, in a letter to the planting community sought to refute the accusation that the fall in labour supply was a direct result of Governmental neglect. Reminding them that the Government had contributed largely towards the protection and medical care of the immigrant, and pointing in particular to the work done after 1843, Tennent went on to make the countercharge that "whatever is to be regretted in their condition could be ascribed not to the State, but to the lack of sympathy and activity of those who invited the coolies, and for whose benefit they worked."[96] The contents of this letter, together with some more specific comments by the Governor were forwarded to the Colonial Office in November 1846. The despatch was a significant one in that it contained the first clear declaration of the principles the Administration had decided to adopt towards the second aspect of the immigrant labour question, i.e. how far the *process* was to be assisted or participated in by the Government. Campbell put the official stand in no uncertain terms. "It was not," he said, "the province of the Government to take any active part either in inviting or promoting the transit of coolies from India to Ceylon," that was the concern of the employers. But once the immigrants had actually arrived in the Island, he would protect them by using public money "for rest-houses and sheds along the roads they had to travel, for peons to afford them assistance and direction on their journey, and for medical treatment wherever it was necessary."

In the course of this policy declaration Campbell met the charges set out in the planters' memorial by emphasizing that the facilities he had described were already being provided, and that the expenditure on those items over the current year and that preceding it had reached £3,000 per annum.[97] In contrast the very planters who complained of Governmental neglect had failed "to contribute in a liberal proportion." The Governor expressed the hope that a sense of their own interest would lead to their being more liberal in future, but should this not occur, he indicated that it was his intention "to introduce a district assessment on coffee plantations for the protection and maintenance of immigrant labourers, and thus remove the reproach which now applies to their neglect and abandonment."[98]

The authorities at Whitehall accepted Campbell's statement of policy as unhesitatingly as they did his strictures of the planting community. In fact, so completely were they in accord with the latter that it was not thought necessary to reply directly to the planters' memorial. The Governor was merely asked to convey to the memorialists the Colonial Office's "acceptance of the sentiments" expressed in Tennent's letter, which in its opinion constituted "a satisfactory reply."[99] The proposal that a tax be levied on plantations if employers continued to fail in their duty was also well received. Indeed, the Secretary of State went so far as to suggest that the time for such an assessment had already come, and advised that it be put up for sanction at the next meeting of the Legislative Council.[100]

In the meantime the planters had called yet another public meeting. Enraged by the Colonial Secretary's suggestion that they were themselves responsible for the fall in labour supply, they met on 19th December 1846 to frame a suitable reply to the charge. The resolution finally decided upon challenged the validity of almost every sentence in the Colonial Secretary's letter. The contention that employers had neglected their workers was met with the rejoinder that the planting community had contributed almost as much as the Government to Dispensaries and Friend-in-Need Societies, and that in addition certain estates provided for medical attendance on the spot at their own expense.[101]

The scarcity of labour, it was held, was due not to the non-payment of wages or any of the reasons suggested by the Colonial Secretary, but to boisterous weather which had prevented some from making the crossing, to abnormal rains which had led others to stay back and cultivate their fields more extensively than usual, and to the privations those who made the journey to Sri Lanka had to endure on the inward march. Also held in question was the view that the planting community benefited exclusively from the immigratory process. "Ceylon's prosperity," said the resolution, "depended on her agricultural interests, and the introduction of Malabar labour therefore contributed to the public revenue and to the benefit of all classes."[102]

On its positive side the resolution took up anew the controversial question of whether or not the Government should participate in the immigratory process. The proposals adopted were more extreme than any suggested earlier. No longer did the planters ask that the prospective immigrant be provided with the cost of his passage; they now demanded that the Government operate a free steamer at its own expense between India and Sri Lanka. Again, no longer was there common agreement on the justice of a tax being levied on plantation owners. It was now contended that the public revenue owed so much to coffee, that it was the duty of the Government to bear the expense of the hospitals, rest-sheds, wells, roads and bridges used by the immigrant labourer.[103] Here was a demand for state-assistance in the fullest sense of the term, making its first appearance in the Island's history. It was being put, moreover, by a group interest which undaunted by previous failures was evidently bent on carrying the fight to the Government. Campbell made no concessions, but it is significant that two days later on 21st December 1846, he initiated what was Sri Lanka's earliest example of an official inquiry into immigrant labour conditions.[104] In one sense this move can be treated as an indication of the importance which the labour question had come to assume in the eyes of the Administration; in another, it can be considered an admission that the Government was ill-prepared to deal with the subject since it lacked an adequate knowledge of the facts and figures pertaining to the life of the immigrant in Sri Lanka. However, it was a step taken in the right direction. So successful did the inquiry prove, that the Government was soon able to dispense with much that was speculative and invest its conclusions and policies with an authority they had previously lacked.

Campbell's inquiry was conducted through a circular addressed to a number of Government officials. The recipients were called upon to submit all the information they could gather on the condition and treatment of immigrant labourers in the districts over which their jurisdiction extended. It is clear that Campbell wanted facts that could be substantiated, not vague or conjectural replies. He asked each official for a full report "drawn from the records of his own office and such other sources of accurate information as were acceptable" and emphatically demanded that the material supplied should be absolutely reliable. "I should particularly enjoin on you that information you supply should be based on documentary evidence or drawn from the most authentic sources, and in any case where you are unable to satisfy yourself as to the accuracy of statements which have reached you, that you will distinguish them from those which you are prepared if necessary, to supplement by proofs."[105]

The circular, accompanied by a questionnaire was directed to a total of five officials, i.e. to Mr J.S. Colepepper, the Superintendent of Police, Kandy; Mr C.H. de Saram, Police Magistrate, Gampola; Mr E.S. Waring, Police Magistrate, Matale; Mr A. Walker, Police Magistrate, Kandy; and Mr W. Morris, Assistant Government Agent, Kurunegalla. It is significant that so few were chosen, for it seems to indicate that the Governor had decided that they were the ones most competent to express an opinion. That he should have so concluded is not surprising. The route from the coast ran for some forty-six miles through territory administered by Morris. Colepepper and Walker were stationed in Kandy, the clearing-house for a high proportion of incoming and outgoing labour, and an important planting district to boot. De Saram in Gampola and Waring in Matale—two other districts of consequence—covered between them a considerable proportion of the remaining plantations.

The queries in Campbell's circular were wide enough in their reference to give a comprehensive picture of the problems immigrant labour had to contend with. Eleven in number, the questions covered the following:

(1) The condition in which immigrants arrived and their treatment at the ferries and on the roads.

(2) The operation of the existing law for the regulation of their employment and the enforcement of their contracts.

(3) The nature of the charges usually brought by employers and labourers against each other.

(4) The personal treatment the immigrants received, and the degree of

attention paid to their wants, food, lodging and general comforts.

(5) The discipline on the estates—imposed with or without the authority of the law.

(6) The general practice as to the care of the immigrants in the event of sickness, the management of hospitals for their relief, etc.

(7) The payment of wages and remedies in case of default.

(8) The amount of protection and security afforded to immigrants by the law; the extent to which they avail themselves of it, and its practical effects.

(9) The amount of immigrant labour in each district, and its proportion to the demands and necessities of the planters.

(10) Causes which were in operation to prevent a more abundant influx of immigrants to Sri Lanka.

(11) The practicability of supplying the deficiency by the employment of the local peasantry.[106]

When replies to the questionnaire came in, they had a harrowing story to tell. The brutalities to which the luckless immigrant was subjected were reported in full by one official after another. In graphic detail they described the use of stocks and whipping posts, the repeated assaults, the neglect of the sick, the overcrowded line accommodation, the frequent non-payment of wages, and the emaciated condition of the labourer when he finally set out on his return journey.[107] Worse still, there was complete unanimity on the failure of the law to provide an effective remedy to these evils. All were agreed that Ordinance 5 of 1841 was by itself a fairly adequate piece of legislation, but they were also unanimous in emphasizing that it was being availed of by the planter alone. The labourer through ignorance and fear seldom sought its protection. The few that did represented merely a tiny portion of the immigrant population, and then the beatings they sometimes suffered at the hands of their employers after leaving the premises of the court, "dissuaded them from repeating, and others from trying the experiment."[108]

The insight gained into the working of the Ordinance of 1841 was one of the more important results of the inquiry. Both the Colonial Office and the local Government had hoped for much when the law had been passed, but it was apparent that the Ordinance had served only to strengthen the hands of the employer. He could ill-treat his work-force in the almost certain knowledge that they would not resort to legal action, yet, if in desperation some deserted, he had only to appeal to the courts to hold them to their contracts.

"The law is in itself a good one, but the Malabar is ignorant of the protection it provides . . . thus he becomes an easy prey to his knowing and unrelenting master" (de Saram, Police Magistrate, Gampola).

"The law operates fully to the satisfaction of the employers, but the labourer seldom avails himself of it, even when it is pointed out to him, and he is advised to do so" (Colepepper, Police Officer, Kandy).

"The Coolies are nearly all ignorant that any law exists for regulating agreements" (Walker, Police Magistrate, Kandy).[109]

Armed with the evidence brought in by the questionnaire, the Administration was at last able to put its case in a positive and forceful manner. The replies were received shortly before Campbell's term of office came to an end, and it was left to Sir James Emerson Tennent who acted as Governor for a period of forty days to prepare the material for submission to the Colonial Office. From his labours emerged one of the most detailed dispatches ever composed by a Government official in Sri Lanka.

Tennent dealt with every conceivable aspect of the labour question. He described the routes over which the immigrants travelled, reported on the harshness of the terrain, explained the workings of the Kangany System, supplied statistical data on the annual arrivals and departures, and discussed the reasons why the indigenous population could not be persuaded to accept employment on the estates. But most of all he set out to prove that the fall in labour supply was due to the failings of the planting community and not to any shortcomings on the part of the Government.

A case against the planters was not difficult to establish. Tennent had merely to describe the deplorable line accommodation on the estates, the forms of physical assault the workers had to suffer, the common tendency to drive the sick off the plantations instead of providing them with medical relief, and the habit of keeping wages in arrear or of withholding them completely, and then link this with the evidence that the immigrant arrived in good health but left in a worn-out and sickly condition. By this means he was able to demonstrate that the employers were themselves the creators of circumstances likely to deter the Indian from continuing to seek his fortune in Sri Lanka, and that the Government was altogether blameless. As a finishing touch Tennent also implied that the failure of Ordinance 5 of 1841 was partially the responsibility of the planting fraternity in that they often crudely discouraged the worker from seeking the law's protection, though they made frequent use of it themselves. "Whilst the employers resorted to it freely upon every occasion, the semi-civilized coolie, unaware of its existence, ignorant of his own rights, or apprehensive of still further annoyance, failed in almost any one instance to appeal to it for protection, or to call on the local Magistrate for assistance."[110] As a result, the immigrant's sense of helplessness was increased and this conduced to the fall in labour supply, "his disposition and habit is to suffer in silence and when at last hopeless of redress, he makes no complaint, but goes back in disappointment to his own country, resolved himself and prepared to warn his companions to return no more to Ceylon."[111]

While thus condemning the planting community, Tennent attempted to show that the Government's record was almost without blemish. "Almost" because it had to be admitted that petty extortion of immigrants often occurred at the ferries on the Northern route. It was claimed that even here there were mitigating circumstances, i.e. that "it was difficult to find respectable parties willing to rent and farm the tolls at these places, whom they knew would observe the regulations exactly," and that "it was difficult to punish them owing to the difficulty, delay and trouble of going to a Magistrate, who in these remote areas were in stations far apart"—but the promise was made that even this single blot would soon be removed.[112]

For the rest, Tennent believed that the Government could not be faulted. It had provided facilities along the Northern route in the shape of rest-sheds and wells; it had appointed peons and petty officers whose whole task it was to aid the immigrant; and above all, it had supplied the following "considerable funds" for medical relief.[113]

Sums expended in medical aid for the exclusive use of Malabar coolies[114]

1843	£186. 10.11d.
1844	207. 5. 2½d.
1845	811. 1. 8½d.
1846	1,590. 0. 3½d.
	£2,794.17.11½d.

Sums expended on Medical and Charitable Institutions to which Malabars were admitted equally with Natives of Ceylon

1843	£1,242. 5. 2½d.
1844	1,185. 11. 9½d.
1845	2,597. 0. 1d.
1846	4,010. 17. 6½d.
	£9,035. 14. 7½d.

When compared to the negative attitude adopted by the planters, the Government's record was indeed an impressive one—but only in this relative sense. It does not appear to have occurred to Tennent that from an absolute point of view the total expended on medical aid was singularly inadequate and out of all proportion to the number of persons it was expected to serve. That Tennent exaggerated the efficacy of the several facilities on which these funds had been spent is also apparent. There is a glossing over of the condition in which many of them were; the state of the Kandy hospital, and of some of the rest-sheds on the Puttlam road being two cases in point.

Given the nature of the available evidence it is easy to accept Tennent's argument that more deaths occurred on the outward journey than on the way in. However, the implication that the planters were *ipso facto* responsible for this mortality does not necessarily follow. It is true that in many instances sick labourers driven out by their employers may well have started off on a desperate journey home, only to succumb on the way, and that others, unpaid for months and hence under-provisioned for the trip may have met with a similar fate. Yet, the prejudice against western medicine and the self-starvation so commonly met with amongst the immigrants must also have taken their toll and have accounted for a number of the deaths which Tennent so unhesitatingly laid at the planters' door.

It has been argued that in his correspondence with the Secretary of State, Tennent intentionally twisted some facts, suppressed others and made much of evidence specially prepared for him, and that he sought in this way to "whitewash" the Government and mislead the Colonial Office.[115] One finds it difficult to accept this view for there was really no reason why Tennent need have done all or any of this. He was a relatively new appointee in the Colony, and it was not his own policy that he was being called upon to defend. Had he believed that the Government was partly responsible for the excessive rate of immigrant mortality he could have said so without hurting his current standing or his future prospects. It was, in fact, far more dangerous to put up a fabricated argument. If the immigrants were mostly dying on the inward march, they would have continued to do so despite any arguments to the contrary, and Tennent would soon have been exposed.

A more plausible explanation of the contradictions in the Colonial Secretary's view, is that he had failed to digest the mountain of information which the Government had gathered on the immigrant labour question. When one studies the sheaf of enclosures which accompanied his monumental dispatch, and which formed the evidence on which his case was based, it becomes clear that Tennent at times quite missed the significance of the information before him.[116] That he submitted these papers in toto however, is significant, for he would certainly not have done so if he had intended to mislead the Colonial Office.

Tennent ended his dispatch by urging upon the Colonial Office the importance of Indian labour to Sri Lanka. For the first time it was officially conceded that if supplies failed and the plantations collapsed, the finances of the Government would receive a severe setback.[117] This admission represented a considerable shift from the earlier line that immigration benefitted the planters alone and was a recognition of the fact that by 1846 coffee had become the main prop of the general revenue—contributing an average of 30% of the annual total. In short, for fiscal reasons the Administration had come to possess a vested interest in the success of the plantation enterprise. Tennent's acceptance of the realities of the situation made it incumbent upon him to advance some positive suggestions as to how labour supplies could be assured in the future. The measures he prescribed went well beyond any the Government had attempted thus far, yet, they were so designed that the principle of an unassisted immigration remained inviolate.

Tennent believed that maltreatment on the plantations could be remedied by the relatively simple expedients of: (1) "assisting and protecting the Cooly in his resort to the authorities for that redress which the existing law has provided," and (2) "by such an alteration in the present system of short contracts as will add to the interest of his employer in promoting his comforts, providing for his health, and ensuring his cheerfulness and contentment."[118] In order to attain the first of these objects it would be necessary to make the immigrant aware of the extent to which the law provided for his protection, and at the same time to facilitate his access to those who administered it. For this joint purpose it was recommended that a special category of officers, known as Protectors of Coolies be appointed. Their duties would include visits to the estates at irregular intervals "to inspect the lines and dwellings constructed for the labourers, with due regard to their cleanliness and salubrity, to ascertain that their contracts are faithfully adhered to, and in cases of infringement to explain to them the nature of the redress, and their means of obtaining it from the nearest Magistrate."[119]

In order to give full effect to the services of the Protectors of Coolies, the number of local Magistrates would have to be so increased as to give the immigrant a readier access to them than he had previously possessed. In 1847, there were several large estates which lay between fifteen to twenty miles or more from the court of the nearest Magistrate, "so that even were the disinclination of the labourer to appeal to them removed, the distance alone would operate to deprive him of their protection."[120]

Regarding the duration of contracts, Tennent was convinced that a much more beneficial influence on the condition of the immigrant than any established by law would originate from the employer himself if contracts were extended beyond the term of twelve months, as specified by Ordinance 5 of 1841. A long-term contract would increase the value of the labourer to his employer. His health would be more anxiously cared for and his willingness to work ensured by consideration and generous treatment. The planter in turn would derive as many advantages from the arrangement. The incompetency of beginners would be done away with, a workforce with experience built up, and the necessity for paying higher wages when shortages arose minimised to the full.

As an additional measure designed to promote a happier atmosphere on the estates, Tennent suggested that small patches of land be allotted to labourers for the cultivation of food and the raising of poultry. Such a step would lessen the difficulty of securing food supplies in remote districts, and more important, there was always the likelihood that in time it would "correct the migrating habits of the Cooly, and attach him to the soil by association and prosperity," a result which in turn would partially relieve the colony from its dependence upon other countries for rice.[121] The idea of settlement on these terms was not altogether new. Individual planters had already tried the experiment as a counter to the growing labour crisis by offering immigrants "a plot of ground for a garden, and a comfortable residence, to locate themselves on the plantations with their families,"[122] but little success had attended their efforts. Tennent must have known of their failure, but he probably believed that the scheme was worth another trial, particularly if carried out in conjunction with his other proposals.

The expense of financing a scheme of the sort proposed by Tennent was comparatively trifling when compared with the expenditure incurred in many other colonies. There was to be no official subsidisation of transport from India to Sri Lanka, the cost of passage being met as before by the immigrants themselves or defrayed out of advances made by the employers. All the same, Government expenditure was likely to increase since the salaries of the additional Magistrates, the pay of the Protectors of Coolies and their establishments, and a fair contribution towards the maintenance of hospitals, rest-houses and other facilities would have to be provided for. To have paid for these out of the general revenue would have seemed dangerously like Government assistance, hence Tennent recommended that the funds be raised by a stamp duty on contracts and by an annual payment per head for each immigrant employed upon any estate.[123]

While he hoped through these expedients to help both planter and immigrant Tennent knew full well that they did not constitute a permanent and conclusive solution to the labour problem. "The measures I have been recommending," he wrote, "however urgent and important at the present crisis, are at best but temporizing with the great question of a permanent as well as a sufficient supply of labour for Ceylon."[124] It had to be accepted that coffee was important to the future of the Island, that an adequate supply of labour was vital to the industry's success, and that the planters had not the slightest assurance that those supplies would be forthcoming. So long as immigration continued to be spontaneous, then so long would it be influenced by uncontrollable causes which could at any time seriously restrict the seasonal flow or even curtail it altogether—"an unusually abundant harvest in India, a sudden and extensive demand for labour on railroads or public works there—a war in the Deccan or an epidemic on the Coromandel coast might exert such an unexpected and extreme influence on the supply of labour usually migrating to Ceylon, as would be all but ruinous to the Colony by the loss of a season's production, or even a continuance of that disaster for years in succession."[125]

With a view to eliminating entirely the probability of labour ever falling so calamitously short, Tennent also submitted for the consideration of the Colonial Office a bold and unusual plan which he believed would provide a long-term solution to the problem. Since the indigenous inhabitants were not disposed to labour on the plantations like the Indians, the Lieutenant-Governor suggested that the latter be made part of the permanent population. This could be achieved he thought, if the Government made available the unoccupied crown lands which lay in the centre and north of the Island, in the immediate vicinity of the coffee districts and on the highway between the northern ports and the Kandyan provinces. These regions were now abandoned and unproductive, but they had once been cultivated and still contained a number of artificial tanks which, if repaired, could bring fertility back to the soil. The climate was similar to that of South India, though less oppressive and the land of equal or superior quality and possessed of "every capability and facility for the location of an Indian community and the establishment of Indian villages, whose inhabitants might be readily induced to settle there, if removed in families and secured in all their accustomed arrangements of village Government under their own potails and village officers."[126]

A race of willing labourers might thus be transplanted into the very neighbourhood of the coffee districts "with the opportunity of restoring the tillage of the district, and raising their own supplies independently of foreign import."[127] Rice and coffee were both seasonal crops and since the slack season of the one coincided with the picking season of the other, the new settlers would find it possible to labour on the plantations for part of the year and cultivate their fields in the remaining months.

This was Tennent's "permanent" solution to the labour problem, one which he hoped would perform the dual role of providing the coffee enterprise with the labour it so sorely needed and of increasing the output of local agriculture. The form of settlement here envisaged differed substantially from that recommended earlier in his dispatch as a counter to the immigratory habits of the Indian. The one was to be left to the private initiative of the individual employer, the other to be undertaken by the Government as a major socio-economic experiment.

Tennent's plan was in keeping with the adoption of the new and realistic attitude that the Colony's finances were now inextricably tied to the fortunes of coffee and that it would be in the Administration's interest to extend to the industry some special marks of favour. It evinced a more accommodating definition of the Government's role vis-a-vis immigration in that an Administration which had previously refused to countenance even a limited intervention in the immigratory process, was now suggesting that it undertake the wholesale transference of Indian villages to Sri Lanka. This is not to say that the Government had abandoned its earlier decision that immigration was not to be financed out of the general revenue. Tennent made it clear that the expenditure incurred on the locating of the Indian communities was to be recovered through a "moderate annual assessment of the lands to be assigned to the new settlers."[128] Nevertheless, it scarcely needs to be pointed out that his scheme went well beyond the "welfare" with which until then, the Government had been solely concerned. Along with "welfare," a degree of intervention in the immigratory process was now being suggested, though significantly, a distinction was drawn between intervention and "financial assistance." To the latter, Tennent remained strongly opposed. This is implied not only by the very nature of the measures proposed but also in a statement of policy made on the very day his suggestions were transmitted to Whitehall. "The duty of the Government," he wrote, "would be fully discharged by the adoption of every precaution to facilitate the arrival of the coolies in the Colony and expedite their journey by safe and healthy roads; to protect them from violence or ill-treatment by the way, to provide them with shelter when weary, and medical care and every requisite comfort when overtaken by illness; to afford them the protection of the law when defrauded or abused; to insist on their humane and becoming treatment when employed on the estates, and to ensure to them every security in returning to their own country with the earnings of their labour. . . . *The charges of their immigration and maintenance are the proper concern of those at whose special invitation and for whose special advantage they resort to the Island.*"[129]

Though he had come round to the view that plantation agriculture required an increased measure of official encouragement, Tennent remained a severe critic of those who ran the plantations. On the very day on which he composed his classic dispatch on immigration, he penned yet another which he devoted exclusively to countering the arguments of the planters' resolution of 19th December. With the facts and figures he now had at his disposal, the Lieutenant-Governor was able to make short work of their complaints. On the charge that the Government had contributed insufficiently to the medical relief of the immigrant he observed that the planters' statistics were wrong and directed the Secretary of State to the returns submitted with his main dispatch. The claim that many an estate provided medical aid at its own expense was similarly dismissed with the scathing comment that "he believed the phrase was used in a very comprehensive sense, and that some items of considerable cost are included, the use of which is more conducive to the comfort of the European Superintendents than the Malabar labourers."[130] The demand for an assisted immigration, at Government expense, was viewed with an equal lack of sympathy. It was admitted again that the Government gained indirectly from the results of the immigrants' labours, but that was not considered sufficient grounds for absolving the planter from the necessity of paying for schemes likely to improve the efficiency of the immigratory process. Tennent also did not allow to pass unnoticed the manner in which the planters contradicted much of what they had previously said. In the first petition they had described in detail the sufferings of the immigrant and sought to blame it all upon the Government; in the second they had shifted their ground and attempted to tone down this particular complaint "since the charges had rebounded upon themselves."[131] Moreover, it was significant that the resolutions, which had been passed in December 1846 were not presented for transmission to the Secretary of State until April 1847. This was due, he said, to the fact that some who had attended the meeting now had reason to be diffident as to the soundness of their case. The "honourable section" of the planting body had had their confidence shaken by "subsequent disclosures" which had satisfied them that the abuses prevalent in some districts were calculated to inflict serious injury on the entire coffee area, by "discouraging the resort of Indian labour to Ceylon."[132]

Tennent's exposure of the disabilities immigrant labour had to endure; his rebuttal of the arguments brought forward by the planters, and his suggestions as to the lines future policy should follow, were accepted in their totality by the authorities at Whitehall. The detailed proofs of ill-treatment on the estates were sufficient to convince them—the protestations of the planters, notwithstanding, that "no doubt there had been cruelty,"[133] and Lord Grey, the Secretary of State indicated that he was prepared to sanction without hesitation any bill the Legislative Council might propose for the protection of the labourer. Moreover, if in order to enforce the law effectively extra Magistrates and Protectors of Coolies were required, he "would gladly apply to the Lords of the Treasury to sanction the increase."[134] Similarly received were Tennent's views on the subject of an assisted immigration. The Colonial Office expressed its agreement that there should be "the continuance of a system of spontaneous immigration in preference to one conducted at the public expense."[135]

The proposals concerning settlement under both private and public patronage were received without any of the protests one might have expected them to evoke. This surprising reaction was the result of a strange coincidence. Whitehall it appeared had on its own, come to the same conclusions regarding the creation of Indian colonies in Sri Lanka! The Colonial Office view, which differed slightly from that held by Tennent, was based on the findings of a committee appointed at the end of 1846 to review the economic affairs of the Island.[136] In the course of its inquiry, the committee had come to realize that the commercial progress of Sri Lanka was intimately connected with the coffee enterprise and that the prospects for coffee were in turn markedly dependent upon the flow of immigrant labour. Hence they apparently considered it within their terms of reference to deal at length with the problem of labour supply.

Pointing to the fluctuating nature of the immigrant population and to the dangers inherent in dependence upon it, the Committee suggested settlement as the only feasible alternative. This could be achieved they believed, if immigrants were granted small portions of land, on a rent almost nominal for the first year or two, but increasing thereafter and reaching its permanent maximum about the sixth or seventh year. If possible, the Government was advised to go even further and induce "whole village communities to immigrate from the adjoining continent, as had been suggested in the case of Mauritius, retaining their peculiar form and modes of self-government, with their native headmen, priest, etc."[137]

The Secretary of State accepted the general principle of these recommendations, though not without significant modifications. In his reply to Tennent's dispatch he intimated that while he agreed for the most part with the Lieutenant-Governor's scheme, he felt it necessary to point out that the immigrants to whom land was allotted might well cease to be labourers: "Experience has shown that a too great facility in obtaining land is in all countries the immediate cause of extreme difficulty in commanding the services of hired labourers. For this reason it is essential that the proposed allottment to the coolies should not be sufficiently large to induce them to devote the greater part of their time to cultivation on their own account."[138] The groupings of the new settlers into communities of their own the Secretary of State looked upon with favour, since other considerations aside, the arrangement would possess certain fiscal advantages to the Government. The difficulty of collecting rents from a number of small occupiers would be removed "by requiring the immigrants to settle upon the land in communities, under their own village officers, according to the custom which prevails in their own country, those officers being made responsible to the Colonial Government for the whole rent of the lands held by the immigrants."[139]

However, while both Tennent and the members of Grey's Committee had regarded settlement primarily as a means of solving the labour crisis, and only secondarily as an instrument for increasing the output of food crops, the Secretary of State proposed that if large numbers responded to the inducements to settle in the Colony, greater allotments might be made available to some "with the ulterior view, suggested by Sir Emerson Tennent, of restoring the cultivation of the deserted districts of the Island."[140] As this was not quite what Tennent had in mind, it is evident that Grey either misunderstood him, or else that he was inclined to push settlement a great deal further than the Lieutenant-Governor had intended.

In addition to urging settlement, Grey's Committee also had other recommendations to make for improving the supply of labour. These in summary were:

(1) That a steam vessel be employed to ply between Rameswaram in India and Arippu in Sri Lanka; or, if the repair of the northern roads should be found too difficult or expensive, to bring the

immigrants to Negombo or Colombo.

(2) That rest-houses, wells and provision bazaars be established along the lines of march.

(3) That officers be appointed to assist and advise the immigrants, and to collect at their port of debarkation all the information available as to places where labour was most in demand.[141]

With these three measures Grey claimed at first to be in full agreement, i.e. in a dispatch of 18th June, 1847. However, on the 7th August, in a dispatch containing a fuller statement of policy, he omitted all mention of the first two proposals. His ignoring of the second can be understood, for Campbell had already made provision for resting-places, wells, etc., but his omission of the first can only be interpreted as an outright rejection of the proposal. Apparently, the Secretary of State had had second thoughts about carrying intervention to the point of sanctioning "the employment of a steam vessel" to ply between India and Sri Lanka; a reassessment not a little influenced perhaps by his receipt of Tennent's dispatches of 21st April.[142]

Along with their recommendations Grey's Committee also suggested ways and means of raising the finances needed to put them into operation. What was favoured was "a system of private contribution among the planters," but it was added that if this failed to materialize, the Governor could "without trenching upon the Colonial revenue . . . obtain funds for the assistance of immigration . . . either by a tax on the employers of coolie labourers, or by some other means which would place the burden on the shoulders of those who benefit by immigration."[143] This proposal was also not officially conveyed to Sri Lanka by Grey in his later dispatch, but there was no reason for him to do so, since he had already agreed to such additional taxation in his instructions to Campbell early in 1847.[144]

The correspondence between Tennent and Grey makes it evident that Colonial Office policy was by no means lacking in flexibility. It is clear that the Home authorities were not unmindful of the interests of the planting body, but it is just as plain that they were not inclined to sanction the application of public money to the solution of the planters' problems. By 1847 they had come round to the view that a limited degree of "intervention" was permissible in Sri Lanka since circumstances, i.e. the future of the coffee enterprise and hence, the state of the Colony's finances demanded it; but of direct "financial assistance" there was to be none. In short, laissez-faire was yet their guiding principle, with deviations from its code permitted only when such departures were merited by considerations of a very special nature. To this "special" category belonged the settlement scheme; but even here it is notable that intervention was not to be carried particularly far. State action was to be limited to providing "inducements," the cost of which was to be borne, not by the general public, but by the immigrant himself through the payment of an annual tax.

It might well be argued that Ordinance 5 of 1841, which regulated the conditions of employment on the estates, was as much a violation of laissez-faire doctrine as the settlement scheme. To hold such a view, however, would be to deny a positive character to the laissez-faire credo and treat it as a synonym for anarchism. Those who supported the theory were not attempting to whittle away all forms of Government control in the belief that an administrative nihilism was a desirable ideal. What they aspired to was a minimum framework of law and order within which the play of economic forces could produce the good of all. With the march of time this relatively simple concept grew in sophistication and content; for official endeavours to apply the theory to the economic life of England tended to erode its earlier rigidity and gave to laissez-faire a practical dynamism it had previously lacked. The philosophy, in other words, matured with age and during the process acquired a more accommodating attitude towards certain facets of the minimum framework it sought to establish. One such embraced its approach to the question of labour legislation. At the turn of the century all forms of interference in this field had been condemned, but by 1802 it had come to be accepted that legislation on behalf of orphan children employed in the factories of Britain was not contrary to the laissez-faire spirit, since this category of labour was too helpless to promote its own advantage. With the passing years the scope of this "helpless" category was extended first, to cover all employed children—whether orphaned or not, and later to include women and "young persons" as well.[145] It is apparent that the Colonial Office had early decided that immigrant labour, even when male and adult, fell rightly under the classification of "helpless," and that legislation in its interests was a duty which the State could scarcely avoid. This being the ruling approach in the 1840s it would be far from correct to consider Ordinance 5 a transgression of the laissez-faire code.

In strong contrast to the policy adopted in Sri Lanka was that followed in a number of other colonies where plantation agriculture was widely practiced. In Mauritius and the West Indies for example, immigration was entirely at the public cost and conducted under the direct supervision of the Colonial Governments. That the Colonial Office should have permitted this is further evidence of the practicality of its policy-makers when faced with circumstances of a "special" nature. In this instance the "circumstances" had their origin in historical events peculiar to the Colonies in question. Slavery there had been abolished in 1835 and the newly liberated slaves, to whom the very word "plantation" had unhappy connotations, refused to convert into wage labourers, preferring to set up as peasant agriculturists, if possible, or else to seek employment in other fields. This was an unforeseen reaction and one which precipitated a labour crisis of such dimensions that an investigating committee of the House of Commons reported in 1842: "that the staple products of the Colonies had fallen off to an extent serious, in some cases ruinous, . . . that its chief causes were the difficulty in getting continuous labour and the high wages that had to be paid for broken and indifferent work, and that an obvious remedy would be to promote immigration."[146]

Within the British Empire it was in India alone that a willing labour surplus was to be found, and accordingly, it was to the sub-continent that the stricken plantation colonies turned for their supplies. Initially, the new traffic was controlled by the planters themselves without any official regulation whatever, but such scandalous abuses were soon uncovered that the Indian Government was obliged to intervene and suspend emigration in 1839. The experience of those few short years was sufficient to convince the Colonial Office that the movement of labour cargoes over great distances could not be humanely effected under laissez-faire conditions. A departure from its stand of "non-interference" seemed justified by the necessity to achieve the dual objectives of ensuring to the planter an adequate supply of workers and of protecting the immigrant against maltreatment. A series of agreements relating to shipping arrangements, the rectification of abuses, lengths of service etc., were therefore concluded with the Indian authorities and immigration resumed under the control and management of the Mauritian Government in 1842, and the West Indian Governments in 1844.[147]

In Sri Lanka the situation was different enough for both Colonial Office and Colonial Government to consider private enterprise more appropriate than public. Tennent neatly summarised their stand when he observed that "the causes which created an obligation on the Imperial Government to facilitate emigration to other colonies, do not operate in the case of Ceylon. The ordinary supply of labour was not interfered with here as elsewhere by the abolition of slavery, nor was any necessity created of providing against a disturbance of the usual course of industry consequent upon an Act of the Supreme Legislature. The distance whence the labourers are to be brought is not, as in the case of our West Indian possessions, so vast as to place their introduction beyond the reach of ordinary capitalists and justify the interference of the State; on the contrary they are so close at hand as to involve little or no expenditure, and to call only for kindness and encouragement."[148] Presumably the Lieutenant-Governor chose to put his settlement scheme under the head of "encouragement," and correctly so perhaps, since it merely provided "inducements" calculated to attract the land-hungry immigrant.

Though the demand for a Government-assisted immigration in Sri Lanka failed to gain official favour, it had one quite unexpected result. The publicity given to the planters' efforts by the local press attracted the attention and what was worse, the disapproval, of the Government of India. In their enthusiasm for a sponsored immigration the planters had inadvertently overlooked the fact that the Indian law strictly prohibited all schemes intended to assist labourers in leaving the country. The law, as we have seen, had been relaxed in favour of Mauritius and the West Indies, but no concession had been made with respect to Sri Lanka. The Indian Government must, of course, have known that immigration to the Island was taking place, but there is ample reason to believe that the authorities on the coast were not anxious to check a movement so manifestly advantageous to their own people. Now that the question had been publicly aired they could no longer continue to close their eyes to what was going on. Overtures to Sri Lanka were therefore made suggesting that the matter be officially taken up by both Governments. In the discussions which followed, the Indian authorities agreed to withdraw the existing prohibition on emigration to the Colony, provided the immigrants were accorded protection by law against re-emigration to other Colonies. These assurances were duly furnished and the agreement given legal form through the passing of Ordinance 3 of 1847.[149]

The implementation of the policies formulated by Tennent and Grey had to await the arrival in Sri Lanka of the Colony's new Governor, Lord Torrington. Before his departure to Sri Lanka Torrington was instructed by Grey to pursue the settlement scheme as effectually as he could, and it seems likely that he was required in addition to make a close study of the recommendation submitted by Grey's Committee.[150] The opportunity to apply these plans, however, was denied Torrington, for his arrival in the Island coincided with a series of events the effects of which dramatically altered the economic and political climate of the country. To begin with, the price of coffee began to fall. Through 1847 quotations on the London market declined by some 31% and before the year was out it was plain that all thoughts of imposing fresh levies on the coffee industry would have to be set aside for a time. With the suggested acreage tax thus ruled out, the financial base of part of the Grey-Tennent reforms was removed and Torrington was left with the choice of either paying for extra Magistrates and Protectors of Coolies out of the general revenue or of dropping the proposals altogether. Considering the current Colonial Office line of "non-assistance" it is not surprising that the Governor chose the second of these alternatives, yet even if he had been inclined to hold that the measures proposed could rightly be placed under the head of' "welfare" there was little point in attempting to convert Grey and Tennent to his view, for the funds at his disposal were soon too limited to permit the added expense. The misfortunes of the coffee enterprise had such immediate effect upon the financial state of the Colony and before long the excess of expenditure over revenue was so great, that it became the Governor's task to curtail spending, not increase it.

The necessity for an increased expenditure on labour had arisen out of the need to off-set the short-fall in immigration, but Torrington found in 1847 that scarcity was a thing of the past, and that an embarrassing abundance of labour was available for employment. This unexpected reversal of conditions was the outcome of famine in South India, which not only dissuaded many of the previous years' immigrants from returning home, but also augmented somewhat the total of those coming in. What was worse, a large proportion of the newcomers arrived well in advance of the picking season, and with no means of support began "dying in all directions on the highways."[151] Fearing that reports of this mortality would deter those upon the march from completing their journey, and thus cause a shortage when the proper time for gathering the crop came round, Torrington decided to put the surplus labour to work on a Government project, i.e. filling up Bogambara Lake in Kandy. The step no doubt was a humane one, but the Colonial Office was fearful that it would set a dangerous precedent and cautioned the Governor against giving the impression that the Government could be expected to provide employment during the periodical cessations of plantation work.[152]

If the problem of labour scarcity had for the time being resolved itself, other more serious questions were not long in appearing. In July 1848, a revolt broke out in the Kandyan districts, the suppression of which imposed a further burden on the strained finances of the Government. The uprising appears to have had little or no effect upon the flow of immigrant labour; a result due in no small measure to the positive steps taken by the Government to prevent any such eventuality. On Torrington's orders, notices were distributed throughout the districts from which the labourers came, to counteract any false alarms that may have spread in those areas. Government Agents were instructed to station officers along the roads and at the ports for the same purpose, and the Madras Government was asked to help by officially dispelling any remaining fears that the immigrant might have entertained.[153] These steps are said to have been attended with so great a degree of success, that Torrington thought it fit to inform the Colonial Office that "people in England, with interests in Ceylon should have no apprehensions as to the effects of the rebellion on the supply of coolies."[154]

The temporary solution to the labour problem which famine in India had brought, came to an end in 1848. By the end of that year conditions had improved sufficiently to remove the threat of starvation and with the disappearance of this positive driving force, immigration began again to decline in an alarming fashion. For this second falling off the non-payment of wages appears to have been mainly responsible. The stringent financial conditions of the time made wage-default so common that Torrington was inclined to treat it as the sole reason for the fall in immigration.[155] In the Police court of Kandy 2,584 complaints arising out of wage default were made within the short period of ten months, and this court it should be remembered was only one of several in the planting districts.[156] The enormous number of actions lodged suggests that immigrants were no longer as reluctant to seek legal redress as before. Certainly, there was no parallel to this in 1845-46, but times were such that only a portion of the complainants were able to recover anything like the arrears due to them.[157] In some cases the owner of the estate had been declared a bankrupt and though according to the law wage claims took precedence over all others on a bankrupt estate, labourers were often unable to afford the stamp fees they were required to pay. In others, the owner of the estate was non-resident and the legal authorities in Sri Lanka were not empowered to seize his property to pay the wages due to his labour force. Torrington rectified matters as best he could by ordering that stamps be issued free to immigrants suing for wages and by passing Ordinance 10 of 1848 which conferred power on the Government Agent to sell the property of absentee owners for the purpose of recovering outstanding costs. Yet, while these steps proved valuable in individual cases they did not altogether allay the immigrants' prejudice against returning to Sri Lanka, and the inflow of labour saw a further decline in 1849. The effects of the fall in supply however, were no longer as serious as they had been, for with scores of estates closing down altogether, and with others being operated on a "care and maintenance" basis, the overall demand for labour had taken a downward plunge. Yet it was a position fraught with danger, for if and when conditions did improve, the planting community could expect to be faced with a labour scarcity of alarming proportions.

On the question of settlement, Torrington at first did nothing, particularly because he was concerned with the problems of depression and revolt, and partly because for the moment "Malabar labour . . . was plentiful."[158] During the uprising, however, the Government's policy of confiscating the property of rebels led to the seizure of land in the vicinity of two important planting districts, i.e. Kurunegalla and Matale. Tennent regarded these as suitable sites for the planting of Indian villages and the Colonial Secretary was not slow to bring this to the notice of the Governor. "The opportunity which now presents itself of locating a race of Malabars . . . on the lands forfeited by the rebels, is one which I trust your Excellency will not allow to pass unimproved."[159] The extent of the land ultimately confiscated proved too limited for the scheme to be given a trial, and though other areas were subsequently examined with this object in mind, it was not long before the scheme was abandoned altogether. This rather sudden demise of a plan from which so much had been expected appears to have been the direct result of an inquiry conducted by a Parliamentary Committee of the House of Commons into the uprising of 1848. In the course of the investigation it was discovered, from more than one source, that "the introduction of Malabar coolies had given the Kandyans much offence." Tennent himself was inclined to believe that the problem could be overcome by keeping the two racial groups away from one another, but apparently the Colonial Office decided that the risks of persevering with the scheme were not worth taking, for no further mention of the project is to be found in the official files.[160]

In June 1850, events arising out of the Commission of Inquiry brought a sudden termination to Lord Torrington's tenure of office. The Governor's departure from Sri Lanka coincided with the beginnings of an economic upswing, which took the coffee industry to a veritable "golden age." One would not be far wrong in holding that 1850 marked the opening of a second phase in the history of plantation agriculture. The first, which stretched from 1836 to 1849 had marked coffee's early rise, had seen it go through boom and slump, and had witnessed its successful emergence from a baptism of fire. The same period had seen also the growth of immigration and the gradual development of an immigration policy on the part of the Government. It seems, therefore, that 1850 is a convenient date at which to pause and take stock of Governmental and Colonial Office attitudes towards the general problems associated with the use of Indian labour.

From what has been said in the earlier sections of this chapter, it is evident that official essays into immigration policy were in the beginning preoccupied only with the provision of a legal framework which would enable plantation owners to hold on to their labour forces. Concern for the immigrant himself was shown in rudimentary fashion by Governor Stewart Mackenzie, but it was with Sir Colin Campbell that a policy towards the Indian worker first emerged in definitive form. Welfare and protection were the watchwords of his approach and his interest in improving the condition of the plantation worker was as firm as his determination to keep the process of immigration spontaneous. To adhere thus to principles of laissez-faire was not in his time a difficult task, for coffee was prosperous and the flow of labour not yet seriously interfered with. True, ominous signs of what was to come were already apparent during Campbell's term of administration, and true also that it was he who first sought a better understanding of the immigrants' socio-economic environment; but it was left to Sir James Emerson Tennent to undertake the further development of immigration policy. Tennent's contribution stemmed as much from his sympathy for the helpless immigrant, as it did from his appreciation of the role that plantation agriculture had come to play in the Colony's affairs. Accordingly, he proposed a degree of interference which his predecessor would probably have refused to countenance. From its earlier preoccupation with welfare alone he moved policy to a position where, by the end of the period under review it accepted a limited intervention on behalf of both immigrant and planter and at the same time rejected the granting of direct financial assistance to the immigratory process.

Perhaps the outstanding characteristic of Colonial Office policy throughout the period 1830-1850, was its flexibility. Though convinced that plantation agriculture like other forms of economic enterprise should generally be left to fend for itself, and though determined that its advance should not be accomplished at the expense of public funds, Whitehall was yet prepared when the need arose—as it did in the late 1840s—to deviate from this stand and sanction such intervention as it believed would save the plantation from extinction. This concern was of course, in part engendered by the stake which the Island's finances had come to possess in the fate of coffee, but one must not forget that the capital threatened was British in origin and this was a consideration the Colonial Office was not likely to overlook. Nevertheless, if Whitehall was disposed to come to the aid of British investment, such encouragement as it was inclined to give was never at the expense of the estate worker. In a sad and depressing epoch of labour history, the happiest portions have to do with the vigilance of the Home Authorities on the immigrant's behalf. Their refusal to sanction the Ordinances of Horton and Mackenzie, their demands for an increased stringency in the penalties applicable to employers, and their insistence that the Indian immigrant should be assured fair health, safety of person, and the opportunity to return home with his hard-won earnings, are notable instances of their concern for the well-being of the labourer. Assessed by the standards of today the totality of these measures may not have amounted to much, but our judgement must be tempered by a sense of the time and the place, and by the realization that the British worker in the mid-19th century did not have a great deal more of either "protection" or "welfare."

NOTES

1. Prior to 1839 those interested in commercial agriculture secured their labour by direct recruitment through agents specially sent over to India for the purpose. The earliest instance was in 1828, when Governor Barnes and a Mr George Bird imported 150 labourers on a wage of 15s. per month or 12s. per month and a measure of rice per day. The experiment, however, proved a failure, for almost all the labourers deserted within a year. C.O.416. 20. G.25. C.R. de Silva, "Ceylon under the British Administration," Vol. II, p. 484.
2. Madras District Gazetteer, South Arcot, p. 75.
3. C.0.54. 227. 11th November 1846—Campbell to Grey; C.0.54. 235, 21st April 1847—Tennent to Grey; Madras District Gazetteers—South Arcot and Madura—p.144 and pp. 162-63 respectively; C. Pridham, "An Historical Political and Statistical Account of Ceylon," p. 102; D. Kumar, "Land and Caste in South India," pp. 138-40; H. Tinker, "A New System of Slavery. The Export of Indian Labour Overseas 1830-1920," pp. 56-57, p. 374; *Statements Exhibiting the Moral and Material Progress and Condition of India*, 1860-61, p. 227, and 1876, p. 87.
4. H. Tinker, *op.cit.*, p. 55.
5. Madras District Gazetteer, Malabar, p. 91.
6. R.L. Hardgrave, "The Nadars of Tamilnad," pp. 52-53; R. Jeffrey, "The Decline of Nayar Dominance," p. 50, p. 131; Dharma Kumar, *op. cit.*, pp. 190-91; H. Tinker, *op.cit.*, p. 54, p. 133, p. 374.
7. D. Kumar, *op. cit.*, p. 139.
8. C.O.54. 235. 21st April 1847—Tennent to Grey; C.O.54. 243. 25th February 1847—Torrington to Grey. These headmen should not be

confused with another group, also known as Kanganies, who for a livelihood intercepted immigrants on the road and undertook to conduct them to certain estates in whose pay they were. This system of recruiting the Indian after he had arrived in Sri Lanka was employed during the first decade of the coffee period, but subsequently fell out of use since it gave rise to various abuses. In particular, it became a practice for Kanganies to procure labourers from the line of march, and then seduce them from one estate to another, drawing an income from every new employer but giving none a steady labour supply—C.0.54. 235. 21st April 1847—Tennent to Grey.

9. The Puttlam route was the main immigrant artery until the middle of the nineteenth century. Thereafter the bulk of the traffic came in via Mihintale. C.O.54. 227. 11th November 1846—Campbell to Grey; C.0.54. 235. 21st April 1847—Tennent to Grey; C.0.54. 243. 1847. Letter to Grey from certain planters. Pridham, *op. cit.*, Vol. I, pp. 397-399. H. Dickman, "An Account of Malabar Coolies in Ceylon" in *The Ceylon Miscellany* of December 1853, pp. 45 and 46.

10. C.0.54. 235. 21st April 1847—Tennent to Grey.

11. C.O.54. 227. 11th November 1846—Campbell to Grey; C.0.54. 235. 21st April 1847—Tennent to Grey; C.0.54. 243—Torrington to Grey. Pridham, op. cit., Vol. 1, pp. 397-99. H. Dickman, "An Account of Malabar Coolies in Ceylon" in *The Ceylon Miscellany* of December 1853, pp. 45 and 46.

12. B.P.P. of 1847. Vol. XXIII. Part IV.

13. Blue Book—statistics relating to the period 1838-42 do not include the acreage under coffee in the Central Province. From 1843 to 1845 a hypothetical figure for that Province has been included. The statistics given are thus little more than a very rough approximation to the truth.

14. Danson, op. cit., pp. 202-3. A.M. Ferguson, Ceylon, *Summary of Useful Information; Blue Books.*

15. See I. vanden Driesen, "The History of Coffee Culture in Ceylon"—Part 1, in *The Ceylon Historical Journal,* July 1953. pp. 31-61.

16. C.O.54. 250. 15th August 1848—Torrington to Grey; B.P.P. of 1849. Vol. XXXVI pp. 191-92.

17. B.P.P. of 1847-48. Vol. XXIII. Part IV.

18. Blue Book—statistics refer to the total area under coffee and not plantation coffee alone. *The Economist* of 12th May 1849 contains the following incomplete return of the acreage under plantation coffee: 1844—25,198 acres, 1845—36,551 acres, 1846—46,150 acres, 1847—50,071 acres.

19. Ferguson, op. cit. Figures for 1849 represent entry through northern ports only. This does not greatly distort the general picture, however, since movements through other ports were of a very restricted nature.

20. Ferguson,*op. cit.*, p. 167

21. *Ibid.*

22. M. Roberts strongly supports this course in "Observations on

computations of the Mortality Rate among Immigrant Indian Labourers 'in Ceylon in the Coffee Period," *Ceylon Journal of Historical and Social Studies*, Vol. 9, No. 2, 1966.

23. C.0.54. 227. 11th November 1846—Campbell to Grey (Encl.).
24. C.0.54. 227. 9th December 1846—Campbell to Grey (Encl.).
25. C.0.54. 235. 21st April 1847—Tennent to Grey. Tennent's first criticism of the planters, a somewhat general indictment, appeared in November 1846 as an enclosure to a despatch of Governor Campbell's (C.0.54. 227. 11th November 1846). This was followed some months later by the more detailed analysis given above.
26. *Ibid.* (Encl.)
27. *Ibid.*
28. *Ibid.*
29. C.O.54. 227. 11th November 1846—Campbell to Grey; C.0.54. 235. 21st April 1847—Tennent to Grey; C.0.54. 258. 13th April 1849— Torrington to Grey; C.0.55. 89. 6th August 1847—Grey to Torrington. H. Suckling, *A General Description of the Island of Ceylon*, Vol. II, pp. 309-10.
30. C.0.54. 235. 21st April 1847—Tennent to Grey. Even as late as 1879, an "expert" on coffee-planting, Mr W. Sabonadiere, recommended that line rooms should measure 12ft. x 12ft. Each room to house 10 labourers. See Sabonadiere, *op. cit.*, p. 77.
31. C.0.54. 235. 21st April 1847—Tennent to Grey (Encl.).
32. *Ibid.* See Colepepper's reference to cases of Sevetiam vs. Dick, and Alagan vs. David Watt.
33. C.0.54. 227. 11th November 1846—Campbell to Grey; C.0.54. 235. 21st April 1847—Tennent to Grey; C.0.54. 351. 5th March 1860— Ward to Newcastle.
34. C.0.54. 235. 21st April 1847—Tennent to Grey.
35. *Ibid.*
36. *Ibid.*
37. *Ibid.*
38. C.0.54. 235. 21st April 1847. Tennent to Grey.
39. *Ibid.*
40. C.0.54. 227. 11th November, 1846—Campbell to Grey (Encl).
41. C.0.54. 351. 5th March, 1860—Ward to Newcastle.
42. C.0.54. 227. 11th November 1846—Campbell to Grey.
43. C.0.54. 235. 21st April 1847—Tennent to Grey (Encl.).
44. *Ibid.*
45. C.0.54. 235. 21st April 1847—Tennent to Grey (Encl.).
46. Sir P.H. Manson Bahr, *Manson's Tropical Diseases*, p. 236.
47. Tennent in a despatch to Secretary of State Grey describes the Anuradhapura Road as "desolate and solitary and unhealthy from Malaria."
48. Manson Bahr, *op. cit.* p. 481.
49. C.0.54. 235. 21st April 1847—Tennent to Grey; *Ceylon Miscellany*, December 1853, pp. 45 and 46., H. Dickman, *An Account of Malabar*

Coolies in Ceylon.

50. The hours of work on the plantations were not inordinately long, being from six to ten in the morning and from noon to half past five in the evening. C.0.54. 235. 21st April 1847—Tennent to Grey.
51. Nominally wages varied from 15s. to 18s. a month, but it was understood that Sunday pay was given only for regular work. For instance, a man marked present for 24 days in the month, when wages were at 15s., was allowed four Sundays, thus giving him 6d. a day for 30 days. If present every working day in a long month, he received 15/6d. C.0.54. 235. 21st April 1847—Tennent to Grey.
52. *Ibid.* (Encl.).
53. C.0.54. 235. 21st April 1847—Tennent to Grey.
54. *Ibid.* The official concerned was Mr C. de Saram, Police Magistrate, Gampola. Mr E.S. Waring, the Police Magistrate at Matale, expressed similar sentiments. "When they are sick their pay is stopped, and there is no medical attendance; when they die they are buried by their friends . . . the Superintendent inspects the lines once a week, but takes no notice of the sick." That the sick labourers were harshly treated was admitted by the Ceylon Agricultural Society in 1843 when it reported that it viewed "with feelings of great pain the destitution of the sick labouring poor." The planters were warned that "unless some internal arrangements be made upon estates, higher authorities will most assuredly intervene to compel the adoption of some system which shall exonerate the agricultural interest of seeing the roads choked with the sick, the dying and the dead." *Proceedings of the Ceylon Agricultural Society*, 3rd Report, pp. 50ff. I am indebted to Dr K.M. de Silva for the latter reference.
55. *Ibid.*
56. See the Blue Book. C.0.59 series; and Ferguson, op. cit.; C.0.54. 227. 11th November 1846—Campbell to Grey; C.0.54. 235. 21st April 1847—Tennent to Grey; C.0.54. 250. 15th August 1848— Torrington to Grey. The impact of the coffee depression was first felt in 1848. The continued fall in labour supply after that date could not, therefore, have presented as many problems as it did earlier, since many estates closed down and a large acreage of land went out of production.
57. *The Economist* of 12th May 1849. Also C.0.54. 235. 21st April 1847—Tennent to Grey (Encl.).
58. C.0.54. 235. 21st April 1847—Tennent to Grey (Encl.). It has been argued that the cholera epidemic of 1845 was largely responsible for the shortfall in labour supplies—K.M. de Silva, "Indian Immigration to Ceylon—the First Phase c.1840—1855," in *The Ceylon Journal of Historical and Social Studies,* IV (2), p. 117. M. Roberts, "Indian Estate Labour in Ceylon during the Coffee Period," in *The Indian Economic and Social History Review*—Vol. III, No. 1, March 1966, footnote 71. It is difficult to agree with this argument, however, since (a) labour supplies had begun to decline *before* the cholera outbreak; (b) the

epidemic occurred during the off-season i.e. November to March, during which the flow of labour from India was always limited; (c) there was no mass exodus of Indian labour to the mainland in 1845; (d) there is no evidence to suggest that cholera was widespread in the planting districts and (e) the planters themselves made no attempt to connect labour shortages with the epidemic. Roberts' argument that "the great influx of immigrants, amounting to a surplus, in 1847 also belies the degree of importance attached to the influence of ill-treatment in 1847" does not hold. There was no "great influx" in 1847. Admittedly, the available workforce in Sri Lanka increased, but this was because a severe famine in India somewhat augmented the number of entries and simultaneously dissuaded many of the previous years' immigrants from returning home. See I.H. vanden Driesen, "Indian Immigration to Ceylon, the First Phase, 1840-1855—A Comment" in *The Ceylon Journal of Historical and Social Studies*, vol. 7, no. 2 (July-December) 1964, pp. 218-29.

59. C.0.54. 227. 11th November 1846—Campbell to Grey; C.0.54. 235. 21st April 1847—Tennent to Grey (Encl.). C.0.54. 250. 15th August 1848—Torrington to Grey; B.P.P., op. cit., 1849, Vol. XXXVI, pp. 191-92; Sirr, *op. cit.,* p. 161. With the depression matters grew infinitely worse. Between June 1848 and April 1849, 2,584 complaints arising out of the non-payment of wages were lodged in the Police Court of Kandy alone. C.O.54. 258. 13th April 1849—Torrington to Grey; C.0.55. 89. 6th August 1847— Grey to Torrington.
60. C.0.54. 235. 21st April 1847—Tennent to Grey; evidence supplied by Colepepper.
61. *Ibid.* Evidence of C. de Saram.
62. *The Economist,* 1846, p. 961; I.H. vanden Driesen, "Some Aspects of the Financing of Commercial Enterprize in nineteenth Century Ceylon," *The University of Ceylon Review,* Vol. XVIII, Nos. 3 & 4. pp. 213- 21.
63. Sabonadiere, *op. cit.*, p. 46. The economic life of the coffee shrub was then put at twelve years.
64. C.0.54. 250. 15th August 1848—Torrington to Grey.
65. C.0.54. 235. 21st April 1847—Tennent to Grey (Encl.).
66. Tennent to the Secretary of the Government of India. C.0.54. 235. 21st April 1847—Tennent to Grey (Encl.).
67. Similarly one can argue that since severe punishments were normal in the Army and Navy in the 1830s and 1840s, the ex-serviceman turned planter was merely pursuing a course to which he was accustomed.
68. C.0.54. 235.,21st April 1847—Tennent to Grey.
69. *Ibid.*
70. *Ibid.*
71. C. Pridham, "A Historical, Political and Statistical Account of Ceylon," Vol. 1, p. 399
72. C.O.54. 156. 3rd October 1837—Horton to Glenelg.
73. *Ibid.* It has been implied that this Ordinance was not drawn up with immigrant labour in mind, and that it was "no more than the introduction

to Ceylon of the main principles of the English master and servant legislation"—see K.M. de Silva "Indian Immigration to Ceylon—the first phase c.1840-1855" in *The Ceylon Journal of Historical and Social Studies*, Vol. 4, No. 2, pp. 112-13. This conclusion is difficult to accept since (a) immigrant labour was in use on the plantations from the very inception of the coffee era; and (b) Horton's dispatch clearly indicates that he had the coffee estates in mind when drawing up the Ordinance.

74. C.0.54. 136. 3rd October 1837—Horton to Glenelg.
75. C.0.54. 156. 3rd October 1837—Horton to Glenelg.
76. *Ibid.*
77. *Ibid.* (encl.).
78. C.0.54. 227. 11th November 1846—Campbell to Grey.
79. C.0.54. 182. 9th December 1840—Mackenzie to Russell.
80. Governor Stewart Mackenzie had to contend throughout his tenure of office with a revenue deficit which averaged £ 16,000 annually. The deficit was caused chiefly by the failure of the pearl fisheries, and by the imposition of an annual payment to the Imperial Treasury of £ 24,000 towards the cost of the Ceylon Garrison.
81. As Dr K.M. de Silva quite rightly points out, this transference from civil to criminal court could have serious consequences for the immigrant. "It followed that breaches of labour contracts would become criminal offences liable to severe punishments." *op. cit.*, p. 242, footnote 2.
82. The new Ordinance was substantially the same as that sent up in 1837, but differed in that it decreed that imprisonment for any offence, with or without hard labour, was not to exceed three months. Included also were clauses which specified how far a labourer engaged for a journey was required to travel per day, the penalties for refusal to perform this task, and a few other minor details besides. C.0.54. 182. 9th December 1840—Mackenzie to Russell.
83. C.0.55. 81. 8th March 1841—Russell to Campbell.
84. C.O.54. 190. 1st October 1841—Campbell to Russell. The limitation of legal contracts signed in Sri Lanka to a period of one year was found inconvenient by the Government. In 1845 the period of contract was therefore extended to three years. C.O.56. Ordinance 14 of 1845. The amendment, however, covered only those who sought employment in the public sector. For a fuller discussion of the details and working of the Act, see M. Roberts, "The Master-Servant Laws of 1841 and the 1860s, and Immigrant Labour in Ceylon," in *Ceylon Journal of Historical and Social Studies*, January-December 1965, pp. 24-37.
85. Proceedings of the Ceylon Agricultural Society. 1st report— 1842, pp. 1-13.
86. *Ibid.*, pp. 30- 31.
87. C.0.54. 227. 11th November 1846—Campbell to Grey.
88. *Ibid.*
89. C.0.54. 227. 11th November 1846—Campbell to Grey.
90. For statistics see pages 19 and 20.

91. C.0.54. 235. 21st April 1847—Tennent to Grey.
92. C.0.54. 227. 11th November 1846—Campbell to Grey.
93. C.0.54. 235. 21st April 1847—Tennent to Grey.
94. *Ibid.*
95. *Ibid.*
96. C.0.54. 227. 11th November 1846—Campbell to Grey (Encl.).
97. Campbell's figure includes expenditure on the "epidemic" hospitals which were open to both local residents and immigrant labour.
98. C.O.54. 227. 11th November 1846—Campbell to Grey.
99. C.O.55. 87. 18th January 1847—Grey to Campbell; C.0.54. 227. 11th November 1846—Campbell to Grey (Encl.).
100. *Ibid.*
101. C.0.54. 235. 21st April 1847—Tennent to Grey. The sums expended on these estates were put at £ 20-£ 40 per annum.
102. *Ibid.* (encl.).
103. *Ibid.*
104. C.O.54. 235. 21st April 1847—Tennent to Grey (Encl.).
105. *Ibid.*
106. *Ibid.*
107. *Ibid.*
108. *Ibid.*
109. C.0.54. 235. 21st April 1847—Tennent to Grey (Encl.).
110. C.0.54. 235. 21st April 1847—Tennent to Grey. Tennent here is guilty of some exaggeration for, as shown earlier, Colepepper could cite instances where immigrant workers had resorted to the courts, though often with disastrous consequences for the complainant.
111. *Ibid.*
112. C.O.54. 235. 21st April 1847—Tennent to Grey.
113. *Ibid.*
114. Statistics from C.0.54. 235. 21st April 1847—Tennent to Grey.
115. M. Roberts, op. cit., p. 10; K.M. de Silva, *op. cit.,* p. 245ff.
116. The enclosures for instance make it clear that self starvation was common on the plantations and that many immigrants showed a strong prejudice against Western medicine.
117. C.O.54. 235. 21st April 1847—Tennent to Grey.
118. *Ibid.*
119. *Ibid.*
120. *Ibid.*
121. *Ibid.*
122. C.O.54. 243. A letter of 25th February 1847 to the Secretary of State, from H. Atchinson, Richard Jefferson and another.
123. C.O.54. 235. 21st April 1847—Tennent to Grey. Tennent considered the tax per head to be more equitable than an assessment per acre. The latter could well have been disproportionate to the labour actually employed, since the size of the workforce would vary with the age and condition of the plantation.

124. C.O.54. 235. 21st April 1847—Tennent to Grey.
125. *Ibid.*
126. *Ibid.*
127. *Ibid.*
128. *Ibid.*
129. C.O.54. 235. 21st April 1847—Tennent to Grey.
130. *Ibid.* Dispatch No. 7.
131. *Ibid.*
132. *Ibid.*
133. C.O.54. 241. The Colonial Land and Emmigration Commissioners to James Stephen—letter of 27th July 1847.
134. C.O.55. 89. 7th August 1847. Grey to Torrington.
135. C.O.54. 241. Letter to James Stephen of 27th July 1847.
136. B.P.P. 1847-48. Vol. VIII, p. 5. Governor Campbell's dispatch of 4th November 1846, on the effects of taxation on Ceylon, had covered so wide a field that the Secretary of State had put all the material submitted before a committee "for their review and consideration." The Committee was made up of four members, viz. Mr Hawes an Under Secretary of State; Mr Tuffnel, a Secretary to the Lands Commissioners of the Treasury; Mr Lefevre, an Assistant Secretary of the Board of Trade; and Mr Bird, a Civil Servant of the East India Company. Their joint report was laid before the Secretary of State on 13th April 1847 and transmitted to Ceylon as an enclosure to Grey's dispatch to Torrington of 18th June 1847.
137. B.P.P. of 1847. Vol. 8, pp. 29-30. Despite the striking similarity between the committee's views on settlement and the plan put up by Tennent—indeed the very language used was almost the same—it cannot be held that one influenced the other. The interval between the presentation of the report and the writing of the despatch was one of eight days, i.e. 13th April and 21st April 1847, a period so short that the committee's views could not possibly have been communicated to Tennent. One cannot, of course, rule out the likelihood that the two had been in touch by private letter, but it seems more probable that both parties had got their ideas from a common source, namely, Grey's plan for Mauritius which envisaged the wholesale transference of Indian villages to that Colony. The Secretary of State's suggestion was strenuously opposed by the Mauritian planting community on the grounds that (1) there was no convincing proof that the immigrants would not set up as peasant agriculturists and cease to be plantation workers, and (2) that the "villages would become sanctuaries for deserters." Consequently, the plan was never implemented. See *Indians in a Plural Society,* by B. Benedict, p. 27. If this was the source of Tennent's ideas, then his scheme was not as "bold and imaginative" as I have held it to be.
138. C.O.55. 89. 7th August 1847—Grey to Torrington.
139. *Ibid.*

140. *Ibid.*
141. B.P.P. 1847-48. Vol. VIII, p. 29.
142. C.O.55. 89. 7th August 1847—Grey to Torrington. The third proposal was partially accepted and the "Protector of Coolies" suggested by Tennent empowered to exercise certain of the functions envisaged by the Committee.
143. B.P.P. 1847-48. Vol. VIII, p. 29.
144. C.O.55. 87. 18th January 1847—Grey to Campbell.
145. The growth of this attitude was reflected in the passing of a series of Factory Acts in 1802, 1819, 1833, 1842, 1844 and 1847.
146. W.L. Mathieson, *British Slave Emancipation,* pp. 106-17; W.L. Mathieson, *The Sugar Colonies and Governor Eyre,* p. 4; P.J. Barnwell and A. Toussaint, *A Short History of Mauritius*, pp. 156-64.
147. C.O.54. 235. 21st April 1847—Tennent to Grey. Immigration in these Colonies was at the "public cost," but this fact is not particularly significant since the planting body comprised the bulk of the tax- paying population.
148. C.O.54. 235. 21st April 1847—Tennent to Grey. Dispatch No.7.
149. C.O.54. 235. 21st April 1847—Tennent to Grey; C.O.54. 239. 11th October 1847—Torrington to Grey.
150. "We would propose to furnish the Governor with copies of the papers which have been presented to Parliament on the subject of Coolie labourers in Mauritius and the West Indies, and to call his special attention to this subject." Page 29 of the Committee's report.
151. C.O.54. 238. 5th August 1847—Torrington to Grey.
152. *Ibid.* (encl.).
153. C.O.54. 250. 15th August 1848—Torrington to Grey.
154. *Ibid.* An enclosed report by Tennent claimed that the only effect of the revolt upon the flow of labour was that immigrants stayed away from the Northern routes. Instead, they followed the coast down to Colombo and then took the main road to Kandy.
155. C.O.54. 250. 15th August 1848—Torrington to Grey; C.O.54. 258. 13th April 1849—Torrington to Grey.
156. C.O.54. 258. 13th April 1849—Torrington to Grey.
157. *Ibid.* Of the 2,584 cases, 1,170 were withdrawn on a compromise being reached "the wages being in most instances paid after much delay and difficulty." In 200 other instances "about a fourth part of the claim was paid." The Police Magistrate of Kandy, Mr S. Hanna, supported Torrington's view that the revolt had no effect on the Indian immigrant and observed that "the rebellion had no influence whatever in inducing the Malabar coolies to leave the estates through fear." C.O.58. 258. 13th April 1849—Torrington to Grey (Encl.).
158. C.O.54. 240. 12th November 1847—Torrington to Grey. In this dispatch Torrington also discussed the prospects of getting Chinese labour to emigrate to Sri Lanka. Hong Kong, Amoy and Singapore were listed as possible sources of supply—particularly the last named. Since Malabar

labour was not then in short supply, the Governor suggested that the Chinese, if brought in, would have to be used, not on the plantations, but for the purpose of rebuilding irrigation works, clearing tanks etc. To induce them to settle, however, they would have to be given land, and this the Government could not do, owing to a "lack of surveys, existing litigation and the difficulty of ascertaining what was Crown property and what was not." Moreover, unlike the Indians, the Chinese would have to be brought over at State expense and this the Government could ill afford.

159. The Third Report on Ceylon. B.P.P. of 1851, Vol. XXI. Tennent's evidence, p. 275. This suggestion gave, as Dr K.M. de Silva puts it, "a diabolical twist" to Tennent's earlier proposal. Matale and Kurunegalla were heavily settled by the Kandyan Sinhalese and were far from the "deserted" lands of the north-central areas. K.M. de Silva, *Social Policy,* p. 261.

160. The Third Report of the Select Committee on Ceylon. B.P.P. of 1851. Vol. XXI, p. 275.

161. For a broad description of these events, see L.A. Mills, *Ceylon under British Rule*, pp. 200-2.

Chapter 3

The Approach to a Publicly-Assisted Immigration—1851-1861

The Economic Background

Though the forces of world depression began to ebb in the middle of 1849, the process of recovery was somewhat retarded in Sri Lanka. Political disturbances and the impoverished state of the revenue had prevented Governor Torrington from satisfying the demand for a greater expenditure on the transport system, hence costs of production on the coffee estates tended to be higher and profits rather lower than they might otherwise have been.

On the other hand, the coffee enterprise emerged from the slump a far more efficient industry. Adversity, it appears, had made apparent the virtues of managerial economics. The useless and wasteful expenditure of former times, the evils resulting from inexperience in the art of cultivation, and the all too frequent ignorance of the importance of proper soil and climate, which had led so many to bankruptcy, were no longer characteristics of the average plantation.[1] It is no exaggeration to say, wrote Tennent, "that there is not a single well established principle which now guides the management of estates, and the conduct of their proprietors, that was not preceded by a directly opposite policy prior to 1845. Observation has since discerned the true tests of soil and aspect, former delusions as to high altitudes have been exploded, unprofitable districts avoided, unproductive estates abandoned; and in lieu of the belief that a coffee bush, once rooted would continue ever after to bear crops without manure, and to flourish in defiance of weeds and neglect, every estate is now tended like a garden, and the soil enriched artificially in proportion to the produce it bears. Expenditure has been reduced within the bounds of discretion; an acre of forest land can be brought under crop . . . for one-tenth what it cost in 1844."[2]

Upon a section of the planting community the depression conferred yet another advantage. Some—obviously the more optimistic—had bought estates at low prices when the slump was at its worst. With the upswing, these plantations, freed at one stroke from the load of debt under which they had been struggling, created anew as it were for a mere trifle, became profitable to the new purchasers and a scale of production which had been totally inadequate to meet the charges on the previous burden of debt became remunerative when those charges ceased.[3]

Fair prices and the continued improvement of the coffee industry characterised the administration of Sir George Anderson, Torrington's successor. But Anderson had been sent out with strict orders to exercise economy, and he only too faithfully obeyed his instructions. Despite a mounting revenue surplus, £85,825 between 1850 and 1854, expenditure on the roads was increased by only a few thousands of pounds per annum, at a time when the acreage under coffee was expanding rapidly. Trenchant criticisms of Governmental policy were not long in coming, but with no satisfactory result. Their protests unheeded, the indignant planters then formed the Planters' Association (1854) to give effect to their complaints regarding the deplorable state of the roads and the failure to construct extensions and spur lines.[4] The Association was barely a year old before failing health led to the resignation of Sir George Anderson, and Sir Henry Ward assumed control of the Administration.

Coffee Prices[5]—Plantation		**Acreage under Coffee**	
	s.		
1850 -	44 per cwt.	1850 -	59,919 acres
1851 -	44	1851 -	64,321
1852 -	41	1852 -	57,885
1853 -	43	1853 -	69,996
1854 -	44	1854 -	70,715
1855 -	44	1855 -	85,505

Sir Henry Ward appeared on the scene at a peculiarly opportune moment, "the man and the hour," it has been said, "arrived together."[6] Coffee was on its feet again with rising prices and frugal methods of production opening up for it a brilliant prospect. All that was needed was encouragement of the proper sort and this encouragement Ward provided. Accepting the simple economic truth that the fortunes of coffee and the condition of the Island's finances were inextricably interwoven, the Governor turned with enthusiasm to the construction of roads, the encouragement of immigration and the pushing of land sales. In an incredibly short time the acreage under coffee saw an immense expansion, exports increased, the general revenue went up, and the Colony enjoyed an era of hitherto unequalled prosperity.

Coffee Prices—Plantation[7]

1856	46 per cwt.
1857	51
1858	53
1859	54
1860	68½
1861	72½

Acreage under Coffee[8]

1856	137,762 acres
1857	154,958
1858	154,958
1859	118,266
1860	119,883
1861	135,422

Land Sales[9]

Year	Acres Sold	Amount Realised	Year	Acres Sold	Amount Realised
1850	1,862	£2,603	1856	11,656	£22,805
1851	939	1,695	1857	19,795	37,047
1852	1,848	2,499	1858	15,752	33,425
1853	2,200	3,324	1859	23,447	38,589
1854	5,392	9,927	1860	33,660	51,628
1855	7,286	16,410	1861	28,329	44,166

Though prices within the period 1850-60 were not as high as those fetched in the early 1840s, the cost of production had fallen so greatly that plantation coffee selling at 44s. the cwt. is said to have brought in handsome profits.[10] The gradual rise in prices above that level after 1856 must therefore have been productive of enormous returns. Unfortunately, this point cannot be further elaborated since hardly any statistical information relating to earnings or investments is to be had, but the official correspondence of the decade often refers to the former as being high, and tells us that this led in the early 1860s to the influx of a great quantity of capital.[11]

If 1850-1860 was a period of prosperity, it was also one in which the supply of labour sometimes fell extremely short. The long-term view which depression had forced upon the planters had bred a more liberal attitude towards the Indian worker and the rising acreage under coffee had created an increasing demand for his services, but time had to pass before the injustices of the previous decade were forgotten and confidence in the good intentions of the planting body built up anew. Throughout the 1850s the Indian worker showed a reticence to voluntarily seeking employment in Sri Lanka and the annual rate of immigration came to be governed by the negative repulsion of Indian agricultural conditions rather than the positive attraction of the relatively high wages available in the colony. When harvests were bad, as they were in 1852 and between 1854 and 1858, supplies showed a marked increase; when food was plentiful, as it was in 1851 and 1853, supplies showed an immediate decline. Moreover, after 1858 a new and complicating factor began to exert an influence upon the flow of labour. The Government of Madras spurred by the frequency with which famines occurred in the Presidency, embarked upon a programme of agricultural improvement which embraced the construction and restoration of irrigation facilities.[12] The offer of employment—virtually on their own doorsteps—was quickly accepted by many who would otherwise have made the journey to Sri Lanka, and even induced a larger proportion than usual of those already in the Island to return home at year's end; hence the sharp fall in arrivals and the abnormal increase in departures in 1859. However, the scope of the public works in India do not appear to have been wide enough to absorb all who sought employment there, for within a year the total number of immigrant entries had once again risen above 50,000 per annum.

Arrivals[13]

Year	Men	Women	Children	Total
1850	37,1155	1,818	499	39,442
1851	28,228	1,003	273	29,500
1852	50,843	2,226	770	53,839
1853	36,582	2,042	653	39,277
1854	54,014	9,006	4,301	67,321
1855	51,979	5,018	1,270	58,267
1856	59,263	6,342	2,399	68,004
1857	60,048	6,974	2,298	69,320
1858	75,172	16,172	4,718	96,062
1859	32,397	5,797	1,911	40,105
1860	41,906	8,946	2,093	52,945
1861	43,147	8,175	2,110	53,432

Departures

Year	Men	Women	Children	Total
1850	20,758	548	303	21,609
1851	16,775	419	191	17,385

1852	22,564	780	284	23,628
1853	27,129	981	378	28,488
1854	21,640	1,422	479	23,541
1855	23,130	573	313	24,016
1856	32,148	1,502	659	34,309
1857	36,887	2,278	772	39,937
1858	45,747	3,277	1,416	50,440
1859	43,900	3,722	1,196	48,818
1860	21,279	1,874	721	23,874
1861	32,636	3,487	1,079	37,202

The Social and Economic Condition of the Plantation Worker

The risks attending immigration appear to have been scarcely less hazardous in the 1850s than they had been in the previous decade. Arrivals for the period under review totalled 667,514 and departures 373,247, leaving 294,267 or 44% to be accounted for. Ferguson holds that mortality in the 1850s was still around 25% and that unenumerated departures and settlement were represented by the remainder.[14] Sir Charles MacCarthy, Governor from 1860-1863,[15] inclined to the view that deaths were somewhat lower, and in July 1861 estimated that up to that time the average death-rate amongst the immigrant population stood at around 20%[16] Settlement in the Island had not increased perceptibly over that of the earlier decade and was thought to be still about 5% of the total emigration between 1850 and 1860. On the other hand, the annual number of unenumerated departures is said to have fallen markedly with the enforcement of a Passengers' Act in 1853. A stricter accounting of entries and exits was thus in force for at least seven years of the period under consideration and it is not unreasonable to suppose that unenumerated departures were somewhat lower than they had previously been. It is evident therefore that the number of Indians who died each year in Sri Lanka must still have been uncommonly high and it is easy to understand why both Colonial Office and local Administration were disposed to consider this a problem of the utmost importance.

If deaths on the homeward journey had been a characteristic of the 1840s the reverse was true ten years later; from all accounts more now died on the way in or as a result of the inward march. The chief author of what one Governor was moved to describe as "this frightful mortality" was a novel method of recruitment employed throughout this period which was quite unlike anything encountered in the past.

When economic conditions began to brighten in mid-1849, renewed planting activity brought with it a quick increase in the demand for labour. The prejudice which past events had created against working in Sri Lanka, however, kept immigration at an uncomfortably low level and it rapidly became apparent that the old method of recruiting the Indian after he had arrived in the Colony would have to be superseded by some new expedient. Refused assistance by the Government, the planting body moved to solve the problem on its own, and capital now embarked upon the almost unprecedented task (for Sri Lanka) of devising ways and means of actively seeking out labour. Of these efforts was born the "Coast Advance System" of recruitment.

The principle upon which the Coast Advance System operated was a relatively simple one. First, an Overseer or Kangany, as he was also designated, contracted to supply a planter with an agreed number of workers. He then received a small sum of money with which to pay advances and purchase rice and other simple necessities for the promised labour force while on the march. With this he left for India, made arrangements with a gang and brought them up to the plantation. The expenses incurred on the journey—usually under 8s. per head—were entered up in the estate "Debt Account" as a charge against the Kangany and his recruits and represented the debt with which every labourer started his life in Sri Lanka.

This account was brought to a close at the end of the season or contract when wages were paid in a lump sum, less the amount originally advanced.[17] The Kangany, whose function it was to manage the workforce, was usually paid between one to two shillings a head on every immigrant who arrived under his influence and £1 per month in addition as a token recognition of his Kanganyship.[18]

The Coast Advance System grew so corrupt that it was soon "characterized by fraud and speculation."[19] The Kangany early discovered that he could spend only a fraction of the original advance by skimping on the food provided on the march. To such a fine art did he develop his technique, that it was estimated that only one third of the amount charged was actually received in kind by the labourer, while the remainder went to swell the private fortune of the Kangany. Again, the Kangany made no allowance for those who through exhaustion or ill health found it difficult to keep pace with their companions. The longer the gang was out on the road, the higher the cost of their food; so the Kangany in order to extract as much profit as he could from the transaction, pressed on with all possible speed. The sick, when they could no longer struggle on, fell behind their fellows and stumbled away into the bordering jungle, there to die, unless by good fortune they were picked up by the road patrol.

The Kangany had no pecuniary reason to regret that a proportion of those who started out from India were unable to complete their journey to the hills. Since only a part of the employer's advance was in fact expended on the immigrant, he could afford to bring over more than the number required and thus make up for the wastage on the march.[20] If a larger number than that contracted for ultimately survived, jobs for the surplus could usually be found on neighbouring estates, but if such employment was not forthcoming the Kangany had nothing to lose as there was no law whereby arrangements made with a worker in India could be enforced in Sri Lanka.[21]

There can be little doubt that the Coast Advance System had disastrous effects upon incoming labour. The official correspondence of that time refers often to its evils and on occasion specifically draws attention to the staggering mortality that it produced. Hundreds are said to have died upon the roads, and those who did not, to have arrived on the plantations in so fatigued and emaciated a condition that many were quite unable to work.

> . . . it is no exaggeration to say that many hundreds of these poor creatures perish annually from want and disease, in spite of the precautions taken both by the Government and individual planters who send over their Kanganies [native overseers] with money sufficient to provide their labourers with rice for the road; though these advances are notoriously misappropriated or the coolies could not reach the planting districts in the state of extenuation which is almost universal.[22]
>
> . . . gangs of coolies . . . are decimated by sickness and fatigue during the long journey from Manaar to the Central Province. . . The coolies do not get the benefit of one third of the advance charged to the employer. Hundreds die of actual starvation upon the road.[23]

If the inherent weaknesses of the Coast Advance System were such as to conduce to an increase in human suffering, the facilities available on the overland march from the coast to the coffee districts in the first half of the 1850s did little to allay its effects. Such evidence as there is suggests that the rigours of the Northern route were even more exacting during these years than they had been a decade earlier. As long as Anderson was Governor no improvements whatever were effected on the road, and the few facilities there already were, barely maintained in a decent state of repair.[24] With Ward's arrival considerable advances were made. Seeing that immigrant labour was beginning to show a preference for the route via Mihintale over that via Puttlam, he took immediate steps to improve conditions upon the former. From 1856 onwards tiled sheds were erected in place of the old thatched structures and in the same year a rest-shed at Kandy and another at Mahiyawa were put up at the joint expense of the Government and the planting community—each party contributing a total of £300.[25] Yet, these measures though valuable in themselves, were hardly calculated to produce much life-saving. What was needed was a strict control of the Kangany system and the provision of adequate medical aid along the entire line of march. Neither of these essentials appeared in the period under review. Anderson did not consider them, and Ward attempted instead to replace the Coast Advance System with a Government operated immigration scheme. The plan was not a success and private recruitment was re-established after two years. Since this ill-fated experiment sought amongst other things to divert the flow of immigration from Manaar to Colombo, on the grounds that labour could then march up to the hills on the main Kandy highway—a well-built road along which water and provisions were easily obtainable—it was not thought necessary to invest heavily in the provision of medical facilities along the overland route. As a result, all that the Government did between 1855 and 1860 was to expend an annual average of a mere £327 on the "cooly hospitals between Dambulla and Manaar."[26] These sums were too limited to do much more than marginally improve the restricted facilities provided by Campbell, and it will not be far wrong to say that over the greater portion of the 1850s the immigrant journeying to the hills had to depend in part upon amenities which were grossly inadequate, and in part upon his own good luck—largely, it would appear, upon the latter.

The hazards of the journey between India and Sri Lanka were further increased by the wide-spread practice of over-crowding the vessels on which the immigrants travelled. Ships which sailed from India were required by the law of that country to carry no more than two passengers per ton, but this was by all standards of hygiene and sanitation an excessive number and could not have conduced to either the comfort or good health of the passengers. On the return journey conditions were even worse. The Indian enactment did not apply in Sri Lanka and there were in addition no local restrictions on the numbers ships were allowed to carry. The appalling results of this shortcoming can barely be imagined until one is given the examples of the schooner "Colombo," a vessel of

29 tons, which carried as many as 201 persons on a single trip; and of another of 80 tons which frequently sailed with over 400 people on board.[27]

Attempts were made to curb these abuses by Ordinance in 1853, 1857 and 1860, but partly because of the lack of personnel to enforce them and partly because of deficiences in the laws themselves, the enactments were unable to exercise an effective control, and the overcrowded vessel remained a characteristic of the 1850s.[28]

Of those who remained after the harsh journey to the hills had taken its toll, a proportion were so weak and diseased that they found employment impossible to get. With no funds of their own, and with the Kangany unwilling to provide any further support, these "masterless men" went into the neighbouring towns and there begged about the streets, "dragging out a miserable existence . . . sleeping under galleries or verandahs of uninhabited buildings or lying in the open air along the thoroughfares," until at death's door, they were picked up by the police and admitted to a hospital—there usually to die.[29]

The more fortunate survivors, whose fitness to work brought immediate employment, found better conditions on the estates than had their compatriots of earlier times. Accommodation was still wretchedly inadequate, the best "line rooms" measured 12ft. by 12ft., and housed an average of ten labourers apiece,[30] but in some respects circumstances had generally been improved. The long-term approach to coffee culture which the depression had forced through to the planting community, appears to have made them conscious of their dependence on an uninterrupted immigration, and to have led them to abandon the previously common practice of physically maltreating labour. For the same reason wage-default was no longer a frequent occurrence. What the planter now most wanted was that his estate should acquire a reputation for fair treatment and prompt payment since experience had proved that this was the best guarantee of a regular labour supply.[31] Moreover, the recent economies in cultivation, fair prices, and relatively handsome profits, had made the shortage of capital a thing of the past. The economic incentive to raise production by driving labour and the desperate need to save on funds by withholding wages were thus removed at a time when a new appreciation of labour's role was beginning to emerge. In other words, circumstances not only compelled the planter to reappraise his attitude to labour—they made it a luxury he could well afford.

This general change for the better on the part of the average planter does not of course, exonerate him from all responsibility for the dire effects of the Coast Advance System. It could not have been very long before employers became aware of what was taking place, yet despite this, they persisted in their patronage of that particular method of recruitment. In a direct sense they could claim to be guiltless, but indirectly they were themselves an integral part of a system "so devised as to almost exculpate the actual employer and throw the blame on the middleman who, whatever his sins, was blessed by the employers themselves for reasons of expediency."[32]

With a larger and generally less healthy population arriving in the Island each year, the need for medical aid on the plantations became more urgent. Despite the increasing prosperity of the times, however, no steps appear to have been taken in this direction and the task of providing almost the totality of available care continued to devolve upon the Government.[33] Official policy in this sphere was itself far from satisfactory. Anderson, in keeping with his instructions to husband revenues, again did nothing, while Ward, blessed with an overflowing treasury and more keenly aware of the shortcomings of the Coast Advance System—which in the interim had had time to develop its more baneful characteristics—spent less heavily on immigrant medical aid than he might have done. This shortcoming was partly due to the Governor's desire to by-pass the Northern road altogether by introducing a steamship service to Colombo, but the scheme proved a failure and the overland route remained the main artery between India and Sri Lanka. A result of Ward's experiment, however, was that less than half of the £8,507 expended on the construction and repair of hospitals between 1855 and 1860 went to institutions frequented by immigrant labour, i.e. £280 and £278 to the Matale and Gampola hospitals respectively, £1,638 to the "cooly hospitals between Dambulla and Manaar," and £1,998 to the Bogambara hospital.[34] The first three were part of the medical arrangements introduced some years earlier by Governor Campbell and the last named the old Friend-in-Need Society hospital in Kandy which the Government took over and enlarged in 1860.[35] Thus, while it is clear that Ward was able on the whole, to effect some improvements in the medical facilities available on the Northern route, it is equally evident that the changes he wrought were not particularly far-reaching. Certainly they were far from sufficient to counter the deadly effects of the Coast Advance System.

Though it is possible to explain why the Administration fell short in its provision of aid to immigrants on the march, no excuse can be found for its failure to increase hospital accommodation in the planting areas. The addition of a wing to the hospital in Kandy was the sole contribution made at a time when the acreage under coffee was spreading with unprecedented rapidity. The new districts open for cultivation after 1855 remained unprovided for in the medical sense and the immigrant population labouring there were in all probability the most neglected in the Island. This failure of the Government to accompany the expansion of the coffee industry with a parallel extension of the hospital system was one of the most serious defects of official policy in the 1850s, for increasing entries at medical institutions elsewhere showed that the prejudice against western medicine was beginning to abate.

Of conditions within the few hospitals available to the immigrant some information exists, but such as there is does not redound to their credit. Ward, writing of the hospital in Kandy, described it as "most horrible and loathsome," and there is no reason to believe that the hospitals at Matale and Gampola were any better.[36] Comparatively large sums were set aside for the provisioning of the existing hospitals during Ward's administration, i.e. £14,649 between 1855 and 1860, but the immigrant case-rate still remained distressingly high. At Kandy hospital for instance, death claimed 36.7% of the 1,571 "Malabar" patients admitted in 1859, and over the entire five year period from 1st January 1855 to 31st December 1859, of 14,958 immigrants who sought medical aid at all hospitals open to them, deaths amounted to 3,047—a case rate of 28%.[37] The latter, though high in an absolute sense, stands in sharp contrast to the case-rates of a decade earlier and is a clear indication that large numbers must now have been entering hospital long before their ailments reached an extreme condition.

For the high mortality in the hospitals explanations are not hard to find. A proportion of the patients were still being admitted "in extremis," being "cold and moribund when brought to the hospital and expiring soon after admission."[38] That this phenomenon was due partly to a deep-rooted prejudice against western medicine and medical institutions and partly to the immigrants' inability to afford the forfeiture of even a day's wages by being absent from the field has already been noticed. To these must now be added the effects of the Coast Advance System. The sick who fell away on the march and those who were too ill to find employment when they arrived in the planting districts were generally well past saving if and when they finally ended in a hospital.

As in the 1840s, it was again contended that the average estate labourer normally subsisted on a minimal diet, practicing the utmost self denial in order to maximise his savings. As a result he was laid open to a host of diseases, many of which proved fatal owing to his inability to resist them. While there is much in this argument, it cannot be given the same weightage as before. On most of the estates of the 1850s it had become the practice to issue the labour force with a monthly ration of rice, the value of which was deducted from their wages.[39] This was the planter's method of compelling the immigrant to eat enough to support life and enable him to get on with his work. By itself this measure was not sufficient to restore a man to perfect health and strength, but it must have gone far to retard the effects of self-induced starvation and thus to have reduced the incidence of disease previously attributed to that condition. Moreover, it also partly explains why mortality on the return journey to India was no longer as high as it had been a decade earlier.

Apart from being directly responsible for deaths on the roads and in the hospitals, the Coast Advance System is said to have made a further contribution to mortality in less obvious fashion. On arrival at Kandy the Indian immigrant who succeeded in securing employment was expected to undergo a great deal of labour as being "fresh from the coast." Many, however, were so weakened by the privations of the march, that though fit in appearance they were really in no condition to meet what was expected of them. Within a short time the strain proved too much and they fell victim to diseases they might otherwise have resisted.[40]

With the extension of the coffee areas into the higher altitudes after 1855, exposure to rain and cold also began to exact a heavy toll. Estate workers were usually poorly clad and frequent chills so undermined their health that some were soon beset with complications which no doctor could possibly cure.[41]

Of the diseases responsible for mortality in the hospitals little information is to be had beyond the single broad statement that deaths were due chiefly to dysentery, anasarca and diarrhoea. Observations have already been made as to the probable nature of the first of these ailments,[42] but the others require some comment.

Anasarca can hardly be described as a disease in itself. Defined as a "generalized infiltration of fluid into subcutaneous tissue,"[43] it is a condition which numerous illnesses can give rise to. It can occur for example, as a result of malaria and since the latter was endemic in Sri Lanka, it is very likely that some deaths from this cause were mistakenly put under the head of "anasarca." Most commonly it is to be found in neglected cases of hookworm infestation, and there are good grounds for believing that this parasite was responsible for a high proportion of anasarcous deaths. The circumstances under which the Indian labourer lived and worked were such as to actively aid infection by the hookworm. Manson-Bahr holds that "infestation is aided by indiscriminate defoecation, moist loamy soil, adequate shade and bare feet. There is special danger in badly used or badly constructed latrines and infected soils in plantations and gardens."[44] All of these conditions were present on the estates of the 1850s and there is every likelihood that a large proportion of the immigrant population were infested with the parasite. Normally, hookworm alone is seldom a fatal affliction, but where the patient is already undernourished or sickly, "any additional cause of malnutrition, such as the small though daily loss of blood caused by the hookworm may be sufficient to turn the scale against him."[45] Since a number of the estate work-force fell within the category of "undernourished and sickly"—the daily issue of rice notwithstanding—most deaths from anasarca could well have been due to hookworm infestation.

Diarrhoea again is a symptom rather than a specific disease and what is more, a symptom which may be due to a vast number of causes. Of those likely to produce a fatal result, malaria, hookworm, enteric, colitis, tuberculous ulceration of the large bowel and food poisoning were probably common on the estates of the 1850s. Malaria, the enteric fevers and hookworm infestations are often diarrhoeic in character, and a proportion of the deaths due to them may well have been entered under the head of diarrhoea. Of the others, i.e. colitis, tuberculous ulceration and food poisoning, it needs only to be said that the poor conservancy on the estates, the weakened constitution of many labourers and their tendency to minimize expenditure on food through the consumption of roots, tubers and herbs, some of which were extremely harmful, created an environment in which these ailments were likely to flourish.[46]

From what has been said about deaths along the roads and the causes of death in the hospitals, it becomes evident that the Coast Advance System had emerged as a new and important determinant of immigrant mortality. Its malignant effects were powerful enough to counter much of the good that might have resulted from the curtailment of factors which had previously produced adverse results, i.e. the decline in physical maltreatment and the prevention of self-starvation by the issue of rice on the plantations. To this it added its own afflictions, and apparently the sum of these pernicious influences was sufficient to sustain a high rate of labour mortality.

Throughout the years 1850-1861 wages remained steady at 18s. per month, despite a rise in the demand for labour and some marked fluctuations in supply. This cannot, however, be taken as an indication that planters had all the labour they required. There is evidence to show that the voluntary settlement of Indians in Sri Lanka was still taking place,[47] particularly after 1854, when an increasing number of women and children began to come over, but the size of the total work-force resident in the Island was far too restricted to make an impression on the market for seasonal immigrants. Moreover, the Coast Advance System had come to exert a novel control over the number of persons actually employed on the estates and in estimating the size of the annual labouring population one has in this period to consider not the total number of entries per year, but the number who arrived on the plantations in a fit condition to work. It is not surprising to learn from the official files that though wage rates continued unchanged, frequent labour shortages were still a characteristic of the plantation sector. This seemingly contradictory phenomenon can best be explained by considering the forces which governed the flow of immigration at that time. When famines were prevalent in India—and during the 1850s they were of frequent occurrence—those who could manage the journey normally set out for Sri Lanka, since what they had before them was a choice between certain starvation at home and a chance of survival in the Colony. The moment conditions improved or alternative employment was available large numbers preferred to stay behind rather than risk the increased hazards which the Coast Advance System had conferred upon the march to the hills. In circumstances such as these, where "negative repulsion" had replaced "positive attraction" the prevailing rate of payment lost much of its power to induce immigration. Other criteria had developed an influence over the immigratory process, which a mere increase in wages by a shilling or two could do nothing to offset. The total number who arrived in search of work each year represented the maximum the planter could expect to get at any reasonable wage and there was therefore absolutely no point in his raising the rate above 18s. per month. A massive increase in remuneration sufficient to overcome all conceivable objections on the part of the immigrant might, of course, had given the Island all the labour it wanted, but that was an expedient the planter could not afford.[48] The only feasible alternative before him was to reduce the risks of the journey to Sri Lanka by effecting a drastic change in that major impediment to immigration, the Coast Advance System. This, the planting community was not slow to see, and during the course of the decade their demands for a Government-assisted scheme which would replace the Kangany grew loud and insistent.[49] Until such a scheme was devised, however, they had no choice but to accept the existing situation and make do with the labour which the yearly traffic provided.

On last matter deserving of comment in this period is the striking change which had occurred in the role of the Kangany. In the early days of immigration he had been the elected leader of the labour gang on whose behalf he had made contracts with employers, and in whom he had had a personal interest since they invariably hailed from the same village. He was their spokesman, their supervisor, their arbiter and generally "in loco parentis" the repository of their trust. The Kangany of the fifties had in a sense changed sides. He was now the representative of the employer and functioned chiefly as a "collector" and "manager" of labour. The men he supplied on contract were not necessarily his kith and kin and the impersonal attitude he consequently adopted towards them removed the old tie between labour and its leadership. Basically the economic interests of the Kangany in both periods had also changed substantially. The earlier sort had a pecuniary interest in getting their entire gangs to the plantations, since they thereafter received from each member a small monthly payment. Provisioning for the journey was the responsibility of those who made it and it is reasonable to suppose that under normal circumstances they would have taken the precaution of ensuring that their stores of food were sufficient for the purpose. When provisioning became the function of the Kangany in the 1850s his economic advantage lay in both skimping on food and in completing the march in the shortest possible time, and unencumbered by personal ties and moral obligations he fell easily into the malpractices which characterised the unsavoury side of the Coast Advance System.

Policy and Legislation

Though difficulties associated with labour began to develop soon after the depression had ended, Governor Sir George Anderson chose for the most part to leave these problems to settle themselves. During his administration the growth of the Coast Advance System was permitted to continue unchecked and the opinions and requests of the planting community allowed to pass unheeded. When he acted, as he did on only one single occasion, it was at the insistence of the Indian Government rather than on his own initiative. This seeming lack of interest in the subject of immigration was partly a result of the general instructions the Governor had received prior to taking up his duties in Sri Lanka. Ordered to practice economy, he did so to such good purpose that at the end of his term of office some £85,825 had accumulated in the coffers of the Colony. Yet, this achievement—if it can be so described—was accomplished at the expense of general social and economic efficiency, and not the least to suffer was the Indian immigrant.

As the evils of the Coast Advance System became manifest in the 1850s the planting body came to realise that an increasing number of immigrants were accepting employment in Sri Lanka only when driven to it by extreme conditions at home. The significance of this new approach did not take long to get through to the planting community. With the acreage under coffee expanding rapidly and with the demand for labour increasing in proportion, it became apparent that a severe labour crisis was in the offing unless immediate steps were taken to improve facilities along the Northern route. These fears were heightened when it was learned that the Madras Government intended to embark upon an extended public works programme which, since it envisaged the employment of large quantities of local labour, would provide immigrants with just the incentive they needed to stay away from Sri Lanka even when bad harvests and famine threatened in India. A meeting of the planters was therefore called in Kandy on 7th October 1854 to consider ways and means of averting the impending disaster, and from its deliberations two demands emerged. The first called upon the Government to repair and augment facilities on the overland route and the second resurrected the old proposal that immigration should be officially assisted.[50] This last was taken up with great enthusiasm by the newly founded Planters Association, which went so far as to suggest that Anderson, who had previously served in Mauritius, should initiate in Sri Lanka the Government-sponsored system which operated in that country.[51]

Neither of these recommendations made the slightest impression upon the Governor. Doctrinaire considerations apart, the expenditure they would involve was sufficient to set him against them. The Northern route was therefore left to deteriorate and the subsidisation of immigration remained a remote and unattainable hope. For similar reasons of economy Anderson made no attempt to increase the number of hospitals or appoint the extra Magistrates and Protectors of Coolies suggested by Tennent and Grey. In fact, no extreme and dogmatic laissez-fairist could have "let things alone" more thoroughly than he, though it must be admitted that there is little evidence to show that the Governor was in any way a convinced supporter of that philosophy. An unimaginative adherence to Whitehall's instructions and a tragic ignorance of what conditions in Sri Lanka were really like, appear to best explain his lethargy. Being in failing health Anderson rarely ventured out on tours of inspection and there is reason to believe that he was not fully aware of the enervating effects of the Coast Advance System and of the connection between mortality and the relative scarcity of labour. One is forced to this conclusion, not only because the Governor failed on even a single occasion to describe the workings of the Coast Advance System in his reports to the Colonial Office, but also because when seeking to explain the high immigrant death-rate he omitted all references to the method of recruitment and travelling conditions. Anderson advanced the simple-minded argument that mortality was heavy since the Indian labourer was inherently prone to disease, "owing to a certain constitutional peculiarity and want of stamina in the Malabars, disease makes a rapid and fatal inroad in the system, with great tendency to disorganisation of the vital tissues, even under comparatively favourable circumstances."[52]

Misguided in this fashion, it is hardly surprising that the Home Authorities made no move of their own to alleviate the misfortunes of the immigrant. If Anderson had given them an inkling of the atmosphere of corruption and death which surrounded the process of labour recruitment it is most unlikely that Whitehall would have continued to advise the Governor to concentrate his energies on the amassing of a favourable balance. By 1854 the deficit induced by the depression had vanished and the Colonial Office if apprised of the situation in Sri Lanka may well have directed the Governor to utilize part of the surplus revenue in the interests of labour welfare. But Anderson's comparative silence on the subject of immigration and his failure to even transmit to Britain the gist of the resolutions passed by the planting community had evidently led Whitehall to believe that there was no longer any need to be particularly vigilant in matters pertaining to labour.[53]

Anderson's single essay into the field of immigration policy was thrust upon him in 1853 when the Madras Government called his attention to the gross overcrowding of the passenger vessels which carried returning immigrants over the Palk Straits to India. Since there was no legislation in Sri Lanka to control this abuse, the Indian authorities suggested that all immigrant traffic be brought under the terms of the Passenger's Act passed in Great Britain in 1852, according to which ships operating in the tropics were not permitted to carry more than one passenger for every 15 square feet of deck space. The proposal was not well received by the Executive Council in Sri Lanka. The members of the Council were agreed that the abuse had to be controlled, but they inclined to the view that the standards laid down in the Passenger's Act were too severe to be applicable to the short voyage between Sri Lanka and the neighbouring coast. Enforcement of the Act they held, would merely damage the interest of the planting industry since smaller loads would lead to a rise in fares and this in turn to a fall in immigration.[54] As an alternative it was suggested that a local Ordinance limiting ships to two passengers per ton displacement would provide the immigrants with adequate protection and at the same time preserve the interests of the planters. The Home Authorities, who in the meantime had also come to believe that the terms of the Passenger's Act were rather stringent, agreed to this compromise and the latter passed into law as Ordinance 8 of 1853.[55]

Though the standards of Ordinance 8 of 1853 left much to be desired, i.e. two passengers per ton was by any measure an excessive number, its enforcement would nonetheless have brought a considerable improvement in conditions aboard immigrant passenger vessels. In practice, however, the law proved to be little more than an ornament upon the statute book, partly because of lack of personnel to apply it, and partly because of deficiencies in the Ordinance itself, i.e. there was no provision for making offences punishable at the ports of disembarkation, where alone evidence of the excess of passengers was obtainable. It was difficult to substantiate charges against Masters of vessels in the absence of witnesses, since the passengers who could give evidence were in India, while the investigation was held in Sri Lanka. The overcrowded vessel thus remained a characteristic of the 1850s and Anderson's sole contribution to immigrant welfare ended in dismal failure.

On the 11th May 1855 Sir Henry Ward succeeded Anderson as Governor. One of those who believed in seeing things for himself, Ward travelled extensively during his first year in office and early grew acquainted with the problems associated with immigrant labour. Altogether unrestricted in the formulation of his policy by the exigencies of finance, the Governor was able immediately to embark upon a programme designed to improve conditions upon the overland route. Yet, though he rescued rest-sheds and medical stations from the dilapidation into which they had fallen in Anderson's time, Ward did not do sufficient to offset the ravages of the Coast Advance System. True, labour supplies rose considerably after 1855, but this was due to famine in India and not to any increase in confidence on the part of the immigrant that his chances of surviving the journey to the hills were likely to be higher. Moreover, as pointed out above, the Governor made no attempt to extend the hospital system into the newly opened coffee districts, and the rapidly growing work-force in those areas, many of whom were already weakened by the march from the coast, were without any form of medical aid. As a result, the immigrant death-rate remained distressingly high. Continued famine in India kept labour supplies at a favourable level, and Ward apparently saw no reason for an increase in the facilities afforded the Indian worker. Indeed he did not even think it necessary immediately to apprise the Colonial Office of the existence of the Coast Advance System and of the dreadful mortality that its operation entailed.

The planting community, though less complaining now than they had been some few years earlier, did not accept the complacency of official policy for long. Economically speaking there were sound reasons for them to feel disgruntled. Despite the stability of wage-rates the enervating effects of the Coast Advance System raised the real cost of labour since a proportion of every gang was incapable of hard and sustained work. Again, the planters were knowledgeable enough to realise that the increase in supplies was only a temporary phenomenon occasioned by adversity in India and most must have known that immigration was bound to decline when conditions in that country improved. It was feared that an alarming situation would then be created, for apart from the large quantities of labour required to satisfy the wants of the expanding acreage under coffee, it was obvious that the Government Public Works Department, which had also become a considerable employer of immigrants, would require an increased recruitment if it was to complete the extended road-building programme it had already embarked upon. Above all, a railroad from Colombo to Kandy, an amenity the planters had long demanded, had at last been sanctioned by the Secretary of State, and it was clear that the Company responsible for its construction would have no alternative but to depend on immigrant labour.[56]

With the prospect of a disastrous wage-spiral before them the planting community began to campaign once more for a Government sponsored immigration. The old demand for a system akin to that established in Mauritius was put afresh in 1857 in the shape of a request for a "Cooly Transport Company" and a "Cooly Agency" having a recognised status with the Indian Government and the power to recruit immigrant labour. In Ward, the planters found a willing listener, for with a heavy road-building programme upon his hands, and with a railway to come, the Governor was as apprehensive of wage increases as they. This coincidence of the Government's interest with that of private capital appears to have convinced the Governor that he could dispense with the advice of the Colonial Office. Without any reference to Whitehall, and on his own conviction that the time had arrived when "a certain amount of Government assistance in aid of private enterprise might be given, as had been done in many other colonies," he set aside £10,000 from the surplus revenue "to be advanced to the Cooly Transport Company, or employed in such a way as the Government found expedient for the purpose of promoting immigration."[57] The only condition attached to this grant was that the Planters' Association would have to subscribe the remainder of the funds needed to put the plan into effect. But the Association positively refused to do any such thing. Heartened perhaps by the partial concessions already made, and aware that the Administration had as much to fear from wage increases and labour shortages, the planters attempted to coerce the Government into meeting the costs of the entire scheme on the grounds that this was a "duty" of the State.

Had the planters got what they asked for, it would indeed have been a resounding victory. But Ward, though prepared to "intervene" and to "assist" was unwilling to subsidise immigration altogether. Instead, deciding on a strong line himself the Governor immediately withdrew his offer, in the hope perhaps that the Planters' Association could be made to see reason and change its mind. But the reaction to this move was a wholly unanticipated one, for the planters now began to oppose the construction of the railway for which they had fought so long.[58]

It was at this point that the Railway Company took a hand in the proceedings. The Construction Engineer, Mr. W.T. Doyne, was confronted by a problem similar to that faced by the planters and the Government. He too needed cheap labour and could see that competition in the existing market would only lead to a higher wage-bill. There was also the danger that growing antagonism to the railway could lead to its construction being totally abandoned. The situation was a delicate one, yet, it was not beyond Doyne's capacity to master it. He put forward the argument that the flow of immigration could be raised to the required level, not by improving conditions along the Northern roads, but by killing the Coast Advance System at its roots and eliminating the march altogether. Embarking immediately for India, the Engineer surveyed such sources of supply as Calcutta and Madras, and then submitted a memorandum to the Government in which was outlined a plan designed to stabilise wage-rates, prevent competition and increase the supply of labour.[59]

Doyne's memorandum quickly impressed Ward, but its implications were so far-reaching that the Governor could not possibly act without the advice of the Colonial Office. The resultant despatch—a long and detailed missive—is remarkable for a number of reasons. It was the first comprehensive document on the subject of immigration that the Governor had written in twenty-nine months; it was the first to carry a full description of the Coast Advance System and its disastrous effects; and it was the first to inform the Colonial Office of the financial ramifications of the unsuccessful experiment in setting up a Cooly Transport Company. The dispatch itself was most cleverly written, the arguments being so arranged that it made it difficult for the Colonial Office to reprimand the Governor for having acted so much on his own authority.[60]

Ward began by reporting to the Colonial Office that opposition to railway construction—a project which Whitehall had enthusiastically supported—had begun to grow in the Colony since the additional demand for labour it would create "was a source of considerable apprehension to the planters."[61] He then went on to describe how this labour was recruited through the Coast Advance System and having condemned its corruption and lamented its cruelty, declared that it was incapable of meeting the augmented demands being made upon it, "instead of seeing the supply of labour increase with the demand, it is admitted that the Kangany System has reached its utmost limits."[62] These were the circumstances, said Ward, which had led him to support the request for the establishment of a Cooly Transport Company. The Indian Government itself seemed disposed at times to discourage immigration to Sri Lanka and it was imperative that some better system be devised. His proposals had ended in failure, but since then the Railway Engineer had put up a plan of his own which seemed to offer a complete solution to the problem. "It appears certain that ample provision may be made for all the requirements of the Colony, without any increase in the rate of wages, provided proper steps be taken, with the assent of the Indian Government for the transmission of the coolies from the Interior to the coast, and for their conveyance to Ceylon at stated intervals. For the first a Ceylon Agency will be required with depots at the most convenient points of embarkation. For the second, two or more steamers which must be bought or chartered, with a central depot at Colombo, to which all coolies will be brought—thus avoiding the route by Manaar—and forwarded, as required, to smaller depots in the coffee districts."[63]

This was the essence of Doyne's proposals, about which the Governor had grown so enthusiastic. The details still needed to be worked out, and Ward proposed that the Government should provide one of the steamers and the Railway Company the other. The cost of setting up depots at Colombo and upon the coast could, he thought, be charged upon the general revenue but all current expenses such as the cost of running the Agencies, working the steamers, supplying medical attendance etc., would have to be met by a capitation tax of 3s. per head on the entire immigrant population in the Colony, whether employed on railway construction, on public works, or on the estates. This charge would be levied not only on those brought in through the official agency, but also on labourers recruited through the mediation of the Kangany, hence a cheaper alternative would not be available, and the Coast Advance System would collapse altogether. The Governor believed that Doyne's scheme would succeed in procuring at least 120,000 immigrants per year, and at 3s. per head this would provide an annual sum of £18,000, "a fund amply sufficient for the purpose." The funds themselves could be placed under the control of a Commission representing the Government, the Railway Company and the Planters, to which "subject to the checks of a Public Audit, and the concurrence of the Governor in Council in all general regulations," large discretionary powers could be given. In the concluding paragraphs of his dispatch Ward attempted to strengthen his case with two further arguments, only one of which was really valid and relevant. First, he emphasized that he was writing on behalf of "all the parties interested" since the Planters' Association had also agreed to support the scheme. This certainly was true, for the Planters' Association had declared in favour of the scheme with an alacrity they had every reason to show. Ward had called their bluff on the Cooly Transport Company and it was evident to the planters that a "free" Government sponsored immigration would never be theirs. Of the available alternatives, Doyne's elaborate proposals were by far the most advantageous. Under the Coast Advance System they paid nothing, but the real cost of labour was high and supplies inadequate; under Ward's plan for a Cooly Transport Company the Government was prepared to put up only £10,000 which was hardly sufficient to purchase and operate two steamers for a year, while they were expected to find the remainder; under Doyne's scheme they merely paid 3s. per employee and left it to the Government and the Railway Company to meet the rest of the charges.

Having established that all interested groups were behind him, Ward went on to his second argument. There could, he said, be no objections to the united request for an assisted immigration since "the principle of such legislation had been repeatedly admitted by Her Majesty's Government." Citing Australia, the Cape, and Mauritius as examples, the Governor pointed out that large sums had been voted from the general revenue of those colonies in aid of immigration, "the object there too, as in Ceylon, being to make the supply of labour a self-supporting system."[64]

The validity of this reasoning is difficult to accept. Emigration to Australia was part of a larger project to colonise the country, and in any case the emigrants sent out were not Indian plantation labourers. In Mauritius and the Cape a subsidised immigration had been permitted on special grounds, e.g. the long sea voyages involved, the abolition of slavery, etc. Ward's comparison was thus a rather foolish one, and seems also to indicate that the Governor was unaware of the correspondence which had passed between Tennent and Grey a few years earlier.

The Colonial Office appears to have been quite unimpressed by Ward's dispatch. Partly, this was due to an unfortunate coincidence which went far to weaken the Governor's case. Famine in India had reached unprecedented heights in 1858 and immigration to Sri Lanka in that year, at 96,062 arrivals, was the heaviest yet recorded. Neither the Public Works Department nor the estates were able to absorb all those who sought employment and ultimately the Government was obliged to appeal to the Railway Company to form its labour gangs somewhat earlier than anticipated in order to prevent untoward distress. Reports of this influx reached Whitehall shortly after Ward's dispatch had been received and apparently led Secretary of State Sir Edward Bulwer Lytton to believe that the Governor had tended to exaggerate the urgency for an assisted immigration. As a result his reply was mainly concerned, not with the details of the scheme, but with questioning the necessity for its very introduction. Drawing attention to what he had heard regarding labour supplies in 1858 Lytton called for an explanation, and in addition in what seems very like an expression of lack of confidence in the Governor's judgement, suggested that the views of the Executive Councillors might also be transmitted to him. The general principles on which Doyne's scheme was based were not questioned at length and Ward's ill-chosen examples justifying official intervention allowed to go unchallenged, but Lytton wondered aloud "whether Government should interfere with private enterprise," and there can be little doubt that the Home authorities were rather uneasy about encouraging such a project.[65]

In the meantime, certain that Colonial Office support would be forthcoming, Ward put his plan into the shape of an Immigration Ordinance and laid it before the Legislative Council.[66] Lytton's response must therefore have come as a shock, but it was not sufficient to undermine the Governor's confidence in either his own judgement or in the necessity for an assisted immigration. In reply he explained again that private enterprise in the immigratory process "had reached its limits"; that this had obliged him "to devote much thought to the subject," and that his proposals were thus not "hastily produced."[67] Of the views of the Executive Councillors he said nothing, but this does not necessarily mean that the Governor had anything to hide; it was probably Ward's way of telling Whitehall that it did not do to cast aspersions on a Governor's ability to arrive at a correct policy decision.

Fortunately for the future of the Immigration scheme, the draft Ordinance, which had already been sent off to London, was accompanied by an explanatory dispatch which put the undertaking in an entirely different light. In this second communication Ward laid greater emphasis than before on the sufferings of the immigrant and made it clear that the Immigration scheme was partly intended as a welfare measure. Having reiterated that the demand for labour was increasing, the Governor explained to the Colonial Office that though some 50,000-60,000 immigrants "driven from their homes by the failure of crops in particular districts, or by the discontinuance of Public Works" could be expected to seek work in Ceylon each year, the evils of the Coast Advance System were such that no permanent increase in this number could be expected unless something was immediately done to reduce the perils of the journey. "The first step therefore, towards any large increase in the supply of labour, must be to diminish the difficulties of transit—to widen the circle in India from which the immigrants come, by giving them the certainty of maintenance, and a passage on reaching the coast—and to hold out to them the assurance that, by landing at Colombo instead of Manaar, they will not only escape the hardships of the overland route, but find the means, at once, of forming engagements with the Government, the Railway Company and the Planters, which will ensure to them employment and food."[68] This, said Ward, was the *object* of the Ordinance, i.e. it was designed to increase the supply of labour and to serve as a welfare measure at one and the same time. The means proposed for its attainment were those he had described earlier, i.e. Doyne's plan, but the Governor had three further comments to offer. The first added further emphasis to the welfare aspects of the project by describing how immigrants were to be dealt with after their arrival in Colombo "Medical assistance and maintenance will be provided until arrangements are made for forwarding them up-country by the main Kandy road, upon which food and shelter in abundance, may be found. . . . A very large amount of human suffering will be put an end to by this arrangement, and a large sacrifice of life avoided." The second assured Whitehall that the general revenue would not have to bear the expense of moving labour from Colombo to their places of employment. "This will be accomplished without cost to the public, as the estates will have their Canganies in Colombo, to engage coolies upon their landing, and like the Government and the Railway Company, will become responsible for the maintenance of those who enter their service, until they reach their destination." The third, which dealt with the financing of the scheme, provided further information on how the funds were to be raised. It was not upon the maximum number of workers employed at any period of the year that the assessment of 3s. per head was to be levied, since this principle, though apparently the simplest, would in practice have worked unfairly, the planters paying as highly for 60-70 days' labour as the Government and Railway Company would have done for 200 or 300 days out of the 365. The estates required a maximum of labour only when in crop, retaining permanently about one third of the work-force then employed. Service in the Public Works Department and the Railway Company on the other hand was continuous and a man once trained was usually kept on as long as he could be induced to remain. In these circumstances it was considered equitable to take 120 days' labour as representing one labourer, and to base the assessment of 3s. per head upon the total number of days work done in the year, subdivided by that amount. Ten thousand days' work, for instance, would give eighty-three labourers, representing £12.9.0d. of assessment, and the total amount to be raised in this manner would run to between £18,000 and £20,000. Moreover, all immigrants irrespective of where they were employed would be required to pay for their return passages, and since some 50,000 persons at least were likely to go back to India each year, a further £7,500 would accrue to the fund. An annual total of about £27,500 would therefore be at the disposal of the Immigration Board, and this it was thought, would be sufficient to cover the working costs of the establishment.[69]

With regard to the provision of steamers, Ward considerably amended his earlier arrangements. The Government undertook to provide one, using as purchase money the £10,000 set aside in the previous year as a contribution to the Cooly Transport Company. The Railway Company was to advance a similar sum for the purchase of the other, but it was now decided that the money was to be considered a loan which the Colony would repay on the completion of the line. This meant in effect that the second steamer was also to be provided for out of the general revenue and the Governor's amendment represented a further commitment of public funds to the Immigration scheme.[70]

Finally, the Government also undertook to advance £20,000 to the Immigration Board during its first year to help set it on its feet. The money was to be recovered "when the Board got working," i.e. out of the first proceeds of the tax in 1860.[71] The Board was to be known as the "Immigration Commission" and was to be made up of four persons; one nominated by the Government and one by the Railway Company with the other two being selected by the Planters' Association and the Chamber of Commerce. The duties of the Commissioners covered the appointment of the Agents to be stationed in India, the control of the steamers, the drawing up of sailing time-tables etc.; in short, they were "to manage and superintend all affairs, matters, and things relating to the immigration of coolies."[72]

It is indisputable that in its final form the Immigration Ordinance made very considerable concessions to both the planting community and the Railway Company. One such was the re-adjustment in the method of taxation on the grounds that it would be unfair to assess planters on the maximum number employed each year. Insofar as funds were being raised to meet the expense of "importing" immigrants, it might well be argued that it cost just as much to bring in a labourer for sixty days' work as it did to bring in one for three hundred and that the planter ought therefore to pay on the maximum number he employed. If Ward's promotion of the Immigration scheme is to be taken as a reflection of his conviction that the additional labour needed by the Colony could be procured in no other way, the alteration in the mode of assessment suggests that, like Tennent before him, the Governor had accepted the dependence of the national finances on the fortunes of coffee and had come to realise that the extension of roads, the construction of a railway, and much else besides, would be quite impossible if plantation agriculture was not fostered and protected.

Ward's appreciation of the role of coffee was quickened by a factor with which none of his predecessors had to contend. This was the growth of the planting interest into something of a political pressure group. They had powerful connections in England, were strongly represented in the Legislative Council, had a strong influence over the local press, and possessed two vigorous organizations in the Planters' Association and the Chamber of Commerce.[73] To the natural sympathy which Ward must have had for the commercial aspirations of his fellow countrymen, was thus added the apprehension which any Governor in a Colony of Sri Lanka's size must have felt of the social and political consequences of opposing the bulk of a limited European community amongst whom he was constantly obliged to move.

The Railway Company appears to have done almost as well out of the Immigration Ordinance as the planting community. The immigration scheme had been their idea, and the general fear of a rise in wages had been occasioned largely by the heightened demand for labour they themselves were expected to create. Their offer of aid in the subsidisation of immigration through the provision of a steamer was thus a fair act of compensation for a situation they had helped to bring about, and was obviously made as an inducement to encourage Ward to embark upon the scheme. The Government's subsequent decision to repay the cost of the steamer, for which incidentally no reasons were given, was tantamount to putting the Railway Company in the same category as the planting community by extending to them a mark of favour for which the general public would have to pay. It is difficult to see why Ward took this step, for the Company did not request it. One possible explanation is that the Governor had decided to hand out inducements which would ensure the construction of the railway. The project was one on which he had set his heart, yet it had hung fire for a considerable length of time. Protracted negotiations had put off construction for a number of years and though work on the line was officially inaugurated in August 1858, little had since been done. By virtually agreeing to cut the company's costs by £10,000 Ward may well have hoped to persuade them to get on with the job.[74]

The Colonial Office took longer to rule on the Immigration Ordinance than it did on any other single piece of legislation emanating from Sri Lanka in the nineteenth century. Ward's first description of the scheme had been sent off to London on 27th May 1858 and the draft Ordinance had followed on the 15th November. It was not until the 8th June 1859 that Whitehall finally conveyed its official assent. This long delay reflected well the reluctance of the Home authorities to sanction so revolutionary a change as that envisaged by the Governor. One side of the scheme evidently appealed to them. Ward's description of the rigours of the Coast Advance System and his emphasis on the welfare aspects of the Ordinance appear to have done much to create a bias in its favour. The Land and Emigration Commission when reporting on the proposals noted with obvious approval that "one of its main objects was to divert the stream of immigration from Manaar, and so prevent the sufferings and mortality inseparable from . . . the overland route."[75] On the other hand, the extent of Government participation in the project seems to have led to a great deal of apprehension. An almost complete break with previous policy in this field was being touted and this was a step which the Colonial Office was naturally hesitant to take.

The final decision to allow the Ordinance probably owed as much to an interest in immigrant welfare as it did to an awareness of what refusal could mean to the country's economy. Ward had stressed that the future progress of the Colony was at stake, and in the concluding sentences of his dispatch had implied that all depended on the approach the Colonial Office would adopt, "if the one thing most to be dreaded in Ceylon be a general rise in the value of labour, which must be the inevitable result of increased competition, in a limited market, for a fixed supply, I shall not I am sure appeal in vain, to your statesmen-like mind, for an indulgent view of the measures to which the apprehension of this danger has led."[76] The truth of this reasoning was difficult to deny, for it was obvious that the country needed an increased labour supply as much as that labour required more adequate protection. The long delay in signifying assent suggests that the Colonial Office had looked for an alternative scheme, but had not found any which combined economic expediency and humanitarian principle as neatly as that put up by Ward. It seems that Whitehall was finally convinced that conditions in Sri Lanka were "special" enough to warrant direct assistance, though there were still some doubts as to whether the Government was not involving itself too deeply in the stimulation of the immigratory process. The extreme caution which characterised Lytton's reply is sufficient proof of how reluctantly the Secretary of State had decided to allow the Ordinance. He strongly emphasized that the scheme was being sanctioned "as an experiment worth trying" and impressed upon the Governor that he was "relying on his judgement" and expected him to exercise a "strict control." On the details of the scheme the Colonial Office had very little to say, and only one change of any significance to suggest. Since the Railway Company were "not to supply either funds or a steamer" it was thought that there was hardly any reason to assign to them the selection of one of the Immigration Commissioners. Ward was accordingly asked to look into the question, and the final discretion in deciding the point left to the Governor.[77]

However grudgingly enacted, the legalization of the Immigration Ordinance was a milestone in the history of labour policy. Hitherto, the accent had been chiefly on welfare and though a limited "intervention" had been mooted by Tennent, direct and open financial assistance had never been previously envisaged. These distinctions vanished in 1858 and official identification with the promotion and control of immigration became an established fact. Short of meeting the entire cost of the scheme the Government could hardly have participated more closely than it now proposed to do. It was represented on the Board of Immigration Commissioners, it was financially responsible for the setting up of labour depots in Colombo and upon the Indian coast, it was to bear the costs of purchasing two steamers, and it was to aid in overcoming the initial problems of the scheme with a loan of £20,000. The sum of these concessions amounted to a victory for the planting community. After some 17 years of campaigning they were at last to get almost everything they had asked for. Moreover, apart from their labour, they were also to have their railway and their roads, and part of the expense of providing for these amenities was to be met by a general public which had little or no use for any of them. The facts of Sri Lanka's economic and political development in the nineteenth century, i.e. the growing importance of the plantation as a revenue-earning asset, and the emergence of the industry's representatives as a force in the political arena, had begun to make concessions to the coffee interest both necessary and inevitable. The political significance of this phenomenon no doubt had greater meaning within the Colony than outside it, but its economic significance had penetrated the doors of Whitehall and won a degree of recognition which, since Lord Grey's time as Secretary of State for the Colonies, had shown a relatively rapid growth.

Ordinance 13 of 1858—the Immigration scheme, was put into force in July 1859.[78] By that date, one small steamer, the "Manchester" was at the disposal of the Board, and since she had cost only £5,500 it was decided to advertise for two more similar vessels.[79] Suitable ships, however, proved difficult to get and the Government was soon obliged to ask Mr George Wall, a member of the Legislative Council and one of the Immigration Commissioners, who happened to be visiting England, to extend the search to Europe.[80] But Wall too could find nothing satisfactory and ultimately it became necessary to ask the Secretary of State to commission an English company to construct two ships of the desired pattern.[81]

In the meantime, the "Manchester" was performing with indifferent success. Her first two voyages had been made at a loss "the time of her arrival and departure not being sufficiently known in the interior, and the permanency of the arrangement being doubted."[82] By the end of August these shortcomings had been rectified and she was bringing over a full complement, but just when it seemed that all was going well the supply of labour began to peter out.[83] Ward at first was inclined to regard this as a temporary setback and explained to the Duke of Newcastle, Lytton's successor, that the long delay in allowing the Ordinance had prevented the Immigration Commissioners from making proper arrangements for bringing labour from the interior to the coast. After confirmation was received it was found that in the meantime economic conditions had improved in India, a larger field of employment having been opened up by "abundant harvests and a more settled state of things."[84] Labour was therefore proving rather difficult to get, nevertheless, it was hoped that matters would improve in the future.

Ward's optimism was shortlived. By January 1860 it was evident that the state of the labour market had been radically altered by agricultural improvements and an extended public works programme in the Madras Presidency, and that "the superabundant supply of surplus labour, on which planters had hitherto relied" was no longer available.[85] As a result the total immigration in 1859 was 58% lower than that of the preceding year and it was estimated that labour supplies fell short of the Colony's requirement by 33%.[86]

The experience of 1859 made it clear that the setting up of an Immigration Agency on the neighbouring cost and the commencement of a weekly steamship service between the two countries, had done little to counter the prejudice against working in Sri Lanka which the Coast Advance System had created. From this it followed that marked fluctuations in labour supply could be expected with every change of economic conditions in India, until with the passage of time immigrants came to realise that the journey was no longer a hazardous venture. Time was a commodity neither the Government nor the planting community could afford to spare and it became imperative that some means of ameliorating the threatened crisis be immediately found. Two methods of achieving this were soon decided upon by Ward. First, he proposed that the recruiting of labour be extended to the northern sectors of the Madras Presidency. These districts had hitherto been untapped and it is probable that the Governor hoped that the indigenous population was too remotely situated to have heard either of the Coast Advance System or of the public works programme in the South. Second, noting that the flow of labour to Mauritius and Demarara, where three-yearly agreements were permitted, was still steady and abundant, Ward decided that similar long-term contracts signed in India for periods of service in Sri Lanka would do away with the prevailing fluctuations in supply.[87] Indeed, such long term agreements were a necessity if a widened recruitment was to meet with success, for the farther removed the prospective immigrant was from his future place of work the more likely he would be to respond to the guarantee of long-term employment.[88]

Since neither of these suggestions could be put into operation without the concurrence of the Madras Government an official communication requesting permission was addressed to the Governor of the Presidency late in 1859. The Indian authorities, however, refused to countenance either of the proposals on the grounds that they seemed "to militate against the interests of the cooly." The immigrant, it was held, must understand what it was he was entering into, and since supervision by Presidency officials in the outlying areas was difficult to ensure, there was every likelihood that "coolies . . . would be imposed upon by those employed to engage them" Again, it was thought that since Sri Lanka was only a trifling distance away there was no reason why agreements should be signed in India "unless it be that a better bargain with the labourer is anticipated than if he were in the Colony to judge for himself."[89]

Disconcerted by this reply, and fearful perhaps that his immigration scheme would collapse, Ward decided to replace negotiations with subterfuge. Suppressing all mention of the correspondence with the Madras Government, he rushed Ordinance 15 of 1859, according to which "contracts could be made in India for periods not exceeding three years for service in Ceylon, and for a period not exceeding one and a half years if the contract be made in Ceylon" through the Legislative Council, and attempted to persuade the Secretary of State to sanction the bill behind the back, as it were, of the Madras Government.[90] Newcastle, unfortunately, decided first to seek the opinion of the Secretary of State for India, who in turn consulted the Madras Government. With this, Ward's little plot was brought to light and though he was not censured for his patent dishonesty in "having deliberately withheld his correspondence"[91] with the Madras Government, Newcastle drew his attention to the objections voiced by the latter, and refused confirmation of the bill.[92]

Owing to this rather embarrassing series of events all questions pertaining to longer contracts and extended recruitment were allowed to rest while Ward remained as Governor. This no doubt was the easiest way out of an awkward personal predicament, but it did nothing to lessen the problems of the Immigration scheme. It meant in effect that the sponsors of the scheme had henceforth to rely on nothing more substantial than the hope that Indian labour would sooner rather than later, realise that the journey to Sri Lanka was no longer fraught with danger and voluntarily begin to come over in adequate numbers. Even worse was to follow. In March 1860 it was discovered that the "Manchester," which was as yet the only steamer in service, was "in a rotten condition" and that essential repairs would amount to £7,000, i.e. £1,500 above her purchase price. Ward rushed off a message to the Searetary of State asking permission to sell the vessel and replace her with two others,[93] but despite the connotations of this request there is evidence to show that the back of the Governor's optimism had been broken. At a private conference with the planting community, called that very month, both parties agreed that "the Ordinance . . . had failed to procure the advantages originally expected from it" and resolved "that it should be continued as an experiment for one year only from that date."[94]

The Immigration scheme limped on, with a singular lack of success, for a further fifteen months. True, the inward flow of labour in 1860 was considerably above that of 1859, i.e. 52,945 as against 40,105, yet this was far short of the effective annual demand. Fortunately for the planter, disagreements between the Government and the Railway Company had led to a staying of construction[95] and the supply of labour to the estates was larger than it might otherwise have been, but this was poor consolation for the failure of an Ordinance intended to solve conclusively the problem of scarcity. Ward was not on hand to witness the disappointments of the closing months of the year. In June 1860 his term of administration came to an end and he was transferred to India as Governor of Madras.[96] Before his departure, however, Ward made one last contribution to Immigration policy. Finding that the regulations governing the overcrowding of Immigrant vessels, as laid down by the Ceylon Act of 1853,[97] were less humane than those of a new bill in India, i.e. the India Act No. 25 of 1859, the Governor revised the law through the passing of Ordinance 1 of 1860. The Ordinance brought local legislation into line with the Indian law by decreeing that no ship "could carry more than one passenger to every four tons of the burthen of the vessel." On paper the new law was a marked improvement on its predecessor which had allowed two passengers per ton, but in practice it did little to check overcrowding since no provisions were included for making offences punishable at the ports of disembarkation. Hence, it still remained difficult to substantiate charges against Masters of vessels, as the persons capable of providing evidence were in India when the inquiry was held in Sri Lanka and vice-versa.[98]

When the "experimental" year decided upon by Ward and the planting community came to an end in March 1861, Sir Charles MacCarthy, the new Governor, found that the Immigration scheme had few supporters left. A deputation from the Planters' Association called for a quick annulment, and the Governor who was himself convinced that "not a single additional coolie labourer had been introduced into the Island under the provisions of the Ordinance," the only results of which had been "that the planting interest was burdened with a heavy and augmented taxation without any corresponding results," made early arrangements for its repeal.[99] When this was done by Ordinance 12 of 1861, MacCarthy expressed the opinion that the Immigration system had collapsed since it attempted "to substitute a complex scheme of Governmental machinery for the full action of private enterprise."[100] One can hardly consider this a particularly enlightened or impartial judgement, for it seems clear enough that the Immigration Ordinance was never given a really fair trial. To begin with, an integral part of the scheme, i.e. the purchase of two additional steamers to ply between India and Sri Lanka was not put into force since the ships ordered by the Board of Commissioners could not be delivered in 1860. Moreover, Ward's impulsiveness and mendacity had effectively ruled out the likelihood of long contracts and widened recruitment being introduced while he was Governor, and without these two features the scheme's chances of success must surely have been reduced. If MacCarthy had been less convinced of the virtues of private enterprise he might well have made a success of the Ordinance by resuming negotiations with the Madras Government and increasing the number of steamers on the Indian run, but the Governor appears to have been so antagonistic to such extended official intervention that he did not even consider the idea.

Apart from "intervention," MacCarthy also made it clear that he disagreed with Ward on the question of "assistance." He objected to public funds being used to support a scheme which would have "served only one class in the country" and suggested to the Secretary of State that in future it would be fairer to follow the principle that all special projects should either be self-supporting or else wholly financed by those whose interests were likely to benefit directly.[101]

Though the Colonial Office accepted the general lines of MacCarthy's proposals and agreed to sanction the repealing bill, it was not forgotten that the Immigration Ordinance had been partly a welfare measure. It was made plain to the Governor that the annulment of the Act did not mean that Whitehall would tolerate a return to the evils of the Coast Advance System. The details of future policy were left in MacCarthy's hands, but it was emphasized that positive steps should be taken to ensure that the welfare of the immigrant worker was not neglected.[102]

With these exchanges a distinct phase in the history of Immigration policy drew to a close. Viewed historically the Ordinance of 1858 marks the largest single step away from earlier policy objectives yet taken by the Colonial Government. The effect was heightened by the inaction which characterised Anderson's term and by the limited interest in the question displayed by Ward during his first years in office. Concentrated into a period of three years was a fury of activity the outstanding characteristic of which was the unprecedented degree of state intervention and assistance that it introduced. That this marked deviation from accepted practice should have occurred at a time when a disastrous shortage of labour was feared does more than explain the enthusiasm with which Ward advocated its acceptance, yet it also leads one to question the motives that underlay the welfare aspects of the Immigration scheme. Had the Governor been sincerely concerned with the shortcomings of the Coast Advance System, he would surely have attempted to redress them in the early years of his administration. Instead, having provided a modicum of relief, he did nothing more until it seemed that labour would run calamitously short unless something was quickly done to counter the hazards of the journey to Sri Lanka. Then, and only then did he inform the Colonial Office of the very existence of the Coast Advance System and suggest measures to alleviate its deadly effects. Ward, it would appear, was not interested in improving the lot of the immigrant on humanitarian grounds alone. To him welfare seems to have been something of an expedient; a necessary instrument without which labour supplies could not be increased to the levels required by an expanding economy. The closing words of his dispatch urging confirmation of the immigration scheme serve as a forceful reminder that the physical well-being of the immigrant was a means to an end, not the desirable end in itself that it should have been, "and if the one thing most to be dreaded in Ceylon, be a general rise in the value of labour, which must be the inevitable result of increased competition, in a limited market for a fixed supply, I shall not, I am sure appeal in vain to your statesmen-like mind, for an indulgent view of the measures to which the apprehension of this danger has led."[103]

Colonial Office policy in the 1850s showed a marked strengthening of a trend which had emerged in the closing years of the past decade. There was on the one hand, a concern for labour welfare which was still maintained; on the other, a growing readiness to intervene on behalf of British capital investment, first displayed by Grey, continued to develop until it reached a point where assistance at the public expense was sanctioned in 1858. Admittedly, Anderson's term of administration saw little "welfare" and less "intervention" but the one was not insisted upon since the Colonial Office were not informed of either the Coast Advance System or of its effects, and the other not encouraged since it was not at any time indicated that the future of capital investment was in any danger. Both these considerations, of course, figured prominently in the Ordinance of 1858, but though they went further than before, their acceptance was consistent with earlier practice and not therefore indicative of a new Colonial Office strategy. What was really significant in the immigration scheme was that it added a third principle to the foundations of Whitehall's policy. Until that time it had been thought that "intervention" was permissible if proof was forthcoming that refusal to allow it would endanger the economic prospects of the Island. Now the same reasoning was extended to cover the provision of "assistance" out of the general revenue. The decision no doubt was reluctantly taken, but the fact that the principle was finally admitted demonstrates that the Colonial Office approach was both elastic and practical enough to allow the only principle of the laissez-faire system which had not been hitherto encroached upon, to be gradually eroded when it became apparent that a strict adherence to it could no longer serve the economic interests of the Colony.

NOTES

1. C.O.54. 307. 6th May 1854—Anderson to Newcastle; C.O.54. 314. 24th January 1855—Anderson to Grey.
2. Tennent, *Ceylon*, Vol. II, p. 232.
3. Speculum, *Ceylon, Her Present Condition*, p. 115.
4. Ferguson, *Review of the Planting and Agricultural Industries of Ceylon*, p. 11.
5. Ferguson, *Ceylon Directory 1866-1868*, p. 284.
6. Ferguson, *Review of the Planting and Agricultural Industries of Ceylon*, p. 11.
7. Ferguson, *Ceylon Directory 1866-1868*, p. 284. For an explanation of coffee price levels in 1860 and 1861 see infra p. 117 and Chapter 4 footnote 4.
8. From the Ceylon Blue Book. The acreage returns show a sudden increase in the area under coffee in the Central Province in 1856, hence the dramatic rise in the acreage under the crop. The returns for that same area show a marked decline in 1860, which explains the sudden fall in total acreage in that year. Thereafter the figures show a consistently rising trend. These marked variations between 1856 and 1859 makes one doubt the accuracy of the returns for those years, as does the fact that an identical acreage is shown for 1857 and 1858. From 1861 onwards the statistics claim to be "complete," i.e. the returns for the North Western Province are included and the figure for the Central Province is no longer a hypothetical one.
9. The Ceylon Blue Book.
10. C.O.54. 335. 5th July 1858—Ward to Lytton; C.O.54. 338. 9th December 1858—Ward to Lytton; C.O.54. 344. 4th July 1859—Ward to Lytton; Ferguson, *Review of the Planting and Agricultural Industries of Ceylon*, p. 12.
11. C.O.54. 369. 27th May 1862—MacCarthy to Newcastle; C.O.54. 377. 15th August 1863—MacCarthy to Newcastle; C.O.54. 379. 1st September 1863—MacCarthy to Newcastle; C.O.54. 392. 17th August 1864—O'Brien to Cardwell; C.O.54. 392. 30th August 1864—O'Brien to Cardwell; C.O.54. 427. 15th September 1867—Robinson to Buckingham.
12. C.O.54. 346. 27th October 1859—Ward to Newcastle; C.O.54. 351. 13th January 1860—Ward to Newcastle. It was reckoned that under normal circumstances, i.e. when harvests in India were not exceptionally good or famines unduly severe, about 50,000-60,000 immigrants could be depended on to make the annual trip to Sri Lanka. C.O.54. 337. 15th November 1858—Ward to Lytton.
13. Ferguson, *Ceylon Directory 1867-1868*, p. 178; C.O.54. 521. 10th September 1879—Longden to Hicks-Beach.
14. Ferguson, *Ceylon—Summary of Useful Information*, p. 167.

15. Sir Charles MacCarthy served as Auditor-General of Ceylon from 1846 to 1850; as Colonial Secretary from 1850-1860, and as Lieutenant-Governor from 18th October 1850 to 27th November 1850 and 18th January 1855 to 11th May 1855.
16. C.O.54. 361. 22nd July 1861—MacCarthy to Newcastle. MacCarthy's estimate was given in response to a questionnaire drawn up by Florence Nightingale and sent out via the Colonial Office. However, since MacCarthy also put immigrant deaths in the hospitals at 20.3% one wonders whether he was confusing total mortality with the hospital case-rate.
17. C.O.54. 334. 27th May 1858—Ward to Stanley; C.O.54. 337. 15th November 1858—Ward to Lytton; Millie, op. cit.; Kondapi, *op. cit.*, pp. 29-30.
18. Millie, *op. cit.*, pages unnumbered.
19. C.O.54. 334. 27th May 1858—Ward to Stanley.
20. Roberts appears to overlook these aspects of the Coast Advance System when he suggests that its impact has been over- emphasized, *op. cit.*, p. 12.
21. C.O.54. 334. 27th May 1858—Ward to Stanley. Though of course the Kangany lost the money spent on the immigrant during the march. Supply, however, was usually short and jobs not hard to find.
22. C.O.54. 337. 15th November 1858—Ward to Lytton.
23. C.O.54. 334. 27th May 1858—Ward to Stanley.
24. A large shed erected at Dambulla in 1848, for instance, was allowed to fall into ruin. In Matale the planters acted on their own and erected a shed in 1854. See K.M. de Silva, *op. cit.*, p. 135.
25. C.O.54. 318. 15th November 1855—Ward to the Rt. Hon. W. Molesworth; C.O.54. 463. 28th February 1871—Robinson to Kimberley (Encl.).
26. B.P.P. of 1861. Vol. 40, pp. 144-45. The "hospitals" referred to were rest-sheds at which rudimentary medical aid was available.
27. C.O.54. 299. 20th May 1853—Anderson to Newcastle.
28. C.O.54. 299. 20th May 1853—Anderson to Newcastle; C.0.54. 371. 29th November 1862—MacCarthy to Newcastle. Similar unsatisfactory conditions were no doubt experienced by the immigrants of the 1840s, but it is likely that matters were not as bad then as they were some years later. Except for two years, i.e. 1845-1846, the total of incoming labourers did not top 50,000. Between 1850 and 1861 this figure was surpassed on eight occasions.
29. C.O.54. 311. 29th December 1854—Anderson to Grey.
30. Sabonadiere, *op. cit.*, p. 77.
31. When one considers that the large numbers who regularly moved between Sri Lanka and the neighbouring coast were drawn from a multitude of villages, it is easy to understand how, by word of mouth, the news that a particular estate had a "bad" reputation, spread rapidly in South India.

32. Kondapi, *op. cit.*, p. 11.
33. "Almost," since the planting community paid a total of £4,891.9.6d., over the 23 years 1837-1859, towards the maintenance of the Kandy Friend-in-Need Society. C.O.54. 351. 5th March 1860—Ward to Newcastle.
34. The rest of the appropriation was spent as follows: £3,000 on the New Civil Hospital, Colombo; £400 on Jaffna hospital; £300 on Trimcomalee hospital; £170.4.9d. on Galle hospital; £162.10.11d. on Colombo hospital and £280 on the Leper hospital; see B.P. of 1861, Vol. 40, pp. 144-45.
35. C.O.54. 351. 5th March 1860—Ward to Newcastle.
36. *Ibid.*
37. C.O.54. 361. 22nd July 1861—MacCarthy to Newcastle.
38. C.O.54. 311. 29th December 1854—Anderson to Grey.
39. Millie, *op. cit.*; Dickman, *op. cit.*, pp. 45-46.
40. Dickman, *op. cit.*, pp. 45- 46.
41. C.O.54. 311. 29th December 1864—Anderson to Grey; C.O.54. 361. 22nd July 1861—MacCarthy to Newcastle.
42. See Chapter 2 under "The Social and Economic Condition of the Indian Immigrant."
43. Usually manifest in swelling of the legs and feet.
44. P. Manson-Bahr, *op. cit.*, p. 791.
45. *Ibid.*
46. *Ibid.*
47. Ferguson, *op. cit.*, p. 167.
48. The offer of an extra shilling or two per month may well have enabled individual planters to attract a sufficiency of labour to their estates. Others, however, would then have followed suit and the danger of sparking off a wage spiral appears to have prevented even the most short-staffed from trying the experiment.
49. See section on "Policy and Legislation," pp. 93-94.
50. *The Colombo Observer* of 7th October 1854 and 18th October 1854.
51. *The Colombo Observer* of 14th December 1854. The Association proposed that the Government purchase two steamers to convey immigrants from India to Sri Lanka. No charge was to be made for the inward passage, but a fare was to be collected for the return journey. See K.M. de Silva, *op. cit.*, p. 136. I am obliged to Dr de Silva for these references.
52. C.O.54. 311. 29th December 1854—Anderson to Grey.
53. Under normal circumstances the Colonial Secretary could do much to keep informed a Governor who chose to remain in Colombo. But feelings between Anderson and Colonial Secretary Charles MacCarthy were so strained that the Governor seldom sought the latter's advice and at one stage preferred to by-pass the Colonial Secretary altogether when dealing with the Home Government.
54. C.O.54. 299. 20th May 1853—Anderson to Newcastle and (Encl.).
55. In August 1853 an amendment to the Passenger's Act was passed in

Parliament allowing Governors of Tropical Colonies "to declare by proclamation that ships sailing in the Tropics from any port within their respective Governments may carry passengers at the rate of one for every twelve square feet of the passenger deck if they be natives of Asia or Africa." Sri Lanka, however, was specifically mentioned as exempt from these arrangements where vessels in the Gulf of Manaar and Palk Straits were concerned. In those areas it "was lawful for the Governor and Legislative Council . . . to regulate by Ordinance the number of passengers to be carried on board." B.P.P. of 1852-53. Vol. V, pp. 333-34.

56. C.O.54. 334. 27th May 1858—Ward to Stanley.
57. *Ibid.*
58. *Ibid.*
59 *Ibid.*
60. *Ibid.*
61 *Ibid.*
62. *Ibid.*
63. *Ibid.*
64. *Ibid.*
65. C.O.55. 100. 29th October 1858—Lytton to Ward.
66. C.O.54. 337. 15th November 1858—Ward to Lytton.
67. C.O.54. 338. 9th December 1858—Ward to Lytton.
68. C.O.54. 337. 15th November 1858—Ward to Lytton.
69. The tax was to be collected in January each year, i.e. over a period of thirty days. It was thought that deception would be difficult since the Government could always examine the check rolls of the Estates and the Railway Company.
70. C.O.54. 337. 15th November 1858—Ward to Lytton.
71. *Ibid*; C.O.54. 338. 9th December 1858—Ward to Lytton.
72. C.O.337. 15th November 1858—Ward to Lytton; C.O.54. 338. 9th December 1858—Ward to Lytton.
73. See I.H. vanden Driesen, *Some Aspects of the Development of the Coffee Planting Industry in Ceylon 1823-1885* (Mss) Ph.d. London 1954, Chapter VIII, "The Economic Background to the Constitutional Reform Movement," pp. 499-503.
74. In earlier negotiations with the Railway Company, the Governor showed so marked a bias in its favour that an Under-Secretary of State was moved to remark that "it would have been more politic in Sir Henry Ward to show less endeavour in advocating the Railway agreement"—vanden Driesen, *op. cit.*, p. 431.
75. B.P.P. of 1860. Vol. 29, p. 53. Twentieth Report of the Emigration Commissioners.
76. C.O.54. 337. 15th November 1858—Ward to Lytton.
77. C.O.55. 100. 9th June 1859—Lytton to Ward.
78. The long interval which elapsed between the transmission of the Ordinance and its confirmation, appears to have created great anxiety in

the Colony. The crop in 1859 was expected to be a large one, and the planting body, probably convinced that the Secretary of State's delay could only be given an unfavourable interpretation, petitioned Ward to use a portion of the £10,000 earlier offered to the Cooly Transport Company and later set aside as a contribution to the Immigration scheme, to purchase a steamer which would be exclusively used to carry immigrant traffic. The Governor was well disposed to the suggestion and immediately sought Lytton's permission to buy the "Manchester," a small steamer which had often run between Colombo and the Indian coast. The Colonial Office dispatch allowing the Immigration Ordinance, however, arrived shortly afterwards and Ward therefore purchased the "Manchester" on behalf of the Immigration Commission. C.O.54. 343. 27th April 1859—Ward to Lytton; C.O.54. 346. 27th October 1859—Ward to Newcastle.

79. C.O.54. 343. 27th April 1859—Ward to Lytton; C.O.54. 346. 26th October 1859—Ward to Newcastle.
80. C.O.54. 345. 29th August 1859—Ward to Lytton.
81. C.O.54. 351. 15th March 1860—Ward to Newcastle.
82. B.P.P. of 1860. Vol. 29. Twentieth Report of Emigration Commissioners, p. 53.
83. *Ibid;* C.O.54. 346. 27th October 1859—Ward to Newcastle.
84. C.O.54. 346. 27th October 1859—Ward to Newcastle.
85. C O. 54. 351. 13th January 1860—Ward to Newcastle.
86. *Ibid;* B.P.P. of 1860. Vol. 29. Twentieth report of the Emigration Commission, p. 53.
87. *Ibid.*
88. Roberts, op. cit., p. 23, appears to overlook this point when he holds that lengthened agreements would not have affected supply. (p. 23) His further argument that there was "no real necessity" for a new "lengthened agreements" Ordinance since such agreements were permitted by the measures of 1847-48, is difficult to accept. The law in India (Act XIII of 1847) did not prevent a three year agreement being signed in that country, but such agreements would have no validity in Sri Lanka where the law (Ordinance 5 of 1841) only recognised contracts of a year's duration.
89. C.O.54. 356. 14th May 1860. Letter from Indian Office to the Secretary of State.
90. C.0.54. 351. 13th January 1860—Ward to Newcastle; C.O.54. 369. 26th April 1862—MacCarthy to Newcastle.
91. This remark was pencilled in by an Under-Secretary of State on the original dispatch—C.O.54. 351. 13th January 1860—Ward to Newcastle.
92. C.0.55. 103. 7th June 1860—Newcastle to Ward.
93. C.O.54. 351. 15th March 1860—Ward to Newcastle.
94. C.O.54. 363. 30th October 1861—MacCarthy to Newcastle.
95. The engineer in charge of construction declared in April 1859 that the cost of constructing a railroad to Kandy would amount to £2,214,000.

The original estimate on which the entire project was based, was £856,537. Construction was therefore stopped until these differences of opinion were inquired into. See vanden Driesen, *op. cit.*, pp. 433-38.

96. Ward did not in fact outlive the Immigration scheme. A month after his arrival in Madras he went down with a sudden attack of cholera and died on 2nd August 1860.
97. The Ceylon Act of 1853 had been extended in 1857 with its provisions unchanged.
98. C.O.54. 371. 29th November 1862—MacCarthy to Newcastle.
99. C.O.54. 363. 30th October 1861—MacCarthy to Newcastle.
100. *Ibid.*
101. *Ibid.*
102. The repealing Ordinance 12 of 1861 was passed by the Legislative Council in October 1861. Confirmation of the Secretary of State was dispatched on 12th January 1862. C.O.55. 106. 12th January 1862—Newcastle to MacCarthy.
103. C.O.54. 337. 15th November 1858—Ward to Lytton. Roberts, *op. cit.*, p. 20, holds a fairly similar point of view.

Chapter 4

The Return to Private Enterprise—1861-1870

The Economic Background

The economic boom which had characterised Sir Henry Ward's administration continued well into the following decade. Under the influence of high and stable prices the acreage under coffee showed a steady increase and the planting area expanded gradually into the higher elevations to the south-east of Kandy. With large surplus balances at hand, Governor Sir Charles MacCarthy was able to re-negotiate and complete the railway project, and by 1867 the line between Colombo and Kandy was officially opened to traffic. The coming of the railroad improved the prospects of the planting industry in dramatic fashion. The cost of transporting coffee from Kandy to Colombo fell by as much as 62%, i.e. from 52/6d per ton to 20s. and similar large reductions were effected in the costs of carrying manure, rice and other stores into the planting districts.[1] Again, a journey which had previously taken eight to ten days, during which "the coffee was subject to the most serious injury to quality and consequent deterioration in price from its exposure to the rains and damp,"[2] was now completed in a single afternoon in secure well-covered wagons and "losses on transit" were cut to a very minimum. The scramble to get the annual crop down to the port of Colombo before the monsoons broke also became past history. Unlike the bullock carts the railway operated efficiently during the rainy season and did away with the need to detain considerable amounts of coffee on the estates until the monsoons were over, "to its great deterioration in quality, and risk of loss and pecuniary inconvenience to the proprietor."[3]

Coffee Prices[4] **Average price of all Sri Lankan Coffee in Great Britian** **s.**	**Acreage under coffee**[5] **Plantation**
1861 - 72.4d. per cwt	1861 - 135,422 acres

1862	-	82.1	1862	-	150,000
1863	-	81.4	1863	-	152,000
1864	-	76.11	1864	-	155,000
1865	-	77.1	1865	-	160,000
1866	-	74.4	1866	-	160,000
1867	-	75.6	1867	-	168,000
1868	-	65.8	1868	-	176,000
1869	-	67.7	1869	-	176,467
1870	-	63.9	1870	-	185,000

Land Sales[6]

Year	Acres Sold	Amount Realised	Year	Acres Sold	Amount Realised
1861	28,329	£44,166	1866	45,546	£72,021
1862	25,302	45,300	1867	44,019	45,257
1863	32,567	72,811	1868	24,492	38,514
1864	34,122	76,567	1869	35,823	57,964
1865	41,150	68,276	1870	29,560	57,206

The profitability of coffee and the facility with which advances could be obtained in London led in time to the return of that reckless expenditure in the management of plantations which had characterised the early 1840s. Optimistic planters, certain in the belief that nothing could halt their run of good fortune grew neglectful of the simplest rules of economy and production costs began to rise until depressed conditions abroad unexpectedly administered a salutary if rather abrupt check.

In 1866 severe financial pressure was felt on the London money market. Prices fell steeply and the advances and loans on which planters had grown dependent became almost unobtainable. That many of these advances had been indiscriminately made and that some investments had been injudiciously chosen became apparent when difficulty was experienced in realising even "safe" investments. As a result, all Sri Lankan securities, good and bad alike, were viewed with suspicion and a large proportion of the planting community were obliged to find their financial requirements out of their own profits. This enforced frugality led immediately to efforts at cost reduction and after 1866 the attention paid to estate expenditure came to be as strict as it had been in 1847-49.[7]

The return of better times was not long delayed. By 1870 the last vestiges of the slump had disappeared. Prices thereafter began to climb and coffee again looked forward to a prosperous future. The prospects for the industry in fact, looked better than they had ever looked before. The railway had been completed and opened to goods traffic in 1867, and Governor MacCarthy's successor, Sir Hercules Robinson (1865-1872) had embarked upon an extended programme of road-building designed to link the newer planting districts with the main highways and the important railroad junctions of Kandy, Peradeniya and Kaduganawa.[8] A fresh wave of optimism now gripped the Colony and stimulated a vast extension of cultivation into the largest remaining forest reserve in the hill-country, known as the "Wilderness of the Peak," which extended from Nuwara Eliya through a succession of upland valleys in Dimbulla, Dickoya and Maskeliya, to the Adam's Peak range, an area covering some four hundred square miles.[9]

The general expansion of economic activity in the 1860s set up a demand for labour which for the first five years at least, was far in excess of the annual supply. True, a marked increase in immigration consequent upon the cessation of the public works programme in India was also recorded over the same period, nonetheless, the combined needs of the estates, the railway contractors and the road department could not be adequately met.[10] With railroad construction now taking place under the auspices of the Government, MacCarthy was doubly anxious to avoid a rise in wage-rates, so rather than compete in the open market for recruits to the Pioneer Corps, he decided to keep wages down by curtailing the road building operations of the Public Works Department.[11] The choice of this expedient proved an unhappy one. Incensed by the Government's failure to provide the newer coffee districts with sufficient outlets and by its inability to maintain the existing roads in a tolerable state of repair, the planting community were soon loud in their condemnation of the "parsimonious" policy of the Governor.[12] The strained relations between Government and planters, however, soon disappeared. The completion of the railway in 1867 so eased the pressure on the labour market that MacCarthy's successor, Sir Hercules Robinson was able to embark upon the heaviest road-building programme yet undertaken in Sri Lanka. At first sight it seems remarkable that a programme of this nature should even have been contemplated; for the flow of immigration was sharply arrested after 1866 by the commencement of railway construction in South India. Nevertheless, the available supply of labour appears to have been sufficient to go round, despite the demands of the road department and the fact that the acreage under coffee was increasing rapidly. This apparent contradiction of the normal order of things was the result of three developments. First, three-year contracts were legalized in 1862. It is thus fair to assume that some of the 68,896 immigrants who entered the Colony that year stayed on till the end of 1865. As the same would be true of those who arrived in Sri Lanka after that time, it is evident that the total number of transcient Indians in the Island in any year after 1862 was always somewhat larger than the year's immigration returns suggested. Second, the voluntary settlement of immigrants which had been taking place since the beginning of the coffee period had created a quite considerable community of resident Indians. At a 5% annual settlement rate, and a (low) rate of natural increase of 1/2 of 1% for each cohort, the size of this resident community at the end of 1870 comes out at 88,633 persons. This estimate compares well with the results of the island-wide census held in 1871. In that exercise the estate population was classified according to their places of birth, and 109,444 were recorded as "born in India."[13] As the census was held in March, a proportion of the year's immigrants must already have entered the Island and have been enumerated on the plantations. Ferguson put their number at 45% of the year's intake, i.e. at 40,281, and if we accept his estimate the resident "Indian-born" workforce comes out at 69,163. To find the *total* resident workforce of Indian origin one would have to add to this figure the descendants of immigrants who had settled in Sri Lanka. The census makes no reference to this category, but the latter must have amounted to some thousands of persons, for at the mere 1/2 of 1% rate of natural increase assumed earlier, over 6,000 locally-born Indians would have been on the plantations in March 1871. One has to take into account also the deficiencies of the census itself. It is generally agreed that there was a considerable undernumeration, of the order of 15.28% in the view of the Island's most authoritative demographer.[14] If this shortfall were to be compensated for in the same magnitude, the number of the "India-born" present in 1871 would increase by nearly 12,500 and the total resident workforce of Indian origin would rise to well above 87,500 persons, a figure not far removed from that earlier arrived at through allowing for settlement and natural increase. Included in the former would be those who had entered the Colony on lengthened agreements in 1869 and 1870,[15] but even when allowance is made for that category and for all possible errors in the census returns, it is still evident that a quite sizeable body of resident workers of Indian origin must have been present in Sri Lanka in the 1860s. This group formed the hard core of most estate gangs and by the end of the 1860s were fast becoming *the* most important element in the total labour supply.[16] As their numbers increased with the passing years, employers grew progressively less dependent on the annual flow from India and in any estimate of the strength of the annually available workforce one must give increasing weightage to the importance of this large and growing category of "resident" immigrants. Third, the post-1866 planter had learned to manage with fewer labourers than his predecessor of a generation earlier. This was due partly to the renewed interest in production costs which had followed upon the depression, and partly to the general improvements in transport which railway construction had brought. Whereas two labourers per acre in.cultivation had been the normal requirement in the 1840s the ratio had fallen to a shade less than one man per acre by 1867. This immense economy of labour combined with the long-term contract and the availability of a resident work-force to reduce the significance of the annual immigration from India, and their joint effects go far towards explaining the diminishing importance of the "labour problem" in the last quarter of the nineteenth century.[17]

IMMIGRRATION RETURNS[18]

Arrivals

Year	Men	Women	Children	Total
1862	51,859	12,502	4,534	68,896
1863	53,828	11,858	5,032	70,718
1864	63,087	14,214	4,499	81,800
1865	66,007	16,831	6,759	89,597
1866	58,488	23,723	6,117	88,528
1867	31,688	18,836	2,255	52,779
1868	41,499	11,540	2,682	55,721
1869	43,998	11,150	2,523	57,671
1870	51,664	10,835	2,735	65,224

Departures

Year	Men	Women	Children	Total
1862	35,577	4,691	1,641	41,909
1863	50,334	7,804	3,627	61,765
1864	54,724	8,526	4,029	67,279
1865	51,504	8,478	4,555	64,539
1866	38,997	6,717	3,515	49,229
1867	35,507	7,293	3,198	45,998
1868	44,820	7,524	2,182	54,526
1869	43,826	8,330	2,175	54,331
1870	44,787	8,035	2,260	55,082

Though a return to the Coast Advance System and the use of the old Northern Route followed upon the collapse of Ward's immigration scheme in 1861, immigrant mortality in the 1860s appears to have been considerably lower than at any other time. In the period 1862 to 1870, 630,934 arrivals and 494,658 departures were recorded, leaving a deficit of 136,276, i.e. 21.6% to be accounted for. As long-term contracts had been legalized in 1862 it follows that a proportion of the post-1868 entries must still have been in the Island in 1870. Their numbers, however, could not have exceeded 13,482 since this figure represents the total difference between arrivals and departures in 1869 and 1870, with no allowance made for either settlement or mortality. The settlement of immigrants at about 5% per annum, i.e. around 31,500 persons in all, has also to be allowed for.[19] Ferguson, writing in 1867, was inclined to put the rate of settlement at 10,000 per year and as justification for this high estimate pointed to the large number of women and children annually arriving in the Island.[20] Subsequently, however, he was obliged to scale down his figure to 5%, for it became apparent that he had erred when (a) the proportion of women and children entering Sri Lanka fell off in marked fashion after 1867, and when (b) the census returns of 1871 showed that settlement in the 1860s could not possibly have been as high as he had imagined.[21]

The passing of two further Passengers' Acts by MacCarthy in 1860 and 1862, the inauguration of a Government-controlled ferry service in 1861, and the appointment of a special officer to superintend immigration in 1862, must have improved the organizational side of immigration in the 1860s and it is unlikely that as many as before slipped out unnoticed. Ferguson for one believed that "the accounts (were) now being well kept."[22] That there was still a leakage, however, is evidenced by the report of the Government Agent of the Northern Province, who in 1872 reported that returning immigrants were leaving the Island unenumerated via Jaffna, and that this traffic had been in existence for some years.[23] One is inclined to believe that the numbers involved could not have been very large and that it was for this reason that these exits escaped official attention. Yet, that such a leakage occurred is sufficient to show that there were still some shortcomings in the immigration returns and that the latter, even if improved, were not altogether reliable.

When allowances have thus been made for long-term contracts, settlement and unenumerated departures, it becomes clear that the rate of immigrant mortality in the 1860s must have been considerably lower than it had been in earlier decades. That it was excessive in the absolute sense is suggested by the evidence cited later in this chapter, nevertheless, there is sufficient reason to accept that relatively speaking the situation with respect to immigrant deaths had decidedly improved.[24]

The Social and Economic Condition of the Plantation Worker

Ward's immigration scheme was superseded by a Government-operated ferry at Manaar which charged so moderate a fare, i.e. 6d. per passenger, that the competition of privately owned vessels was almost completely eliminated.[25] This could not but improve the conditions under which the immigrant travelled on the first stage of his journey to Sri Lanka since these small private boats had been notoriously overcrowded and devoid of all sanitary precautions. The few that were able to remain in business were brought under strict control, being henceforth obliged to ply their trade under the supervision of a Government officer, the Superintendent of Immigration, who after 1863 had behind him the authority of a new Passengers' Act which at last effectively enforced the provision that no vessel "could carry more than one passenger to every four tons of the burthen of a vessel without a licence."[26] Licences to exceed this limit were issued only to ships which possessed sanitary and other facilities, i.e. sufficient ventilation, safety precautions, etc., which the Administration thought adequate, and those that met these specifications were permitted, like government operated vessels, to carry two and a half passengers to the ton. This ratio was by no means a satisfactory one, two and a half persons per ton being by any standards an excessive number, but it cut by half the load these boats were accustomed to carrying, and in a relative sense was thus a decided improvement upon the past.

Measures to ameliorate conditions along the second stage of the immigrant's journey, i.e. the march from Manaar to the coffee districts, were concentrated upon the route which ran through Madawachchi and Dambulla. In 1862-63 eighteen wells were sunk at suitable places on the drier sections of the route and thereafter water was plentifully available all along the way.[27] At the same time repairs were effected to existing rest-sheds, a number of new sheds were built, and three "cooly" hospitals were established at Dambulla, Mihintale and Combansandekulam.[28] The hospitals and wells proved of lasting value, but not all the sheds, for within a year many of the new and of those refurbished had so deteriorated that Mr P.A. Dyke, Government Agent of the Northern Province, was led to observe that of the twelve halting stations in the Manaar and Nuwarakalaviya districts "there is scarcely a shed now habitable."[29]

This state of neglect appears to have persisted until 1869. Dyke's successor, Mr W.D. Twynam, who was regarded by the Administration as the country's foremost authority on immigration, reported at the end of the decade that "the cooly sheds at Manaar and on the Manaar-Madawachchi road, which were erected in 1863 have never been habitable. Three tumbled in, and the others were in such a dangerous state, that the coolies were not allowed to go into them."[30] The Government Agent of the Central Province, Mr H.S.O. Russell, referring to the same question in 1871 expressed a similar point of view.[31]

Governmental indifference to the problem of immigrant accommodation in the last half of the 1860s was reflective of its attempts to launch yet another scheme which would re-route immigrant traffic through Colombo. It was when this also ended in failure and it became apparent that the Northern route would be difficult to replace that attention was once again directed to the provision of amenities on the road and in 1870 a heavy expenditure of £2,410 was incurred on the construction of halting places and hospital sheds.[32]

Despite the neglect of the later 1860s, there can be no doubt that conditions along some stretches of the Northern route were better than they had been a decade earlier. No criticisms were levelled at the state of the halting places south of Mihintale, and the new hospitals and the increased number of wells must have done much to reduce the rigours of the march to the plantations.

Yet, reports continued to come in that the average immigrant was in poor condition when he finally arrived in the coffee districts.[33] The main reason for this was that the return of private enterprise in the field of labour recruitment had brought with it a resurrection of the Coast Advance System, and there is no evidence to suggest that the Kangany had undergone a change of heart. The old practices of skimping on food, abandoning the sick, and defrauding both employer and worker were revived, and perhaps contributed more than any other single cause to the rate of immigrant mortality.[34] It must not be forgotten that incoming immigrants were assured of employment only if they stayed with the gang the Kangany had under contract and that they had no alternative but to do so since the latter controlled the supply of food. The sick and the hungry therefore marched with their fellows for as long as it was humanly possible, refusing prolonged treatment at the stations on the way, until their strength gave out and they could go no further. That this was the "normal" course throughout the decade of the sixties is made apparent by Major-General O'Brien's comment in July 1864 that "under even favourable circumstances the mortality on the North road is considerable and the coolies who travel it arrive generally in a weak and sickly condition."[35] Similarly, Lieutenant-General Hodgson, in April 1869, observed that "after a painful tramp of two hundred miles without sufficient food, and overcome by fatigue and exposure they sink down to die at the door of . . . hospital."[36]

Hospitals, medical stations and rest-sheds even if efficiently run could do nothing to combat hunger. They could save a proportion of those who might in earlier times have died on the march—and no doubt they did—but their mere proliferation could not possibly eradicate all the shortcomings of the Coast Advance System. One of the Under-Secretaries of State in the Colonial Office put it well when reporting on the facilities available to the immigrant on the Northern Route, remarked: "I do not understand that he finds rice, and resting-places are of little use if he is urged on till he drops of starvation."[37]

Apart from the trials of the journey, the estate worker of this period, like his counterpart of earlier times, had to contend with the problem of poor accommodation on the plantations. The lines were overcrowded and unsanitary and in the higher elevations into which the plantations were gradually penetrating, the convenience of securing an unfailing supply of water often led to the lines being sited in unhealthy proximity to the marshes and swamps which abounded in the valleys.[38]

The availability of medical aid in the planting areas was, until 1865, confined to the hospitals at Kandy, Matale, Kurunegala and Gampola. Labourers in the newer coffee districts to the south and east of Kandy were too far removed from these centres to make much use of their facilities and for all practical purposes were altogether unprovided for in the medical sense. An effort to rectify this shortcoming was begun by MacCarthy in 1862[39] and continued by Robinson with the construction of hospitals at Badulla, Ratnapura and Nuwara Eliya, and with the extension of that at Kurunegala, but the planting areas expanded more rapidly than did the extension of the hospital system, and throughout our period a substantial part of the immigrant population was totally without the most rudimentary forms of relief. Where hospitals were situated within reach of the estates a Government regulation that a charge of 6d per day be entered against the plantation for every labourer sent in, tended in practice to work against the immigrants' interests. Reluctant to bear the expense of hospital charges, many planters took to doctoring their sick themselves,[40] often with such disastrous results that the Officer-in-Charge of the Matale Hospital once complained that "the terrible death-rate is easily accounted for by the well-known fact that the majority of the patients are moribund on admission, having been experimented on by the planters till past hope of recovery, and brought in by the police, dying of starvation and disease."[41]

Though most of the Colony's medical institutions were either new or else had been frequently improved, the conditions within them were still far from satisfactory. Repeated complaints were made that the water supply was poor, that sewage, ventilation and drainage were inadequate, and that facilities for bathing were far from sufficient. The hospitals, moreover, were small, overcrowded and grossly understaffed and were hardly the sort of place to which a patient would voluntarily go.[42]

More information than was previously to be had on the subject of mortality in Government medical institutions is available for the period 1861 to 1870. In 1863 a report on the three hospitals lying on the Northern Route, i.e. at Dambulla, Mihintale and Combansandekulam, recorded a relatively low case-rate of 11.3%, and it appeared that the terrors of the march were well on the way to being conquered. Two years later, however, a second report showed an increase to 20.4%[43] and though this rate was lower than those recorded at Kandy, Matale, Gampola etc., in previous decades, it was sufficiently high to induce the Government to issue a circular to all civil hospitals asking for the fullest information on mortality. When the replies to this circular came in, it was seen that generally speaking case-rates were indeed somewhat lower than they had been, but it was also evident that the Government had no grounds for complacency and that much more remained to be done.

Civil Hospital	**Percentage of Deaths**[44] *1866*
Kandy	25%
Matale	45%
Gampola	9%
Badulla	15%
Kurunegalla	18%
Ratnapura	16%
Puttlam	16%

After 1867 it became Government policy to submit an annual medical report to the Colonial Office. As these returns covered only the major Government civil hospitals and omitted all mention of the "cooly" hospitals and medical stations on the Northern Route, it is likely that they presented a more favourable picture than actual conditions warranted. Again, the case-rates given were an average of all deaths, no attempt being made to distinguish between immigrant and local inhabitant, and this must also have done much to mask the true state of affairs. Yet, what the returns had to show about important planting stations like Matale and Badulla was bad enough, and it was clear that despite some quite considerable improvements in other centres, the problem of an excessive immigrant mortality was still a long way from being conclusively solved.[45]

Civil Hospital	Percentage of Deaths		
	1868[46]	1869[47]	1870[48]
Kandy	15.25%	17.90%	13.2%
Matale	40.01%	23.20%	25.8%
Gampola	16.10%	21.50%	15.0%
Badulla	17.47%	21.80%	22.0%
Kurunegalla	19.70%	10.90%	9.0%
Ratnapura	19.00%	15.50%	11.2%
Puttlam	17.40%	13.40%	13.7%

The high case-rates, particularly those at Matale and Badulla, were once again said to be due to the estate workers' antipathy to Western medicine, and to their tendency to avoid the hospitals until veritably at death's door. It cannot be denied that there was a great deal of truth in this view, but in the light of the available evidence one can scarcely assign to it full responsibility for the immigrant's tardiness in seeking medical aid. On the one hand, the hospital returns make it clear that the decline in the prejudice against Western medicine, first evident in the 1850s had continued to grow.[49] On the other hand, we have it from the doctors themselves that employers were loath to bear the expense of sending their labourers to hospitals, and we know also that a fair proportion of the plantations were far removed from the major towns in which these medical institutions were situated. The "economy" of the planters and the inability of the Administration to keep hospital expansion abreast with the extension of the planting area must therefore be allotted some share of the blame, even if that portion be a restricted one.

Though the medical reports cover no more than a small fraction of the total immigrant population, their descriptions of the ailments common to this class of patient are capable of general application, there being no reason to believe that those who died outside were the victims of afflictions not encountered in the hospitals.[50]

In all the institutions to which Indian labour was admitted, bowel complaints, i.e. diarrhoea and dysentery still exacted the highest toll. Observations on the probable cause of these diseases have already been made (in Chapters 1 and 3), yet, since the opinions of the medical men in charge of the Colony's hospitals in the 1860s are available in the report issued in 1869 some further comments will not be out of place. Every doctor who chose to discuss the incidence of bowel complaints drew no distinctions between the several forms of dysentery and diarrhoea. It was also not suggested at any time that a bacillus might have provoked the one or that the other might well have been a symptom of some less obvious ailment. The two were always treated as though they were specific diseases in themselves. This approach had to do with the prevailing state of medical knowledge and does not signify that the doctors in Sri Lanka were inferior practitioners of their profession; it merely helps one to understand why they unanimously declared that all diarrhoeas and dysenteries were the end result of an ill-chosen diet.

"The nature of his food is insufficient for his support. His staple food is rice and water with dry chillies for a relish. Of this he will eat a large quantity. . . . On feast days he will indulge in many dishes of curried meats and vegetables, but from his habits of greediness and parsimony, he will eat the flesh of vermin, putrid meats, wild herbs and fruits—hence bowel complaint is his most frequent disease. . . . The enormous quantity of food he eats causes a strain on the digestive system and its indiscriminate quality irritates the bowels. These causes combined with his constant life of toil, exposed to every degree of heat, cold and rain, renders him most liable to this class of disease."[51] (Medical Officer in Charge, Kandy Hospital)

"They eat to repletion and are far from discriminating in the choice of their food. There is indeed nothing short of poison, with which a low-caste Malabar will not try to appease his hunger. Putrid meat, entrails, reeking hides, roots, leaves, nothing comes amiss to him. He will exhume the buried carcass of a sheep to feast on its decomposed remains, and if there is any dainty to which he is partial, it is a kind of ferruginous clay which he will chew and eat with as much relish as if it were some sweet confection. . . . Hence, it is not surprising that the chief complaint from which the Malabar cooly suffers and to which he generally succumbs is diarrhoea, or its co-genitor dysentery."[52] (Medical Officer in Charge, Gampola Hospital)

These two extracts are sufficient to demonstrate that many deaths generally classified under diarrhoea might well have been due to food poisoning, and that a proportion of the deaths put down to dysentery must have been of bacillary origin. The partiality to "ferruginous clay" suggests hookworm infestation since perverted appetites and a desire in particular to "gratify an unnatural craving for earth, mud and lime"[53] are well known characteristics of the disease. The high incidence of ailments of this sort bears out what has heen said earlier about overcrowded and insanitary line accommodation and, of course, serves also to show to what lengths the necessity to save can drive the recipients of poor wages.

In every hospital in the coffee districts Anasarca and Asthenia ranked second in the list of death-dealing afflictions. The probable nature and causes of the first have already been noticed (Chapter 2) but the latter appears in the medical reports for the first time and requires some comment. The term "Asthenia" seems to have been used in nineteenth century Sri Lanka as a synonym for any form of anaemia which later produced a dropsical or anasarcous condition. The doctor at the Kandy hospital, for example, observed that "the system is ill-nourished, the body wastes, there is deficiency of red corpuscles, and dropsy is a frequent accompaniment of other diseases,"[54] and his counterpart at Gampola reported that "the continued weakening of the system often brought on dropsy. Hence, . . . anasarca or more comprehensively asthenia, of which anasarca is only a symptom, fills the hospital wards. Dropsy in Malabar coolies is never acute, . . . and usually occurs as the most prominent symptom of general debility."[55] It follows therefore that asthenia has to be regarded not as a specific ailment, but as a general condition analogous to diarrhoea, fever, etc., which might have been brought on by a variety of causes. It could well have been dietary in origin, i.e. the result of a deficiency of iron, vitamin B12 etc., or else the outcome of diseases like malaria and tuberculosis; or again, it might even have been produced by such parasites as the hookworm or the roundworm. Whatever its origin, it is clear that the incidence of asthenia traces back to the social and economic environment of the Indian worker. It provides a commentary on the food he both ate and did not eat, on the primitive sanitary arrangements of the lines he lived in, and on the general hardship that characterised his working life.

As in earlier times "fever" was named again as being responsible for a proportion of the deaths in every hospital and, as before, no attempt was made to break this category down into its several forms. A large number of ailments must therefore have been included under this head, though there is every likelihood that malaria, typhus and enteric still continued to account for the majority of cases.[56]

Of special interest in the medical reports is the inclusion of three previously unmentioned infirmities, i.e. rheumatism, ulcers and venereal disease. The mortality rates produced by these complaints were not high, but they are nevertheless important because of the insight they give into the social and economic conditions of the time. The increase in the incidence of rheumatism appears to have accompanied the penetration of the plantations into the higher elevations. For the convenience of securing a cheap and steady supply of water, it became normal practice to site line accommodation in the valleys, and there, "miasmatic influences" are said by the doctors to have effectively completed what "exposure to all the inclemencies of the weather had begun."[57]

The ulcers from which immigrant labour frequently suffered were said to have been brought on by the "slightest abrasion of the skin" and to have been large, foul-smelling and disposed to turn gangrenous.[58] This description corresponds so closely to what Manson-Bahr has to say about the aetiology of ulcus tropicum, i.e. tropical sloughing ulcer, that there seems little doubt as to the identity of the ailment. "Sloughing (ulcer) is apt to attack the half-starved malaria stricken pioneers in jungle lands, over-driven labour gangs, and soldiers campaigning in the tropics. In such circumstances a slight wound, an abrasion, even an insect bite . . . may serve as the starting point for one of these terrible sores. The sloughing process rapidly extends in all directions until the skin . . . over an area of one to many inches in diameter is converted into a . . . horribly stinking slough. In bad cases, muscles, tendons, nerves, vessels, and even . . . the bones have shared in the gangrenous process."[59]

Though the descriptive portions of the medical reports tend to emphasize the widespread prevalence of syphilis, the statistical returns always group gonorrhoea and syphilis under a common head, and it is likely that the former was more generally to be found on the estates. One inclines to this view since (a) deaths from the venereal diseases were extremely low in an age when there was no known cure for syphilis, and because (b) the doctors complained that the disease was difficult to eradicate "as patients returned again and again to hospital, not infrequently with fresh disease added to the old one."[60] In the nineteenth century such recurring attacks accompanied by a low death-rate was possible in the case of gonorrhoea, but certainly not of syphilis, where infection was invariably followed by a fatal result.

The high incidence of venereal infection was the inevitable outcome of the immigration of too few women. The doctor at the Kandy Hospital summarised the socio-economic aspects of the question particularly well, "migrating from his native shore the Malabar leads a wandering life. Seeking labour where he can command the highest price, with the fixed idea of ultimately returning with his savings, he is little inclined to contract marriage. He seeks the indulgence of his passions and has little regard for the consequences. Hence the syphilitic taint is widely prevalent among this race."[61] There is every likelihood that venereal disease was widespread amongst the immigrant population from the earliest days of Indian immigration, for the masculinity ratios were then a great deal higher. That it attracted attention in the 1860s suggests that immigrants had become more willing to seek medical aid and rather contradicts the official argument that they did not do so until "in extremis."

As there is every reason to believe that the diseases discussed above were also prevalent amongst those who either would not or could not enter the hospitals, it is very likely that deaths on the plantations must have been considerable. However, one has to be rather circumspect about accepting such evidence as there is on this question. To begin with, it is of a rather restricted nature, being limited to an abstract of mortality returns based on information supplied to the Planters' Association by 325 estates for two years only, i.e. 1868 and 1869.[62] The returns put mortality at 3.4% in 1868 and 2.8% in 1869, but as the number of persons covered was only 39,609 and 45,476 respectively, they are representative of no more than about 25%-30% of the estate workforce at peak. Again, it is significant that the planters as a body bitterly opposed an effort made by the Government to collect similar information at an official level in 1862 and that no returns at all were submitted then.[63] The information later supplied to the Planters' Association came at a time when Whitehall was strenuously maintaining that immigrants deaths were excessive and that remedial action was necessary[64] and the coincidence in timing is difficult to overlook. One seems justified therefore in holding that the available evidence is too restricted and too obviously supplied by interested parties to be accepted as trustworthy.

Despite a heavy increase in the demand for labour and some marked fluctuations in supply, wages continued to remain steady at 18s. per month.[65] In the early years of the decade this stability was due in part to a happy coincidence. Railroad construction and an extension of the planting area in the Colony commenced at a time when the cessation of the public works programme in India had created a large pool of workers prepared to seek employment in Sri Lanka. A rise in the annual immigration thus took place when it was most needed, and effectively prevented the sort of wage spiral which might have resulted if the railroad contractor and the planting community had had to contend with a limited market.

Such competitive bidding could quite easily have occurred, for unlike Ward, neither MacCarthy nor Robinson had made any special arrangements for the direct recruitment of railway gangs in those parts of India not normally tapped by the Kangany. Again, deliberate Government policy also played some part in keeping wages at their former levels. MacCarthy chose to sacrifice part of his road building programme as an alternative to strengthening the ranks of the Pioneer Corps,[66] and when he ultimately found himself obliged to increase the size of the force, imported recruits from Northern India in an effort to curtail competition in the local labour market.[67]

The falling off in immigration in the last years of the 1860s made no impression on the prevailing wage-rate partly because the coming of the long-term contract rendered the decline more apparent than real, and partly because the railway works were in the last stages of completion and did not require a large supply of labour. Moreover, it should be remembered that the resident immigrant community was steadily growing in number and that fluctuations in the annual arrivals from India were no longer as significant as they once had been. Finally, with reference to the entire period, should be reckoned the influence of the Coast Advance System. The dangers it imposed on the march to the hills were still sufficient to deter many Indians from seeking employment in Sri Lanka unless conditions at home gave them no choice. In these circumstances they came because they had to, and since the recruiting kanganies rarely competed against one another, wages tended to remain undisturbed at their traditional levels.

Policy and Legislation

Once the Immigration Ordinance of 1858 had been repealed it became Governor Sir Charles MacCarthy's task to devise a system which would simultaneously meet a number of objectives. It had to satisfy the needs of those dependent upon Indian labour by ensuring that supplies were large; it had to protect the immigrants to the satisfaction of the Colonial Office by making adequate provision for their welfare; and it had to safeguard that section of the population whose economic interests were independent of an imported workforce by not trenching upon the general revenue.

With the first of these ends in view a permanent ferry was established at Manaar in 1861 for the conveyance of immigrants between Sri Lanka and the neighbouring coast. A packet service consisting of three vessels chartered by the Government at a moderate expense was stationed at that port and placed under the direction of an officer specially appointed to superintend its working.[68] The cost of the entire undertaking was put at £2,352 per annum, and it was estimated that the number of immigrants who annually availed themselves of these facilities would at 6d per head be large enough to render the system a self-supporting one and thus remove any semblance of Government "assistance."[69]

Having made arrangements for the actual physical transference of labour to Sri Lanka, MacCarthy turned next to the controversial question of the long-term contract. In January 1862, observing that it was of paramount importance to the planting interests, he presented for sanction Ordinance 20 of 1861 which repealed the earlier law restricting labour agreements to a year's duration and henceforth permitted employers of agricultural labour to enter into contracts for periods ranging between one month and three years.[70]

Remembering perhaps the earlier allegations made by the Madras Government that the signing of long-term agreements in India would "militate against the interests of the cooly" since he "would not be in Ceylon to judge for himself" and could therefore "be imposed upon by those employed to engage him,"[71] MacCarthy was careful to include in the new Ordinance a clause which insisted that all long term contracts should be entered into after the immigrant had arrived in the Island. Moreover, in order to prevent him from being exploited by unscrupulous employers, it was also decreed that agreements could only be entered into "in the presence of a Police Magistrate or some other person expressly authorised by the Governor, whose duty it would be to see that the contract is fully explained to, and understood by the parties, and that they enter into it of their own free will."[72]

Despite MacCarthy's precautions the new bill did not receive the immediate approval of the Colonial Office. Recalling perhaps the questionable tactics used by Sir Henry Ward in connection with this very issue in 1859, the Secretary of State adopted an attitude of extreme caution. Confirmation was refused until the Secretary of State for India had examined the Act and pronounced an opinion, and to enable this to be done it was suggested that the Colonial Government should supply a fuller explanation of certain aspects of the Ordinance. For example, it was pointed out that the proposed bill did not seem to afford Indian labour the same amount of protection as had been considered necessary in other colonies where they were employed under indentures for long periods. True, these other colonies were far removed from the source of emigration, but in the opinion of the Colonial Office, the mere affinity between Sri Lanka and India was "scarcely sufficient ground for dispensing with precautions similar to those which have been adopted in Mauritius and the West Indies, where officers appointed specially for the protection of the Indians are invested with exceptional powers to visit estates and enquire as to the treatment of the labourers, as well as make special provision for securing the labourers access to the officers."[73] Again, the Government in each of these colonies was empowered in case of the ill-treatment of a labourer, to cancel his indenture and where there had been gross or repeated ill-usage, to cancel the indentures of all labourers on a particular estate. It appeared to the Secretary of State that in Sri Lanka functions of this kind could be performed by the Police Magistrate, and he enquired whether there were reasons why such provisions should not be introduced in the Colony. Since answers were required to these and a number of similar questions, it was thought best that confirmation of the Ordinance should be deferred until the Governor had submitted a comprehensive report on the amount of official protection the immigrant could expect while in the Island.[74]

With the fresh problem of allaying Whitehall's suspicions now on his hands. MacCarthy took what proved to be the wise step of comunicating directly with the Governor-General of India and of forwarding to him a copy of the new bill. In an accompanying letter the measures taken for the protection of the Indian immigrant were described and it was specially emphasized that all contracts were to be signed in Ceylon, "so that the labourer is free after his arrival in the Island, to make the best bargain he can for himself."[75] In practice, of course, there was little in this last concession. The labourer was indebted to the Kangany from the moment he left his village and with his destination decided in advance could not survey the market after his arrival in Sri Lanka prior to entering into an agreement. These subtleties of the Coast Advance System were either unknown to the Governor-General or else ignored by him for he not only expressed his satisfaction with the bill, but went on to comment that "the legislative measures . . . taken by the Ceylon Government seem to be ample to secure the liberty and fair treatment of Indian labourers who migrate to the Island, and the Ordinance indeed affords them even a greater degree of protection than they would receive if they migrated to any other part of India than that in which they reside."[76] That the law in Sri Lanka was in some respects less demanding than that enforced in Mauritius and the West Indies was not thought to be of much importance. This aspect of the question may have perturbed the Secretary of State, but not so the Governor-General of India, who declared that any further stiffening of the legal code was altogether unnecessary since "there is this great difference between Ceylon and the other British possessions in which there is a demand for Indian labourers, that in the latter there exist a negro population and the traditions and associations of negro slavery while in the former they have no existence."[77]

After this most favourable reaction to his policy there was little left for MacCarthy to do. He merely transmitted to the Colonial Office the reply received from the Indian Government, with the accompanying comment that "he hoped that after such unqualified expression of approval of the Ordinance by the Government of India, the Ordinance would be confirmed."[78] His hopes were not ill-founded, for Newcastle, his fears apparently put to rest, immediately allowed the bill, and the long-term contract passed into the law of the land in July 1862.[79]

With the final acceptance of Ordinance 20 of 1861 an important part of MacCarthy's general scheme was complete. Through the legalization of the long-term contract and the setting up of the ferry service at Manaar, he had provided for the interests of those dependent upon the supply of immigrant labour. What yet remained to be done concerned the labourer himself. Facilities along the roads to the hills had to be improved sufficiently to satisfy the Colonial Office that the return to the overland route would provide the immigrant with at least as much "welfare" as that afforded by Ward's immigration scheme, and the immigrant, in addition, had to be convinced that he no longer had reason to entertain a prejudice against seeking employment in Sri Lanka. As a first step towards achieving these dual ends, MacCarthy made it part of the duties of the newly appointed Superintendent of Immigration to supply all labourers on arrival with "such information as they required" pertaining to their journey to the plantations, i.e. the fares normally payable at ferries, the current price of provisions, etc.[80] Next, the Governor turned to the problem of the overcrowded transport vessel and finding that existing legislation did not effectively control the few private boats still plying between Sri Lanka and the neighbouring coast, passed Ordinance 10 of 1862, "to extend the provisions of Ordinance 1 of 1860 and to make offences against the Indian Act No. 25 of 1859 punishable in Ceylon." Ordinance 1 of 1860 had attempted to prevent boats in the Gulf of Manaar and the Palk Straits from carrying more than one passenger to every four tons of the displacement of a vessel without a licence to do so. The corresponding Indian Act No. 25 had a similar provision, but the enactments were found to be defective in that they did not contain any provision for making the offences committed punishable at the ports of disembarkation, where alone such evidence of the excess of passengers was obtainable. It was therefore proposed that a law should be passed in both countries, providing for the punishment in India and Sri Lanka respectively of Masters of vessels carrying passengers in excess of the specified ratio. With this in view an Act was passed by the Madras Government No. 2 of 1862, extending the provisions of the

Indian Law of 1859 to vessels from Sri Lanka. MacCarthy's new Ordinance was a corresponding measure on the part of the Government in Colombo, by which all offences against the Indian Act were made punishable in Sri Lanka.

In order to improve conditions on the second stage of the journey to the hills, MacCarthy decided that it would be more practical to concentrate his attention on the road which ran through Madawachchi and Mihintale. The other route, via Arippu, Puttlam and Kurunegala, being less direct and more difficult to travel, had fallen out of favour in the 1850s and the Governor quite rightly concluded that a better use of resources would be made if work on this line was immediately curtailed.[82] Between 1862 and 1864 therefore a number of wells were sunk at strategic points along the Central Route, new rest-sheds were built where necessary and those already constructed put into a decent state of repair. To provide sick immigrants with better medical attendance on the road, additional hospitals were built at Dambulla, Mihintale and Combansandekulum and that at Matale enlarged. New medical stations were also to be erected where required, their staff of attendants was to be increased and two supervisors appointed to take charge of all such institutions sited on the route to Kandy. Finally, Government officials stationed in the districts through which Indian labour moved were directed to consider it an essential part of their duty to attend to all matters relating to the comfort of the immigrant.[83] Many of the rest-sheds and medical stations, as pointed out earlier, were never put to use because of their faulty construction and some of the latter were not built until the decade was out but it is unquestionable that the other features of the programme were a decided advance upon the facilities previously available on the line of march.

The third and last section of MacCarthy's programme concerned the welfare of those who had already arrived on the plantations. This was by far the weakest part of his general scheme, being much less elaborate in its details that his other welfare arrangements. In all, three measures were introduced under this head, and of these, two were legal in nature. The first was a special clause in the Ordinance legalizing the long-term contract, by means of which all wages due to the labourer for a period of six months were made a first charge against the estate, with summary means provided for their recovery in the Court of Requests. The second, which was also brought in as a special clause in Ordinance 20 of 1861, took up the question of the incapacitated labourer and made employers liable to "furnish labourers rendered incapable of service, with adequate means of returning to their country."[84] The third step was of a very different character and had to do with the medical amenities available in the planting districts. With the extension of the coffee area, large sections of the immigrant population had come to be so far removed from the existing hospitals that they were virtually denied all forms of medical aid. To rectify this shortcoming, MacCarthy in 1862, began the construction of a hospital "for coolies and paupers" at Badulla. The choice of location was a wise one, for situated on the further side of the central mountain massif, the new hospital catered to a rapidly developing area which was then the most remote of the coffee growing districts.[85]

This then was MacCarthy's programme for the general promotion of immigration. Its virtues certainly were manifold, yet, it is true that its defects were also numerous. There can be no doubt that the Ordinance legalizing the long-term contract was of immense benefit to the plantation owner but against this it can be shown that the protective clauses of that self-same bill were not always of value to the immigrant. The insistence on contracts being signed in Sri Lanka in the presence of the local magistrate was rendered meaningless by the Coast Advance System, through the working of which de facto agreements were made in India and the prospective labourer held to his contract through the simple device of being put in debt to the recruiting Kangany. The de jure agreement finally entered into upon arrival in Sri Lanka was reduced to the level of a mere formality, for a dissenting immigrant had not the funds with which to pay off the Kangany for expenses already incurred. There was no question of the immigrant "seeing for himself" before concluding what the Government of India hopefully described as "the best bargain." His terms of service were decided for him well in advance of his departure from his native village.

The decision to make wages a first charge on the estate was less important in fact than it appeared to be on paper. The prompt payment of dues had become normal procedure throughout the plantation sector, and there is no evidence to suggest that employers were inclined to jeopardize their future labour supply by reverting to the earlier short-run practice of defaulting on wages. Nevertheless, the stipulation was a valuable insurance to have in times of depression, and though bankruptcies were few and far between in the 1860s, MacCarthy's foresight was destined to prove its worth in later years.

The clause which rendered employers liable to provide incapacitated labourers with funds sufficient to take them back to India, can best be described as a mere theoretical improvement in the immigrant's terms of service. Having resorted to Sri Lanka with the avowed intention of making as much money as he could, the Indian labourer even when ill, tended to work for as long as was humanly possible. When he had reached the point of being "incapable of work" he was usually in no condition to undertake the tedious tramp to Manaar, or for that matter, even fit enough to make the journey to the hospital. One can argue, of course, that after 1867 the sick immigrant could go down to Colombo by rail and then proceed to India by sea, but since the law made no mention of the method of transport to be used in such cases, it seems reasonable to suppose that few employers would voluntarily choose to subsidise the patient's use of a more expensive route.

In contrast, the installation of the ferry service at Manaar, the chartering of three well-appointed vessels and the employment of a special supervising officer must be recognised as a substantial contribution to the immigrants' well-being. The grossly over-crowded dhoney on which the immigrant had been previously obliged to travel and the extortion he had often suffered at the hands of unscrupulous boat-owners were virtually abolished by this part of MacCarthy's programme. It is unfortunate that the full advantage of these improvements should have been watered down by the clause in the Passenger's Act which permitted licensed vessels to exceed the specified limit of one passenger to every four tons' displacement, nevertheless it cannot be denied that the comparative advances made in this field were enormous.

Though some of the new facilities on the Northern Route must have eased the problems associated with it, it is not difficult to see that MacCarthy's policy did not offer a permanent solution to the basic questions associated with this stage of the journey. The root of the problem here lay in the semi-starvation induced by the Coast Advance System and though the facilities offered by the Government could do much to alleviate its effects, they were powerless to counteract this evil at its source. In other words, the measures introduced by the Administration were not designed to prevent the immigrant from falling ill, they sought instead to assist him *after* he had reached that condition. Mortality on the Northern Route could therefore be reduced, but only reduced up to a point. To go beyond this a more far-reaching programme than that launched by the Governor was needed. The Coast Advance System had either to be abolished altogether, or else controlled effectively enough to prevent semi-starvation from being its constant companion.

MacCarthy's extension of the hospital system to the newly opened coffee districts was a good beginning, but his efforts were too restricted in their scope to make much impression on the general problems associated with health on the plantations. The limitation of his programme to the construction of a single institution was probably a result of his having been sent out with instructions to practice the strictest economy,[86] and it cannot be denied that hospitals were expensive amenities to provide; that at Badulla, for example, cost £1682 when completed.[87] Yet, one cannot help but feel that the Government's approach to the question was mistaken. There appears to have been no reason why a system similar to that proposed for the Northern road should not have been introduced into the coffee areas. A number of medical stations, strategically located would have cost less and have been productive of more good than one distant hospital.

Though it is possible so to criticise MacCarthy's immigration programme, one must be careful not to allow its shortcomings to obscure the extent of his achievement. The ferry service at Manaar and some of the facilities on the Northern road were far in advance of all earlier arrangements, and the measure of their effectiveness can best be seen in the decline in immigrant mortality. Moreover, the overall expenditure on medical facilities in the Island was higher in MacCarthy's time than it had ever been before. Between 1860 and the end of 1864 over £46,000 was expended on hospitals and some £54,000 on the medical establishment.[88] These amounts it is true were spent on institutions shared equally by immigrants and local inhabitants, and though the exact proportions cannot be worked out, it is obvious that the former were now better catered for.

Despite his strictures of Ward's attempt to introduce a system of immigration which would not "be paid for by the class that benefitted only," MacCarthy was never able to attain his professed goal of setting up a "self-supporting" scheme.[89] We are to be sure, not quite certain what exactly he meant by the term, i.e. whether it was intended to cover all aspects of immigration or only the operation of the ferry service. But it can be reasonably assumed that the Governor accepted Campbell's view that the immigrant, though a temporary resident in the Colony, had the right to a modicum of welfare at official expense and excluded the cost of all welfare projects from his calculations. On this assumption it follows that only the maintenance of the ferry service and its attendant establishments was to be met by the income from fares, and that it was MacCarthy's desire to balance this account without trenching on the general revenue. Even this limited goal was never reached. The Governor had estimated that £2,352 per annum would be sufficient to cover the expenses of his scheme, but by 1863 the yearly expenditure had risen to £4,691, and by 1864 to £4,821.[90] No returns relating to the proceeds from passage money are available for these years,[91] but since the Government vessels ferried 69,347 immigrants in 1863 and 84,000 in

1864, the total receipts from this source would have amounted to only £1,734 and £2,100 respectively. Thus, despite MacCarthy's declared antipathy to any form of "assistance," immigration was in reality being subsidised by the general public, to the tune of £2,957 in 1863 and £2,100 in 1864.[92]

In his endeavours to raise the annual migration to Sri Lanka, MacCarthy sought to do more than merely improve the amenities available to labour. Believing that immigration "might be injuriously affected by a misapprehension which existed in some quarters that the rate of mortality was high among the coolies," and convinced himself that the disproportion between arrivals and departures had been erroneously ascribed to deaths, "whereas there were good grounds for supposing that a large number of immigrants have not returned to India, but settled in Ceylon with their families," the Governor in 1862 passed Ordinance 17 of that year "To ascertain the proportion of mortality amongst the natives of India employed in agricultural and other labour in Ceylon."[93] The Ordinance called upon all employers of Indian labour "to furnish quarterly returns of the number of coolies employed by them, showing the number of deaths during the quarter, the probable cause of death and other particulars." It appears to have been MacCarthy's intention to publicise the results of this inquiry, in the hope perhaps that it would set at rest any lingering fears still entertained by the Government of India and the Colonial Office.[94]

The new Act was not destined to prove a success. The planting community, some of whom had at first been favourably disposed towards the general motives underlying the bill,[95] objected strenuously to the clause demanding the inclusion of the cause of death and suggested that it be dropped from the returns. This the Governor refused to do on the grounds that the particular item would, if included, "induce increased care in the attention paid to the coolies," and with the Secretary of State's approval the Ordinance was brought into force unchanged.[96]

The Administration's refusal to delete the offending clause was sufficient to kill the effectiveness of the bill. The planters, condemning its "inquisitorial character," refused to co-operate and MacCarthy was left with the choice of either penalising those who failed to send in their returns, or of allowing the law to become a dead letter.[97] Prudence led him to adopt the latter course. The legal prosecution of the entire planting fraternity was a step even the boldest of Governors would have hesitated to take, and with feelings between the opposing factions already strained by disagreements over official policy in a number of other spheres, i.e. over constitutional reform, the road-building programme, and Sri Lanka's contribution to the Metropolitan Military Fund, the Governor could hardly have wished to induce a further deterioration in relations.[98] Ordinance 17 of 1862 was therefore allowed to remain upon the statute book, but no effort was ever made towards its practical application.[99]

Apart from his attempts to augment the supply of labour through the active promotion of immigration, MacCarthy also sought to prevent that increase in wage-rates which both public and private sectors so constantly feared. Believing that the combined demand of the planters and the railway contractor would strain the existing market to the full, the Governor decided in June 1863 that all future recruits to the Pioneer Corps should be obtained "from a fresh source of supply in more northern India." With the assistance of the Indian Government, five hundred men were recruited in Calcutta, and it was agreed a like number should follow before the year was out.[100] The experiment proved a disastrous failure, for soon after their arrival the new pioneers refused to perform the work required of them, claiming that they had been recruited as soldiers, not labourers.[101] MacCarthy denied the allegation, and it could well be that a genuine misunderstanding and not sharp practice was responsible for this rather unfortunate affair. It was sufficient to prevent any further adventures on the Governor's part, and for the remainder of his term he attempted to make do with the existing strength of the Pioneer Corps.[102]

The Administration of Major-General Terence O'Brien, Acting Governor for the relatively long period of 1st December 1863 to 31st March 1865, was remarkable for the development of a movement to abandon the Northern Route in favour of returning to an arrangement not unlike that introduced by Sir Henry Ward. Apparently the planting body had discovered by 1864 that MacCarthy's welfare measures had done little to improve the physical condition of those immigrants who finally arrived on the plantation. Despite the low wages paid, the real cost of labour therefore continued to be high, and though more efficient methods of labour utilization were being introduced there was still a relative waste of resources because of low individual productivity. In other words, the planting body had come to realise that on economic grounds, as distinct from humanitarian ones, the Coast Advance System stood condemned as a most wasteful form of recruitment. That this was the thought uppermost in their minds becomes evident when one considers that the total immigration in 1863 at 70,718 was greater than at any previous time, with the exception of 1858 when owing to an abnormal famine in India the annual arrivals reached 96,062.[103] Not the supply of labour merely, but also the physical state of the worker had become important, and seeing that the villain of the piece was not difficult to identify, it is hardly surprising that the planters should have decided to settle the problem by rooting out the evils of the Coast Advance System. With this object in view, the Planters' Association privately commenced negotiations with the Madras and Colombo Steamship Company for the establishment of a regular link between Colombo and the Indian coast. After some correspondence the Company finally agreed to introduce a service making two calls per week between Colombo and Negapatam, and one call per week between Madras and Colombo, touching intermediate ports in the course of both rounds. Once this offer had been made the negotiations were brought into the open, and O'Brien was strongly urged by the Planters' Association to accept the Company's offer.

The Acting Governor proved sympathetic from the very outset. Plainly he was at one with the planters in believing that his predecessors's policy had not touched the real core of the difficulties encountered on the Northern Route, for writing to the Secretary of State he observed that while it was gratifying to find that the Manaar ferry had proved successful, it still remained true that "under even favourable circumstances the mortality on the north road is considerable, and the coolies who travel by it arrive generally in a weak and sickly condition. It is therefore very desirable to provide if possible a more healthy route, and if the coolies can be induced to come by the steamers, they will be landed in Colombo where there are excellent roads to the estates passing through a cleared and healthy line of country, and when the railway is completed they will be forwarded to their destination with much more ease and expedition than at present."[104]

If O'Brien was enthusiastic in his support of the planters' proposals his Executive Council was at first inclined to be more cautious. The advantage of doing away with the shortcomings of the Coast Advance System were not denied, but the councillors felt that a firm understanding with the shipping company should not be entered into until the ferry service at Manaar had been discontinued. The Planters' Association clearly wishing to keep all its options open, immediately objected to the suggestion. The route by which the immigrant travelled could not, they held, "be changed at pleasure," hence it would be unwise to discontinue the Manaar ferry, "until it had been ascertained that the coolies take readily to the more expensive route by the coasting steamers."[105] This argument sufficed to convince the Executive Council that both ferry and shipping service should operate simultaneously for a period and with their unanimous support O'Brien sought Whitehall's permission to grant the shipping company a subsidy of £3,000 per annum for five years, in return for the setting up of a regular steam service between Colombo and the Indian coast.[106] An important feature of the proposed arrangement was that the subsidy was to be met out of the general revenue and not through the sort of tax that Ward had earlier levied on the planting body. O'Brien, it is evident, did not share his predecessor's view that immigration was best left to private enterprise, or that the expense of conducting it should be met by those who benefitted directly.

The Secretary of State, rather surprisingly it may seem, expressed approval of the Governor's plans. One can only take this as an indication that the Colonial Office had also come to believe that MacCarthy's immigration policy despite its many advances, was not really capable of conclusively solving the problems associated with immigrant labour. Their support of O'Brien's proposals was tantamount to an admission that in their view "welfare" could not be effectively practiced along the Northern road and that £3,000 per annum was a small enough price to pay for a more humane method of importing labour.

It was left to Sir Hercules Robinson, Sri Lanka's new Governor, to complete the arrangements begun by O'Brien. A quick settlement of the agreement with the Madras and Colombo Steamship Company proved difficult to reach, there being some differences of opinion on a number of details, and after a prolonged correspondence it was finally decided to break off negotiations. Nevertheless, the decision to set up a direct service between Colombo and India was persisted with, and at last in October 1866 Robinson was able to announce that a contract had been signed with another group, the Bombay Coast and River Steam Navigation Company, for the establishment of a regular steam connection between Colombo and the Indian coast. The terms agreed upon were identical in spirit with those authorised by the Secretary of State, i.e. a subsidy of £3,000 was to be annually paid by the Government, but with the difference that the contract was to run for three years and not five. In addition, for a further subsidy of £1,000 per annum, the shipping company also undertook to operate the round-the-Island service hitherto performed by the Colonial Steamer, "Pearl."[107]

In spite of the hopes held out for it the new immigration scheme was as ill-fated as that experimented with by Sir Henry Ward, for the reaction of the average immigrant followed the lines the Planters' Association feared it would. To the Indian labourer a rise in the cost of transport meant an increase in the size of the advance he would have to work off on the estate and there were not very many prepared to concede that the decline in total earnings was compensated for by the ease and convenience of the voyage by sea. The vast majority continued to take the Northern Route and with so few availing themselves of the steamer service the Bombay Coast and River Steam Navigation Company soon found themselves in desperate financial straits.

In September 1867, Messrs. Armitage and Company, the local agents, represented to the Government that the shipping line had sustained severe losses on the contracts and asked that they be annulled. At the same time they urged that in consideration of the losses incurred, no penalties should be imposed for non-fulfillment of the agreements. The Governor was disposed to deal liberally with the Company so far as penalties were concerned, but he insisted that the round-the-Island service be continued until alternative arrangements were made. The link between Colombo and India he allowed to be immediately suspended as the Manaar ferry was still in operation and no inconvenience to immigrant traffic was envisaged.[108]

With the failure of this second attempt to channel the flow of immigration through Colombo, the Administration turned again to the improvement of the Northern route. Conditions there had deteriorated somewhat after 1864 as a result of the Government's pre-occupation with the sea route to Colombo. The ferry service had been kept going between 1864 and 1867, but as shown above, little else was done within that period to augment or even adequately maintain the other amenities provided to lessen the hazards of the march.

With the return to the overland route the Colonial Office began once more to press upon the Governor's attention the need for an extended policy of "welfare" at Government expense. Clearly the Secretary of State was far from satisfied with what had been achieved by MacCarthy, for while commending the improvements already effected, he went on to observe that "the endeavours made by Government to mitigate the evils attendent on the annual immigration of Malabar coolies have not produced all the results which might be desired. It is by the labour of these people that the colony is enriched, and the expense necessary to prevent a scandalous mortality amongst the immigrants on their passages to Ceylon must be considered as part of the cost of that labour and as such devolving upon the Colonial revenue."[109]

Robinson's policy towards immigrant labour did not differ substantially from that followed by MacCarthy. After the attempt to institute a steamer service had ended in failure, the Governor approached the labour problem in much the same way as his predecessor and concentrated his attention on rendering the ferry service more efficient, on improving conditions along the Northern road, and on extending the hospital system.

Where the ferry service was concerned it was decided to improve the existing facilities by increasing the number of vessels in operation. To the three already employed, five smaller boats were added and officers directly responsible to the Superintendent of Immigration were appointed to the ports of embarkation in India, i.e. Divipatam and Paumben, to exercise a more effective control over the augmented fleet.[110]

Upon the Northern road there was much to be done. The neglect of the years 1864-1869 had to be corrected, and arrangements had also to be made for an expansion of the amenities provided by MacCarthy. A first step was the repair and construction of rest-sheds and medical stations, a task to which Robinson addressed himself so energetically, that by the end of 1870, £2,410 had been expended on this one item alone and nineteen halting stations, each with a separate hospital shed for the sick had been put up on the Manaar-Matale highway. An overseer was placed in charge of each with two patrolling officers under him and it was their daily duty to go out upon the road and bring in those who may have fallen ill on the way. In addition, two itinerant medical practitioners were appointed for the special purpose of visiting these halting stations and attending upon those brought in by the patrols.[111]

Hospital construction during Robinson's administration took place both in the coffee areas and along the line of march. Two new general hospitals were put up at Manaar and Anuradhapura and work was begun on a third at Vavuniya. In the planting districts, Kurunegala, Ratnapura and Nuwara Eliya were provided with general hospitals, a second hospital was built at Gampola and additions were made to the institutions at Kandy, Badulla and Matale.[112] As one can well imagine, the total expenditure on medical facilities reached a new peak during this period. Between 1865 and 1870, £66,470 was spent on hospitals alone, and £87,242 expended on the medical establishment.[113]

In addition to continuing MacCarthy's policies, Robinson also broke fresh ground. Seeing that the expansion of the coffee industry had in many instances made the march from Kandy to the point of employment almost as difficult as the march from the coast to Kandy, the Governor made provision for the maintenance of "five or six cooly bungalows . . . in various places where experience had shown them to be necessary."[114] This was a step the importance of which his predecessors had failed to appreciate. Without exception they had concentrated their attention on the first stages of the immigrant's journey, on the assumption that rest-sheds were unnecessary once Kandy had been reached. This reasoning was realistic so long as the bulk of the planting area was centred around the Kandy district, but with the expansion of the coffee enterprise from Ward's time onward the ultimate destination of the incoming labourer grew progressively more distant from Kandy. The final stage of his march, often through wet, cold and mountainous country, became quite as hazardous as the journey through the plains, and that it was often productive of fatal results was emphasized by the Assistant Government Agent of Nuwara Eliya, who once observed that "the presence of a suitable shed and a patrol on the line between Nuwara Eliya and Wilson's bungalow might during the inclement weather of the early part of the year, have humanly speaking, saved several lives of coolies who apparently died of cold and exhaustion."[115]

Since Robinson's general policy on immigration was not fundamentally different from that adopted by MacCarthy, most of the criticisms levelled at the one are equally applicable to the other. The criticisms, however, do not apply with quite the same force. Like his predecessor, the Governor may have failed to see that a permanent solution to the difficulties of the Northern Route could only be found in a strict control of the Coast Advance System but it is nevertheless true that he went a great deal further towards allaying its terrible effects. Similarly, the extension of the hospital system to the coffee areas brought three, and not just one, of the newer planting districts within its scope, and to that extent at least, was a marked improvement on the earlier position. The provision of "cooly bungalows" in the hill-country was a most imaginative step, likely to prove useful whether the Coast Advance System existed or not. Yet, one cannot help but observe that the measure might have been productive of even better results had the Governor had the foresight to attach a medical station to each, with overseers and patrols similar to those appointed to the Northern road.

In the field of labour legislation Robinson was called on to deal with a problem which arose out of MacCarthy's Ordinance of 1861 "permitting employers to enter into contracts for the hire and service of persons . . . for a period . . . not exceeding three years."[116] According to that bill, no contract with Indian labour was considered legally valid unless it had been signed *after* the immigrant's disembarkation in Sri Lanka. There was thus nothing to prevent a man who had entered into a verbal engagement with a Kangany in India and had accepted an advance, from refusing to honour that agreement once he had arrived in Sri Lanka. No evidence exists to show that this had actually occurred and there is no reason to suppose that an ignorant immigrant would take such a step. He usually went where the Kangany directed and there worked off the debt he owed. The Kangany, however, could fictitiously claim that a batch of immigrants had refused to honour their obligations, and they could then be switched over to another employer for a financial consideration—perhaps a second advance! This was a risk which the planters were not prepared to take, particularly because the railway works were in progress again and offered a ready source of alternative employment. The Planters' Association in 1865 therefore asked that fresh legislation be prepared, making agreements concluded in India legally valid in Sri Lanka. Robinson proved sympathetic to the request, but remembering the earlier objections of the Government of India on this very issue, submitted the draft Ordinance to the Indian Governor-General for his approval, before putting it up to the Secretary of State. The draft Ordinance was partly a consolidating law, bringing together in one Act the provisions of a number of earlier bills.[117] In addition, it decreed that "all contracts entered into in India for service in Ceylon were valid and binding, provided the contract be in writing and that it be valid and binding according to the laws in force in India." This clause gave the planting community what they had asked for,[118] but it is important to notice that Robinson at the same time tightened up on the relations between master and man. Clause seven of the proposed Act declared that "no servant was liable to punishment for neglecting work, or refusing to work, if his wages had been unpaid for one month." This was a condition to which the planters strenuously objected, and attempts were early made to have the period at the end of which an unpaid labourer could legally break his contract extended from one month to three, i.e. made equal to the period for which wages were a first charge on the estate. But the Governor refused to delete the offending clause, it being his opinion that such a step would have aroused the suspicions of the Indian Government and probably have proved fatal to the whole Ordinance.[119]

Surprisingly, the Government of India, which must surely have been aware of the Madras Government's earlier objections to contracts signed in India being made binding in Sri Lanka, accepted the draft Ordinance without protest. MacCarthy and Robinson it seems had together done enough to dispel the doubts which Ward's questionable tactics had earlier given rise to and had convinced the Government of India that the protection of the immigrant was as important to the Administration in Sri Lanka as was their desire to secure an adequate supply of labour. The new bill, as Ordinance 11 of 1865, consequently had a relatively easy passage when it ultimately reached the Colonial Office, and was confirmed without the delay which had come to characterise the sanctioning of legislation relative to the legal position of the Indian in Sri Lanka.[120]

While MacCarthy had sought to make the ferry service a self-supporting system, Robinson does not appear to have regarded this as a necessary goal. The yearly outgo on this facility rose somewhat during the later 1860s, yet Robinson was inclined to push expenditure still further and suggested to the Secretary of State that it would be desirable to increase the number of boats in operation at Manaar. This too, in spite of the fact that the income from fares must in the meantime have declined considerably, for the total of arrivals and departures showed a marked falling off after 1865. The increased degree of subsidisation which these events brought seems not to have disturbed the Governor, and did not evoke from him even the merest of comments.

Year[121]	Maximum number possibly using ferry £	Maximum income at 6d per head per voyage £	Total expenditure £	Minimum degree of subsidisation £
1865	154,136	3,853	4,680	827
1866	137,757	3,443	5,212	1,769
1867	98,777	2,469	5,928	3,459
1868	110,247	2,756	5,450	2,694
1869	112,002	2,800	5,596	2,796
1870	120,306	3,007	5,619	2,612

On reading through the many dispatches on immigration written by Robinson between 1865 and 1870, one is left with the impression that he was never really aware of the problems immigrant labour had to face. Not once during this period did he mention the Coast Advance System, and not once did he ever concede that that method of recruitment was productive of distressing results. Indeed, from first to last the Governor appears to have believed that Indian labour had little to complain of.[122] For example, commenting on the housing provided on the estates he observed that "coolies as a rule have good accommodation, being housed in well-built lines which are clean and comfortable,"[123] and this despite the opinions of the Colony's doctors and even of one veteran coffee-grower, Mr W. Sabonadiere, that the condition of the lines was far from satisfactory.[124]

Of the welfare measures introduced along the Northern Route Robinson wrote in glowing terms, and when called upon to explain why, in spite of what had been done, the rate of immigrant mortality still remained unconscionably high, came up with the reply that "the supposition was incorrect" and that "deaths were by no means excessive."[125] The arguments in favour of this contention are so questionable that one is frankly amazed at the extent of the Governor's naivete. Taking the immigration returns for the ten years 1859-69, he began by agreeing that arrivals were in excess of departures by 26.3%. It was then assumed (admittedly by guesswork) that 17.3% of the total entries had settled in Sri Lanka and that the remaining 9% therefore represented mortality. This percentage was next divided by 3½, on the grounds that the average Indian labourer normally remained in Sri Lanka for that length of time and the resultant answer of 2.5% was claimed by Robinson to represent the annual immigrant death-rate. That his assumptions were open to question, and that the latter part of his calculations was at best a mathematical aberration seems not to have occurred to the Governor. In fact, he went on to apply the same reasoning to the years 1843-1869, and arrived at the conclusion that deaths over the entire period were a mere 7.04% per annum.[126]

On the allied question of why the case-rates annually recorded in the hospitals were so high, the Governor took the conventional stand that the immigrants were entirely to blame. "Owing to caste prejudices and distrust of European medicine, the cooly as a rule refuses to enter a hospital until he collapses and has to be carried there. The hospitals are in consequence, filled with the worst cases, and as long as this state of affairs continues so long will the death-rate as compared with the admissions be excessive in hospitals so circumstanced, and it is hopeless to expect any other result."[127] That the semi-starvation induced by the Coast Advance System was partly responsible for a decline in the immigrant's health; that the charge of sixpence per day per patient was an expense plantation owners were not prepared to incur, and that the hospitals were so few and far between that the journey to them was likely to affect adversely even those who were not at death's door, were evidently not considerations to which any thought was given. Indeed, there is nothing to suggest that Robinson ever attached particular importance to analyzing the question, for it was his practice to send in the annual hospital returns *without* comment.[128]

The peculiar nature of the fallacies and shortcomings of Robinson's reports may well lead some to believe that he was trying intentionally to mislead the Colonial Office, but it would be difficult to make such an accusation hold. The very frankness with which he laid the basis of his extraordinary calculations before the Secretary of State seems sufficient to clear him of that charge. Rather, it would be more accurate to argue that his attitudes were fashioned partly by his own limitations, particularly his mathematical ones, and partly by his failure to analyze with care the many facets of the Colony's immigrant labour problem.

The history of Government policy in the 1860s makes it apparent that MacCarthy was the last of the laissez-fairists. The grounds on which he condemned Ward's immigration system and his declared objective of making the ferry service a self-supporting one are enough to indicate where the Governor's doctrinal sympathies lay. That he failed to achieve his ideal is true and it is a fact also that he took no positive steps to reduce the degree of subsidisation that his scheme imposed on the general revenue, but one cannot take this to mean that the Governor had abandoned his earlier convictions. The accounts of the ferry service first showed a deficit in 1863, i.e. in its second full year of operation, and it was at this very juncture that ill-health forced MacCarthy to leave Sri Lanka. Had he remained, there is every likelihood that some adjustments might have been made in the working of the ferry, or perhaps in the charges levied for its use, with a view to balancing income and expenditure. If these expedients had failed, the introduction of a tax on the planting community, similar to that levied by Ward may well have followed.

MacCarthy's efforts to improve the Northern Route, his Passengers' Act, his labour law etc., were in keeping with the prevailing belief that welfare and laissez-faire were not mutually contradictory. Moreover, apart from the urgings of the Colonial Office and the Governor's own humanitarian sentiments, it must not be forgotten that "welfare" was intended to serve the utilitarian purpose of increasing the annual immigratory flow. With railway construction under way and with the plantation sector expanding rapidly, a large inflow of labour had become a vital necessity and there were sound economic reasons for a heavy investment in facilities on the Northern road. To have organized that inflow through some form of Government agency would have constituted an infraction of laissez-faire principle, and this may well have been the reason why MacCarthy did nothing to break the back of the Coast Advance System. Not once for that matter, did any of the dispatches he wrote on the subject of immigration even carry a description of that system's working, let alone a critical appraisal of it. Recruitment through the Kangany was an essential part of the "free action by private enterprise"[129] which the Governor recommended, hence outlawing the practice was altogether out of the question. At best, steps could be taken to minimise the evils which followed upon its use, and this precisely is what the Administration sought to do If it be true that this really was the conviction which dictated the Governor's approach, then our earlier charge that MacCarthy had failed to recognise the shortcomings of the Coast Advance System must needs be withdrawn and in its place must be put the rather more serious criticism that though aware that halting-stations and wells were no substitute for food, he had persisted in applying a policy which could never bring complete success.

Major-General O'Brien's decision to give up the Northern Route was a virtual vote of no confidence in MacCarthy's labours. He made no attempt to conceal his belief that his predecessor had failed and openly expressed the opinion that medical-stations and rest-sheds notwithstanding, mortality on the North road was still unecessarily high.[130] Yet, it must be emphasized that O'Brien did not advocate a change in the method of private recruitment. There were to be no Government-appointed recruiting agents on the Indian coast and no Board of Immigration Commissioners such as had been set up by Ward. All that was attempted was a channelling of the flow of labour through Colombo, in the hope that this would reduce the rigours of the journey to the hills. An arrangement of this nature would have violated MacCarthy's concept of "free action" and was not an experiment he could have tried, but his successor was obviously no firm supporter of any such doctrine. That this was so was made even clearer by his decision to subsidise the steamship line out of the general revenue. Here, he was going much further than Ward, who though willing to provide a fair degree of assistance, insisted that the beneficiaries of his scheme should meet its working expenses through the payment of a tax. It would seem then, that it was during O'Brien's administration that the final break with laissez-faire first became apparent. True, the private enterprise of the Coast Advance System was allowed to remain basically intact, and true also that the amount of interference employed was not as extended as that adopted in 1858, but the provision of financial assistance without the merest suggestion that even a moiety of the funds supplied should be recovered from those the new scheme was intended to serve was something altogether new and reversed a practice which until then had been regarded as axiomatic. If O'Brien's stewardship had followed upon that of Sir Henry Ward, the break with the past would perhaps have appeared less startling and its significance may well have been missed. MacCarthy's return to a stricter application of the laissez-faire credo separated the two, and what might otherwise have seemed a minor change in policy has been so highlighted that it can be seen for what it really was—the final rejection of what remained of laissez-faire.

Robinson's decision to pursue the negotiations which O'Brien had begun with the steamship company, make it evident that he too was no laissez-fairist. That he chose to follow this line because of his conviction that it offered the best solution to the question at issue and not out of a desire to preserve the continuity of Governmental policy was made apparent when those negotiations failed. Rather than allow the scheme to lapse, the Governor sought out and concluded an agreement with an alternative group, and this surely he would not have done unless the plan enjoyed his full support. Moreover, if Robinson had adhered to the belief that public funds should not be utilised to benefit the interests of a particular section of the population, he would certainly have taken steps to tax the planting community, but no move in this direction was made and there is no evidence to show that he entertained any misgivings on the subject.

The forces which prompted Robinson's return to the Northern road after 1867 were not those which had motivated MacCarthy. The latter had gone back to the development of the overland route since it was integral to the system of private enterprise he wished to re-establish, but the latter reverted to it only because he had no feasible alternative before him. Once the change had been made Robinson demonstrated yet again his indifference to the tenets of laissez-faire. The accounts of the ferry service were by then showing a heavy annual deficit, and if the Governor had considered it objectionable that public funds should be used to subsidise an amenity which catered to the economic interests of a restricted group, he would doubtless have attempted to balance the loss through a tax on the planting community. But no such step was ever suggested; on the contrary, it was proposed that the degree of subsidisation be increased still further by the appropriation of funds from the general revenue for the purchase of an additional vessel. Similarly, Robinson's acceptance of the Coast Advance System was not as in MacCarthy's case based on any devotion to private enterprise. The Governor appears to have persisted with that particular method of recruitment because he believed it more sinned against than sinning. His effort to prove that mortality was lower than was commonly believed, and his tendency to hold the immigrant responsible for such deaths as there were, implies that he saw no glaring faults in the Coast Advance System *per se*, and that he retained it, not for doctrinaire reasons, but only because he did not think badly enough of it to desire its abolition.

If it was in O'Brien's time that the first signs of the final break with laissez-faire became discernible, it was during Robinson's administration that the departure came to be consolidated as normal Government policy. After the 1870s "assistance" became as much a part of the official approach to immigration as "intervention" and "welfare," and never again was the ideal of a self-supporting immigratory process regarded as a commendable objective. MacCarthy's failure to establish such a system was thus more than an unsuccessful experiment—it marked the end of an era.

In the sphere of general immigration policy the relations between the three Governors of the 1860s and the planting community were remarkably strife free. Every important request put up to the Administration was almost immediately granted and such disagreements as there were, arose over details the significance of which were of little consequence. The only matter over which serious discord appeared likely to arise was MacCarthy's bill of 1865 which laid down that the causes of mortality on the estates should be annually submitted to Government. Yet, as we have seen, the hostility of the planters was sufficient to dissuade the Governor and his successors in office from insisting on the provisions of the Ordinance being met, and with this the threatened rupture was avoided.

The solicitude shown to the planting interests in the field of immigration policy was no doubt partly due to the Government's appreciation of the role of the coffee industry vis-a-vis the Island's finances; partly too, it was accidental, i.e. MacCarthy's belief in the self-supporting system and the disdain of his successors for that very same principle ended in the planters coming fiscally unscathed through the entire decade; partly, it was a result of the growing political influence of the planting community. Of these considerations the first two have been earlier discussed, but the third requires some further elaboration.

Among the three Governors concerned, MacCarthy alone seems to have been uninfluenced by the course of political events. Admittedly his term of office was characterised by a series of sharp disagreements between the Administration and the coffee-growing interest over the Government's road-building programme and the annual payments made to the Imperial military exchequer, but his Ordinance allowing the long-term contract was introduced two years before these controversial issues began to build in intensity and his concession cannot therefore be regarded as a measure even partially induced by a desire to placate the planting community. The problems of MacCarthy's time came to a head when O'Brien was in office and eventually thrust upon him the unenviable distinction of being the first Governor in colonial Sri Lanka to have a vote of censure passed against his administration.[131] The deterioration in relations between coffee-grower and Government which accompanied these events gave O'Brien ample reason to wish to avoid any further embarrassment, and his concern for the physical condition of the incoming labourer may well have been influenced somewhat by an anxiety to keep the planters satisfied. The request for a steam connection with India was put by the Planters' Association when the controversy over the military contribution was at its height, and viewed against this background, it is difficult to accept that the Executive Council's decision to allow the demand that the ferry service and the shipping company should operate simultaneously was in no wise induced by a desire to conciliate.

Ten days after his arrival in Sri Lanka, Sir Hercules Robinson witnesses the founding of the Ceylon League, a political association brought into being by the incidents of the early 1860s and dedicated to the winning of constitutional reforms which would seriously curtail the financial powers of the official members of the Government. Observing that the League was composed of two major elements, i.e. the planting community and the indigenous middle class, and realising that the former were in the alliance out of a sense of economic frustration, the Governor effectively destroyed this embryonic political opposition by the simple expedient of giving the planters all that they wished for. By 1870, more had been spent on the roads than ever before, the export duty on coffee had been repealed and arrangements had been made to extend the railroad. These measures proved sufficient to cool the ardour of the planting community for political reform and within four years the Ceylon League had faded into insignificance. The passing of Ordinance 11 of 1865 which acceded to the request that contracts signed in Sri Lanka should be regarded as legal, may well have owed something to the Governor's strategy of wooing the planters away from their political allies. The demand for the bill originated in the Planters' Association and Robinson went so far as to invite that organisation to draw up the draft Ordinance. True, this was later amended by the Government with the intention of stiffening some aspects of the law, but the initial gesture was an unprecedented one and might reasonably be interpreted as an indication of the Governor's wish to placate the planting community.

Colonial Office policy throughout this period exhibited two outstanding characteristics. On the one hand the standards set in the sphere of immigrant welfare assumed a more searching and exacting level than in previous years, and on the other the gradual drift away from laissez-faire culminated in the total abandonment of that philosophy before the decade was out. On the side of welfare, Whitehall's ever increasing preoccupation with the subject became apparent at the very outset of MacCarthy's term. When the Governor suggested the abolition of Ward's immigration scheme, the Secretary of State's dispatch sanctioning the change made it a point to emphasize that Ward's system had had its welfare side, and it was impressed on MacCarthy that a return to the Northern road should be accompanied by a wide application of welfare measures.[132] This note of warning took on a more positive note in the correspondence over the Ordinance allowing the long-term contract. The bill, first sent up on 8th January 1862, was not confirmed until MacCarthy had written three long dispatches explaining in detail the degree of protection afforded to the Indian immigrant,[133] and the nature of the questions which he was called upon to answer demonstrated that the Colonial Office was becoming increasingly difficult to please.[134] The Governor's accounts of what was being done on the Northern Route were accorded similar treatment. The Passengers' Act, the provision of well-appointed vessels, the building of rest-sheds etc., met with immediate approval, but in the same breath it was suggested that reports on the effects of these improvements on the health and mortality of the immigrant should also be submitted.[135] The tone of the Secretary of State's replies leaves one with the impression that mere descriptions of the facilities extended to labour no longer satisfied him, but that he wished to discover whether the measures taken had proved successful or not. Evidently, such proof of success was not to be found in MacCarthy's policies, for O'Brien's proposal that the steam connection with India be re-established was assented to with remarkable alacrity. This sudden reversal of Colonial Office favour could not have been caused by any dissatisfaction with MacCarthy's scheme as a system of supply, for the annual inflow of labour between 1860 and 1863 had risen from 52,945 to 70,718, an increase of over 33%. What appears to have convinced Whitehall that a change was necessary was O'Brien's observation that there was still a great deal of suffering on the Northern Route, i.e. that the scheme had failed on its welfare side. The Secretary of State's support of Governmental interference with the "free flow" of labour was thus a manifestation of his concern for immigrant welfare and is comparable to the attitude adopted towards Ward's experiment in 1858. The same, however, cannot be said of the decision to allow the new arrangements to be financed out of the public funds. In Ward's time the interest in welfare had been just as great, but it was not forgotten that the Immigration scheme was also a system of supply and that part of the expenditure incurred had been raised through a tax on the planting community. In 1864 no objections were voiced against the proposal that a scheme which was as much a system of supply as Ward's had been, should be entirely "assisted." out of the general revenue. Clearly, the Colonial Office had finally resolved to break with the one laissez-faire principle it had always sought to maintain.[136] The principle, it is true, had been violated in 1858, but then only in part, and with extreme reluctance. Moreover, the expansion of the coffee industry and hence, the future of the Island's finances were at stake and the Colonial Office had no alternative but to permit a measure of assistance. In 1864, on the other hand, the plantation sector was not in similar straits, yet the Secretary of State showed no reticence in allowing the subsidisation of the shipping line. The rupture with laissez-faire became all the more apparent during the administration of Sir Hercules Robinson, the increasing degree of subsidisation which followed upon his return to the Northern Route being allowed to pass without comment. The concern for immigrant welfare was even more prominent, and Robinson's every statement on the question subjected to the closest scrutiny. The Governor was strongly pressed to submit periodical reports on the condition of immigrant labour,[137] and though this was not regularly done, at least the yearly hospital return became a regular feature in the annual Ceylon Blue Book. The high case-rate which these hospital records showed quickly convinced the Colonial Office that "the endeavours made by the Government to mitigate the evils attendant on the annual immigration of Malabar coolies have not produced all the results which might be desired."[138] Robinson was therefore reminded that it was "a matter of obligation" for the Administration to improve the lot of the immigrant, particularly because Sri Lanka "was without the appliances usually to be found in civilized communities for the relief of the labouring classes of the population."[139] Of course, not all of this concern sprang from humanitarian sentiments alone. Welfare was also a means to an end, it being economically expedient to encourage the immigrant to resort to Sri Lanka. That this was a consideration on which Whitehall kept its eye is evident from the closing sentences of a dispatch to the Colony, "It is by the labour of these people that the Colony is enriched, and the expense necessary to prevent a scandalous mortality amongst the immigrants on their passages to Ceylon, must be considered as part of the cost of that labour and as such devolving upon the Colonial revenue."[140]

Robinson's description of what had been done to ease the rigours of the march to the hills do not appear to have been taken at their face value by the Colonial Office. When the Governor wrote of the numerous halting-places which had been set up, an Under-Secretary wished to know whether they were in a state of good repair; and when assured that they were, inquired whether steps had been taken to prevent them from falling into disrepair.[141] Similarly, the Governor's view that the hospitals were filled with "the worst cases" and that immigrant mortality in general was low does not seem to have been accepted. No official statement to this effect was conveyed to Sri Lanka, but against the margin of the original dispatch to Whitehall is pencilled this cynical comment, "What about deaths outside the hospitals, e.g. on the estates and the roadsides?"[142]

By the end of 1870 the Colonial Office was far from satisfied with the state of immigrant labour policy. It had by then become too aware of the details of the Coast Advance System to be unduly impressed by the mere proliferation of rest-sheds, wells etc., and official circles had begun to cast around for some more drastic solution to the question of labour mortality. This decision was eventually conveyed to Robinson and though no definite suggestions were put up to the Governor, it is significant that he was not cautioned as to how far he should go in interfering with the mechanisms of supply.[143] Evidently Whitehall was prepared to intervene, assist, or even abolish private enterprise in this field if it was likely that such a policy would produce the results they sought.

Superficially viewed the increasing enthusiasm of the Home Government for labour welfare may seem to have sprung from a number of sources. One can claim that it was an extension of earlier humanitarian policy, or point to the influence of the India Office, or give part credit to the ever-watchful Evangelical Societies.[144] This line of reasoning would no doubt be broadly true, but what is really important is that the policy-makers of the Colonial Office, the Indian authorities and the Evangelicals had had their views revised by the disintegration of the laissez-faire credo in the course of the 1860s. It was in that decade that the axioms of the philosophy were mortally undermined by opposing intellectual forces, and an early result of this process was the rapid collapse of the prejudice against all forms of intervention. The limits of permissible State action in the cause of welfare, already wide, were now made broad enough to include spheres of economic activity previously regarded as sacrosanct. To all those interested in the fate of the Indian immigrant this represented the removal of a barrier which had hedged about the policies they had hitherto advocated. There was nothing now to prevent their demanding a comprehensive programme of Governmental interference, and what is more, they could do so in the knowledge that the Colonial Office was prepared to listen with a sympathetic ear.

In the same way the foundering of laissez-faire sufficiently altered the attitude towards the rules of public finance to remove "assistance" from the category of unscientific economic conduct. The State was now free to assist the immigratory process if the conditions of the time seemed to warrant such a policy, for the new theories which replaced the older approach were inclined to the view that assistance could often stimulate development. This change in assumptions does not, of course, necessarily justify Colonial Office support of the assistance extended by O'Brien and Robinson to the planting community. The latter were not economically speaking in difficult straits and all that subsidisation eventually did was to increase their margins of personal profit. The motivation in this instance may well have been of a political nature, born of Whitehall's desire to see an end to the coalition between the planters and the Sri Lankan middle-class. One cannot argue though that these events were altogether unconnected with the new trends in thought, for in a period of laissez-faire triumphant, the early 1850s for example, it was most unlikely that assistance of this sort would have been countenanced, however great the provocation. It was the breaching of the walls of the old system that undermined the objections to what was done after 1864 and permitted it to go unquestioned.

The breakdown of laissez-faire was of wide significance in the field of immigration policy. With the presumption against Governmental action now completely removed, the stage was set for the introduction of measures which identified the Government more closely with all aspects of immigrant life in Sri Lanka. Officialdom was not slow to follow this course and the crop of bold experiments which characterised the approach to the labour question throughout the remainder of the coffee era were a natural result of the changes in outlook which accompanied laissez-faire's demise.

NOTES

1. C.O.54. 233. 13th February 1847—Campbell to Grey. Higher fares were charged by carters for the journey up to the hills, i.e. 80s. per ton, and this made a formidable addition to the cost of rice, manure and stores taken up to the plantations. The railway made no such differentiation in rates and the cost of the upward trip came down by 75%. See vanden Driesen, *op. cit.*, p. 409 and pp. 480-81.
2. C.O.54. 233. 13th February 1847—Campbell to Grey.
3. *Ibid.*
4. This rather general price series has been used in place of one specifically related to plantation coffee, since exports from that sector were valued at a fixed average price of 54s. per cwt., between 1858 and 1872. This figure no doubt reflected the state of the marktet in 1858 but it grew increasingly unreal as the years progressed. The discrepancy between fact and valuation had become so apparent by 1872 that the Customs

Department was compelled to revise its valuation and soon after to abandon fixed valuations altogether. Other sources of information on coffee prices exist, yet it is difficult to construct an accurate price index for plantation coffee as the Sri Lankan crop was marketed under three classifications, i.e. ordinary to fine ordinary, fine fine ordinary to middling, and good middling to fine, and the records do not indicate how much of each sort was sold annually. The best one can do in the circumstances is to use the British Customs returns which show the average prices of *all* coffee annually imported from Sri Lanka, since these can at least serve as a useful indication of coffee prices current in general. These total imports were made up of both plantation and peasant coffee. The latter, which accounted for a maximum of 21.7% and a minimum of 9.8% of total coffee imports during these years, usually fetched lower prices on the British market, the average price being between 15s. and 25s. the cwt. below the average of the plantation varieties. Their inclusion in the British figure must therefore reduce somewhat the average price of the plantation crop. That these are merely British prices is true, but they are of major significance since it was to that country that the bulk of Sri Lanka's coffee went. Of the total plantation crop exported between 1868 and 1872, 94.9% was shipped to Great Britain.

5. The figure for 1861 is taken from the Blue Book and those for 1862-1870 from Ferguson's Directory. The latter estimates have been preferred over the former since there is ample reason to consider them more accurate. The Government returns are incomplete and make no differentiation between plantation and peasant coffee. Ferguson, on the other hand, estimates separately the area under plantation coffee, and after 1866, denotes the individual acreage of each holding. See Directory of 1866, 1874, etc.
6. Ceylon Blue Book.
7. C.O.54. 415. 12th October 1866—Robinson to Cardwell; C.O.54. 427. 14th September 1867—Robinson to Carnarvon.
8. See vanden Driesen, *op. cit.*, pp. 392-96.
9. C.O.54. 467. 14th September 1871—Robinson to Kimberley; Ferguson, *Ceylon in the Jubilee Year*, p. 64.
10. C.O.54. 377. 6th July 1863—MacCarthy to Newcastle; C.O.54. 378. 26th August 1863—MacCarthy to Newcastle.
11. *Ibid.* The Pioneer Corps was the permanent work-force attached to the Public Works Department.
12. Vanden Driesen, *op. cit.*, pp. 508-9.
13. The Ceylon Census of 1871, table XXI, p. 113.
14. N.K. Sarkar, *The Demography of Ceylon*, pp. 19 and 57.
15. By the end of 1870 those on lengthened contracts could not have exceeded 13,482 persons. This figure represents the difference between entries and exits in 1869 and 1870, with no provision made for mortality or settlement.

16. They usually formed the permanent force on the plantation and were considered a valuable asset owing to their experience and ready availability. A small number took employment as domestics, gardeners and horsekeepers etc., or else set up on their own as traders, shopkeepers etc., but there is no evidence that such a movement away from the plantations had reached any magnitude during the 1860s.
17. Ferguson, *The Ceylon Directory 1874*—note on "The Coffee Enterprize" pages unnumbered.
18. Blue Book. C.O.59 series.
19. One is encouraged to stay with the 5% rate of settlement owing to the similarity in the estimates of the resident Indian population arrived at via computations based on the settlement rate and the census returns respectively (see pp. 118 and 120 above)
20. Ferguson, *The Ceylon Directory 1867-68*, p. 178.
21. Ferguson, *The Ceylon Directory 1867-68*, p. 248, 311 and 414.
22. Ferguson, *The Ceylon Directory 1867-68*, p. 178.
23. 1872 Administration Reports, Jaffna District and Northern Province, 2nd June 1873, p. 103. I am indebted to Dr. Michael Roberts for this reference.
24. Ferguson at first put the death-rate at 4%, i.e. in his Directory of 1867-68 because of his belief that settlement in the 1860s was exceptionally heavy. In his revised estimates of 1874 he made no specific reference to deaths in the period 1860-1870, but held that mortality from 1839-1874 must have been around 20%. Since he had earlier concluded that mortality from 1839 to 1850, and 1850 to 1860 was equal to 25% in each period, it follows that he must have put deaths between 1862 and 1870 at 10%.
25. C.O.54. 370. 30th August 1862—MacCarthy to Newcastle; B.P P. of 1863, vol. 15. Report of the Emigration Commissioners, p. 55.
26. C.O.54. 371. 29th November 1862—MacCarthy to Newcastle; Mr. T.J. Reidy was appointed Superintendent of Immigration at a salary of £400 per annum. C.O.54. 370. 30th August 1862—MacCarthy to Newcastle.
27. B.P.P. of 1864-66 (I.U.P.) Vol. II, pp. 295 and 584
28. B.P.P. of 1864-66 (I.U.P.) Vol. II, pp. 295 and 584.
29. B.P.P. of 1864-66 (I.U.P.) Vol. II, p. 901.
30. C.0.54. 463. 28th February 1871—Robinson to Kimberley (Encl.). Roberts, *op. cit.*, Part I, p. 29, holds that conditions on the road were satisfactory in the late 1860s since amongst other things, there were "15 sheds with hospitals attached to most" between Manaar and Dambulla. But Twynam points out that these hospital sheds were in "a most unsatisfactory state" and that some were never built. Roberts also quotes the Assistant Government Agent at Anuradhapura, Mr. L. Liesching as a man "on the spot who gave a much better report." Liesching, however, based his impressions on the fact that neither the planters nor the immigrants had made any complaints, and made no direct reference to the state of the sheds. Significantly, Robinson in his dispatch of 28th

February 1871, implicitly accepted Twynam's strictures by assuring the Colonial Office that many of the former's "suggestions had been carried out and that others were now in progress."

31. C.O.54. 463 28th February 1871—Robinson to Kimberley (Encl.).
32. B.P.P. of 1871-72 (I.U.P.).
33. C.O.54. 391. 15th July 1864—O'Brien to Cardwell; C.0.54. 444. 10th April 1869—Hodgson to Granville.
34. C.O.54. 444. 10th April 1869—Hodgson to Granville.
35. C.O.54. 391. 15th July 1864—O'Brien to Cardwell. Major-General Terence O'Brien was Officer Administering the Government in the interim between the departure of Governor MacCarthy and the arrival of Sir Hercules Robinson.
36. C.O.54. 444. 10th April 1869—Hodgson to Granville. Lieutenant-General Hodgson was the Officer Administering the Government when Sir Hercules Robinson was away on leave from 2nd July 1868 to 13 June 1869.
37. C.O.54. 463. 28th February 1871—Robinson to Kimberley. This comment was pencilled in on the original dispatch.
38. C.O.54. 444. 10th April 1869—Hodgson to Granville (Encl). C.O.54. 463. 28th February 1871—Robinson to Kimberley (Encl.).
39. In 1862 Governor MacCarthy began the construction of the Badulla hospital. The institutions at Kurunegalla and Ratnapura were begun in the following year and that at Nuwara Eliya in 1870. See the Blue Book for those respective years.
40. On estates remote from the hospitals the Superintendent had no alternative but to "doctor" his work-force. Such attention even if unskilled was certainly better than no treatment at all.
41. C.O.54. 444. 10th April 1869—Hodgson to Granville (Encl). Something of an exaggeration this comment. It is difficult to accept that the majority of patients admitted in a moribund condition had first been experimented upon by their employers.
42. C.O.54. 425. 24th May 1867—Robinson to Carnarvon (Encl.); C.O.54. 457. 6th August 1870—Robinson to Granville.
43. C.0.54. 392. 17th August 1864—O'Brien to Cardwell; C.O.54. 415. 4th October 1866—Robinson to Cardwell.
44. C.O.54. 423. 24th May 1867—Robinson to Carnarvon. The hospitals listed above are the seven medical institutions normally frequented by Indian labour.
45. While the returns of 1866 showed that sanitation, water supply, drainage, accommodation and staffing were poor in all Government hospitals, those of 1869 and 1870 recorded a gradual but steady improvement in these essentials.
46. C.O.54. 444. 10th April 1869—Hodgson to Granville.
47. C.O.54. 464. 21st June 1871—Robinson to Kimberley.
48. *Ibid.*
49. Ceylon Blue Book.

50. Cholera and small-pox were dealt with in separate institutions. It is difficult to discover how many immigrants died of these two diseases each year since isolation hospital returns give no indication of the patient's ethnic origin. Small-pox appears to have been more common than cholera, but there is no evidence to suggest that either was ever responsible for a high proportion of immigrant mortality, i.e. sufficient to account for a significant share of the discrepancy between arrivals and departures.
51. C.O.54. 444. 10th April 1869—Hodgson to Granville (Encl.).
52. *Ibid.*
53. Manson-Bahr, *op. cit.*, p. 794.
54. C.O.54. 444. 10th April 1869—Hodgson to Granville.
55. *Ibid.*
56. *Ibid.* C.O.54. 457. 6th August 1870—Robinson to Granville; C.O.54. 464. 21st June 1871—Robinson to Kimberley.
57. C.O.54. 444. 10th April 1869—Hodgson to Granville (Encl.); C.O.54. 463. 28th February 1871—Robinson to Kimberley (Encl.).
58. C.O.54. 444. 10th April 1869—Hodgson to Granville (Encl.).
59. Manson-Bahr, *op. cit.*, pp. 646-47.
60. C.O.54. 444. 10th April, 1869—Hodgson to Granville (Encl.).
61. *Ibid.*
62. C.O.54. 463. 28th February, 1871—Robinson to Kimberley.
63. C.O.54. 371. 22nd December 1862—MacCarthy to Newcastle.
64. C.O.54. 463. 28th February 1871—Robinson to Kimberley.
65. C.O.54. 425. 6th March 1867—Robinson to Carnarvon. Female labourers and boys were paid at rates ranging from 9s. to 14s. per month.
66. C.O.54. 377. 6th July 1863—MacCarthy to Newcastle; C.O.54. 378. 26th August 1863. MacCarthy to Newcastle.
67. C.O.54. 376. 25th June 1863—MacCarthy to Newcastle; C.O.54. 379. 1st September 1863—MacCarthy to Newcastle; C.O.54. 380. 30th September 1863—MacCarthy to Newcastle.
68. C.O.54. 367. 27th February 1862—MacCarthy to Newcastle; B.P.P. of 1862 Vol. 22—Report of the Emigration Commissioners, p. 58.
69. C.O.54. 367. 30th August 1862—MacCarthy to Newcastle; B.P.P. of 1863, Volume 15—Report of the Emigration Commissioners, p. 55. Of the three vessels employed, the Governor had this to say, "Two, the 'Sarah Armitage' and the 'Geraldine,' the former of 165 tons and the latter of 87 tons, are first-rate vessels. The other, the 'Adiletchimy' is being fitted up to bring her to a level with the other two."
70. C.O.54. 367. 8th January 1862—MacCarthy to Newcastle.
71. C.O.54. 356. 14th May 1860. Letter from the India Office to the Secretary of State.
72. C.O.54. 367. 8th January 1862—MacCarthy to Newcastle.
73. C.O.55. 106. 20th March 1862—Newcastle to MacCarthy.
74. *Ibid.*
75. C.O.54. 369. 26th April 1862—MacCarthy to Newcastle.

76. *Ibid.* (Encl.)
77. *Ibid.*
78. *Ibid.*
79. C.O.55. 106. 19th July 1862. Ordinance 16 of 1863, confirmed in March 1864, extended the provisions of Ordinance 20 of 1861 to labour other than agricultural. Railway construction had begun again and the contractor, like other employers, desired to make long-term agreements with his employees. C.O.54. 396. 11th March 1864—Newcastle to O'Brien (Encl.).
80. C.O.54. 367. 27th February 1862—MacCarthy to Newcastle.
81. C.O.54. 371. 29th November 1862—MacCarthy to Newcastle.
82. C.O.54. 367. 27th February 1862—MacCarthy to Newcastle. In 1871, the Government Agent of Jaffna, Mr W.C. Twynam, pointed out that about 7,000 immigrants per year used the road through Puttlam and that the neglect of that route was productive of much suffering. In reply, however, the Government maintained that this was not ordinarily so, and that the Puttlam road had only been used by a limited number between 1864 and 1866 because of cholera outbreaks on the Central Route. It was suggested that Twynam was generalising on inadequate evidence. C.O.54. 463. 28th February 1871—Robinson to Kimberley (Encl.). C.O.54. 468. 26th November 1871—Robinson to Kimberley.
83. C.O.54. 367. 27th February 1862—MacCarthy to Newcastle; B.P.P. of 1866, vol. 49, p. 117.
84. C.O.54. 367. 8th January 1862—MacCarthy to Newcastle; C.O.54. 367. 27th February 1862—MacCarthy to Newcastle.
85. B.P.P. of 1864, Vol. 40—Report on the Blue Book for 1862.
86. See vanden Driesen, *op. cit.*, pp. 508-9.
87. B.P.P. of 1871, Vol. 47. Report on the Blue Book.
88. Ceylon Blue Book. MacCarthy left Sri Lanka in December 1863, but the expenditure for 1864 has been added to the total given above, since there was no change in policy under the Acting Governor, Major-General Terence O'Brien.
89. C.O.54. 363. 30th October 1861—MacCarthy to Newcastle.
90. Ceylon Blue Book.
91. The earnings from all Government vessels, i.e. the India ferry and the Round-the-Island service were entered under a common head.
92. Roberts, *op. cit.*, p. 26.
93. C.O.54. 371. 22nd December 1862—MacCarthy to Newcastle. This represents a marked change of view on the Governor's part. Eighteen months earlier, i.e. in July 1861 he had held the view that "Malabar deaths" amounted to 20%. See C.O.54. 361. 22nd July 1861—MacCarthy to Newcastle.
94. B.P.P. of 1862, Volume 15, Report of the Emigration Commissioners, p. 55.
95. The need for such an Ordinance was first brought to the attention of the Governor by Mr. A. Nichol, who from October 1860 to April 1862 had

represented the Planters' Association in the Legislative Council. C.O.54. 371. 22nd December 1862—MacCarthy to Newcastle.

97. Ferguson, *The Ceylon Directory. The Labour Laws of Ceylon.*
98. See vanden Driesen, *op. cit.*, pp. 387-90 and 508-10.
99. Ferguson, *op. cit.*
100. C.O.54. 376. 25th June 1863—MacCarthy to Newcastle. MacCarthy described these workers as Punjabis and Sikhs, but the evidence suggests that they were from Bengal.
101. C.O.54. 379. 1st September 1863—MacCarthy to Newcastle; C.O.54. 380. 30th September 1863—MacCarthy to Newcastle.
102. This was one reason why MacCarthy was unable to expand Sri Lanka's road system. The shortage of workers so alarmed Major Skinner of the Road Department that he suggested the import of Chinese labour, but the proposal was not approved by the Colonial Office. C.O.54. 378. 26th August 1863—MacCarthy to Newcastle (Encl.). Soon after MacCarthy's departure Acting Governor O'Brien decided that a partial solution to the problem would be found in the extension of Pioneer Corps contracts to five years instead of three. This was agreed by the Secretary of State and was legalised through the passing of Ordinance 15 of 1863. C.O.54. 385. 7th January 1864—O'Brien to Newcastle.
103. Blue Book.
104. C.O.54. 391. 15th July 1864—O'Brien to Cardwell. Roberts, *op. cit.*, p. 26 holds that as O'Brien was strongly disposed to support the steamship company's proposal, his comments on the Northern Route should be taken "with a grain of salt." But why would O'Brien have supported the steamship company if such support was undeserved? Moreover, it was not O'Brien but the planters who first mooted the scheme.
105. *Ibid.* (Encl.)
106. *Ibid.*
107. C.0.54. 415. 12th October 1866—Robinson to Cardwell. The Government transferred the "Pearl" to the shipping company as an equivalent for the first £5,000 of the combined subsidies, i.e. in lieu of the Government subsidy for fifteen months.
108. C.O.54. 437. 2nd October 1868—Major-General Studholm Hodgson to Buckingham. Major-General Hodgson administered the Government while Robinson was on leave from 2nd July 1868 to 13th June 1869.
109. C.O.55. 117. 26th June 1869—Granville to Hodgson.
110. C.O.54. 463. 28th February 1871—Robinson to Kimberley.
111. *Ibid.*
112. *Ibid.*—also Ceylon Blue Book.
113. Ceylon Blue Book.
114. C.O.54. 463. 28th February 1871—Robinson to Kimberley.
115. *Ibid.* (Encl.)
116. Ordinance 20 of 1861. C.O.54. 367. 8th January 1862—MacCarthy to Newcastle.
117. The new bill brought together (a) Ordinance 5 of 1841, a law which

insisted that contracts beyond one month and not exceeding twelve, should be in writing, and did not provide for long engagements; (b) Ordinances 14 of 1845 and 3 of 1849, both of which covered Pioneer labour; (c) Ordinance 20 of 1861, MacCarthy's bill which allowed long-term contracts signed in Sri Lanka.

118. '"The new Labour Ordinance will make advances safe and give a better hold on our coolies," said one (planter); "it's an immense boon" said another'—quoted by Roberts. "The Master and Servant Laws of 1841 and the 1860s and immigrant labour in Ceylon" in *The Ceylon Journal of Historical and Social Studies* January-December 1965, p. 35.

119. C.O.54. 405. 30th November 1865—Robinson to Cardwell; Ferguson, *Ceylon Directory 1866-1868. The Labour Laws of Ceylon.*

120. C.O.54. 405. 30th November 1865—Robinson to Cardwell; C.0.55. 112. 6th March 1866—Cardwell to Robinson. When officially consulted by the Secretary of State on the terms of the new bill, the Indian Government suggested that "additional means should be taken for ascertaining the actual conditions of the Indian labourers," and that periodical reports should be sent in. This proposal was passed on to Robinson, and one such report was submitted in March 1867. After that date, however, the practice was dropped and only the annual hospital reports transmitted regularly. C.O.55. 112. 23rd March 1866—Cardwell to Robinson; C.O.54. 425. 6th March 1867—Robinson to Carnarvon.

121. Statistics from the Ceylon Blue Book. In the first column it has been assumed that all arrivals and departures in the period under consideration were made via the Manaar ferry. Since some must have made the journey on privately owned vessels, the real annual rate of subsidisation must have been considerably above that given in column four.

122. C.O.54. 463. 28th February 1871—Robinson to Kimberley.

123. C.O.54. 425. 6th March 1869—Robinson to Carnarvon.

124. C.O.54. 463. 28th February 1871—Robinson to Kimberley (Encl.).

125. *Ibid.*

126. *Ibid.* What is more surprising though is that Under-Secretary Murdoch of the Colonial Office accepted Robinson's mathematics! The obvious errors in his calculations, however, do not appear to have passed unnoticed for long, for Whitehall was soon concerning itself again with the question of immigrant mortality. Murdoch's comments are to be found in the margin of a letter to the Governor from Dr. W. van Dort of Gampola Hospital; submitted as an enclosure with the dispatch cited above.

127. *Ibid.*

128. The only full description of mortality in the hospitals together with reports from the doctors in charge was submitted by Lieutenant-General Hodgson in April 1869, when he was Officer Administering the Government. C.O.54. 444. 10th April 1869—Hodgson to Granville.

129. C.O.54. 363. 30th October 1861—MacCarthy to Newcastle.

130. C.O.54. 391. 15th July 1864—O'Brien to Cardwell.

131. Dissension over the annual military contribution waxed hot in 1863 when the total of military payments demanded of Sri Lanka was raised to £126,000 per annum. In protest the unofficial members of the Legislative Council in their reply to the Governor's speech opening the sessions in August 1864 inserted a clause which read, "The Council desire to record their dissatisfaction and discontent that revenues have been exacted for several years so far beyond the requirements of the public service, and so much larger than could be devoted to public purposes; and they further complained that whilst the revenues have been so abundant the efficiency of nearly every public department has been seriously impaired by the parsimonious policy of the Government." The amendment happened by chance to be debated when three official members of the Council were absent, and the unofficial members who were at full strength succeeded in obtaining a majority of one. B.P.P. of 1867-68. Vol. XLVIII; C.O.54. 392. 30th August 1864—O'Brien to Cardwell.
132. C.O.55. 106. 12th January 1862—Newcastle to MacCarthy.
133. C.O.54. 367. 8th January 1862—MacCarthy to Newcastle; C.O.54. 367. 27th February 1862—MacCarthy to Newcastle; C.O.54. 369. 26th April 1862—MacCarthy to Newcastle.
134. C.O.55. 106. 20th March 1862—Newcastle to MacCarthy; C.0.55. 106. 9th May 1862—Newcastle to MacCarthy.
135. C.O.55. 106. 9th May 1862—Newcastle to MacCarthy.
136. Though laissez-faire theories of public finance did not specifically state that all special projects should be wholly financed by the interests likely to benefit directly, the principle seems to have been quite strictly adhered to in practice. To have failed to have observed it would in fact have been contrary to the spirit of the philosophy, for it would have been tantamount to "assisting" a particular group at the expense of the others. The levying of a tax was obviously regarded as a means through which the assistance given could be "cancelled out" and the device was normally used when Government was obliged to perform some service for an interest which for some reason was unable to act collectively. This principle appeared in different guises in a variety of economic fields, a good example in the sphere of purely private enterprise being that of the Turnpike Trust in Great Britain where users, i.e. those who benefitted directly and not the general public, paid for the upkeep of the roads.
137. C.O.55. 112. 6th March 1866—Cardwell to Robinson.
138. C.O.55. 117. 26th June 1869—Granville to Robinson.
139. C.O.55. 120. 16th September 1870—Kimberley to Robinson. By "appliances found in civilized communities" the Secretary of State indicated that he meant work-houses, almshouses, infirmaries etc.
140. C.O.55. 117. 26th June 1869—Granville to Robinson.
141. C.O.54. 463. 28th February 1871—Robinson to Kimberley (Encl.).
142. *Ibid.*
143. C.O.55. 120. 7th October 1870—Kimberley to Robinson.

144. One of those who evinced an interest in the condition of the immigrant labourer in Sri Lanka was Florence Nightingale. Early in 1861, through the Secretary of State, she submitted a questionnaire to Governor MacCarthy requesting information on the rate of immigrant mortality, the causes of death etc. MacCarthy's reply was short and rather general in nature. C.O.54. 361. 22nd July 1861—MacCarthy to Newcastle.

Chapter 5

The Last Phase: Experiments in the Principle of Subsidisation—1871-1886

The Economic Background

By 1870 the Sri Lankan coffee industry had reached its zenith. Prices were high, exports stood at over a million hundredweights per year, and the acreage under the crop was rapidly expanding. The prosperous state of the enterprise reacted favourably upon the revenue and with large surplus balances to its credit, it seemed that there was literally no limit to what the Government could do to further the development of the Island's resources. A Golden Age in short, appeared to lie ahead. Yet, barely fifteen years later coffee was no longer Sri Lanka's most important product, former growers of the shrub were desperately attempting to salvage their fortunes by turning to the cultivation of other crops, and the rate of national economic growth had been sharply arrested.

This catastrophic decline of the Colony's most important export was caused primarily by the ravages of Hemileia Vastratrix, a fungoid affliction popularly known as the coffee leaf disease. First noticed in Madulsima, one of the younger planting districts, in 1869, the blight spread rapidly over the entire coffee zone.[1] Initially, its evil effects passed unnoticed. Output tended to drop off slightly, but such decreases were credited to seasonal influences rather than to the pest. Other considerations, moreover, served most effectually to blind the eyes of all concerned to the insidious progress of the fungus and to the gradual but sure decline of the annual output. Short crops in Java and Brazil combined with an increased demand for the Sri Lankan product on the American market to raise prices by 67.8% in the decade 1870 to 1879 and the concomitant increase in profits was sufficient for a time to delude the planting community into believing that nothing was seriously amiss.

Average Price of All Sri Lankan Coffee in Great Britain[3]	Average Price of Plantation Coffee	
Year s. d.	Year s. d.	Year s. d.
1870 - 63.9. per cwt.	1873 - 88.0. per cwt	1877 - 106.0. per cwt.
1871 - 64.9.	1874 - 90.0.	1878 - 107.0.
1872 - 72.0.	1875 - 100.0.	1879 - 107.0.
	1876 - 106.0.	1880 - 104.0.

Under the stimulus of rising prices, the 1870s witnessed a vast expansion of the acreage under coffee.[4] A cycle of favourable seasons brought quick success to the new districts in the higher elevations, and it was found that a crop which had previously been supposed to find its suitable limit at 4,000 or 4,500 ft. could be cultivated with profit at 5,000 or 5,500 ft.[5] The competition for land became so keen that forest areas which ten or twenty years before would not have fetched as much as £1 per acre, were sold for over twenty times as much and even at these prices investors were confident of profitable results.[6]

Acreage under Coffee Plantation[7]

1870	185,000 acres	1876	260,000 acres
1871	195,627	1877	272,243
1872	206,000	1878	275,009
1873	219,974	1879	265,000
1874	237,345	1880	252,431
1875	249,604		

Despite the opening up of thousands of acres of fresh land, however, the annual export of coffee was never again able to surpass the peak reached in 1870. The deadly effects of the leaf disease so weakened its host that no affected bush could bear heavily for two consecutive years and even when in crop, attained a level of productivity far below that of earlier times. A fluctuating output thus came to characterise the coffee trade of the 1870s.[8]

Coffee Exports—Plantation[9]

1870	921,506 cwts.	1876	585,783 cwts.
1871	775,454	1877	892,085
1872	582,432	1878	585,372
1873	634,180	1879	725,324
1874	634,180	1880	611,842
1875	809,835		

After 1877 serious notice of the leaf disease was forced upon the planting community. It became apparent that the pest was not just a passing phenomenon, but one which could spell disaster to the entire industry. Chemical sprays, heavy manuring and a variety of other experiments were hastily tried in a desperate effort to halt the progress of the fungus.[10] Yet, all was in vain, for the disease continued to spread rapidly from one estate to another and before the decade was out not one plantation is said to have been free of infection.

A lavish governmental expenditure on communications which greatly improved the quantity and the quality of the roads in the Central Province, and which carried the railway into the heart of the new planting districts did much in the 1870s to balance the rising costs of production by introducing economies in transport. Coffee prices, in addition, continued their upward march, hence the industry despite its travails was able to remain a profitable enterprise. The day of reckoning, however, was not far off. By 1880 a veritable flood of low-grade coffee from Brazil had begun to make its presence felt on the international market and for the first time in years, quotations for the Sri Lankan product showed a tendency to decline. Worse was to follow. With the setting in of the Great Depression falling incomes led consumers to substitute cheaper descriptions of coffee for the more expensive varieties, and with this the higher prices which had hitherto shielded Sri Lankan coffee from the full effects of Hemileia Vastatrix fell precipitously.[11]

Coffee Prices—Plantation[12]

1880	-	104s. per cwt.
1881	-	100s.
1882	-	81s.
1883	-	81s.
1884	-	80s.
1885	-	80s.
1886	-	91s.

Though the decrease in prices in the 1880s was not as severe as that experienced between 1845 and 1849—quotations in fact did not fall below the comparatively high level of 80s. per cwt.—the leaf disease had so curtailed output and pushed up the cost of production that even at this high figure estates were unable to pay their way, and a large number of producers had no alternative but to abandon or sell their plantations.

The prospects for coffee took on an even gloomier complexion as the depression worsened in England. Early in 1880 the City of Glasgow

Bank was forced to close its doors and the financial difficulties which followed reacted disastrously through the Oriental Bank in Colombo upon local commercial enterprise. The Oriental Bank, an institution with wide planting connections, after a vain attempt to restrict operations, was itself forced to shut down in May 1883,[13] and with its closure the resultant curtailment of credit hastened scores of planters into the bankruptcy courts. With the acreage under coffee diminishing rapidly, and with the leaf disease restricting output on estates still in production, a cultivated area of 174,000 acres was able in 1883 to export only 290,593 cwts., or less than the amount shipped thirty years earlier from one third that acreage. The economic consequences of these misfortunes were felt throughout the Colony. The Government saw its revenues decline by over half a million sterling within the short period of ten years and was forced to discontinue a number of important undertakings. Carpenters, carters and numerous other categories of local labour associated with the coffee trade soon found themselves out of business and many of the Agency Houses which handled the export of the crop collapsed for want of work.[14]

Acreage under Coffee—Plantation[15]		**Coffee Exports—Plantation**[16]	
1880	252,431 acres	1880	611,842 cwts.
1881	252,431	1881	407,222
1882	220,000	1882	429,203
1883	174,000	1883	290,593
1884	150,000	1884	287,509
1885	127,000	1885	295,038
1886	98,000	1886	169,163

By 1883 it was plain the King Coffee's reign was drawing to a close. The yearly output continued to fall and none of the preventive measures showed even the slightest success in counteracting the spread of the leaf fungus. A proportion of the planting body, their resistance broken, gave up the struggle and attempted to sell their estates. But buyers were not easy to find, for there were now few left who were optimistic enough to believe in the future of coffee. "All around me" wrote a contemporary, "there seemed to be an air of expectation of disaster . . . the crisis was acute; the Colony was practically in a state of paralysis."[17] This pessimism was well founded. To administrator and planter alike it had become apparent that Sri Lanka was providing the world with a classic example of the hazards of monoculture. With every estate confined to the cultivation of a single staple it had required only a short time for the leaf disease to engulf the entire planting area, and it was now patently clear that nothing could be done to resurrect coffee.

Despite the gloom of the 1880s there were some who were far-seeing enough to realize that the demise of coffee did not herald the end of the plantation system. They recalled now the advice of Dr Thwaites, Superintendent of the Botanical Gardens, who had consistently called for a diversification of the country's agriculture and had proved by experiment that tea, cocoa and cinchona could easily and profitably be grown in the Island.[18] It was to the cultivation of these, in what has been described as the "era of new crops" that the planters turned after 1882.

Of the new products tea showed the most sustained signs of promise and so enthusiastically was its cultivation taken up that by 1886 the acreage planted with tea had surpassed that under any other plantation crop. Indeed, for a while it appeared that a monoculture would appear again, but this happily was prevented by the introduction of rubber in the last decade of the nineteenth century and by a rapid extension of the coconut industry in the lower elevations.

Acreage under tea[19]		**Exports of tea**	
1880 -	9,273 acres	1880 -	162,575 lbs.
1881 -	13,500	1881 -	348,157
1882 -	22,000	1882 -	697,258
1883 -	32,000	1883 -	1,665,768
1884 -	70,000	1884 -	2,392,973
1885 -	102,000	1885 -	4,372,722
1886 -	150,000	1886 -	7,849,888

The collapse of coffee and the transference to the new products did not effect any radical changes in the basic economic structure of Sri Lanka. Tea, rubber, cinchona and cocoa were cash crops which, like coffee, required for their successful cultivation a steady supply of labour, good roads, railways, ports, banks etc. The new products simply took over the economic edifice which had been built up over the course of the nineteenth century and became the instruments through which plantation agriculture continued to exert as strong an influence on the Island's history as it had earlier done.

A notable feature in the last phase of the coffee era was the reversal of conditions in the market for labour. The perennial shortage was replaced by an embarrassing plenitude and there were times when the annual supply was greatly in excess of the Colony's needs. The general improvement in facilities and the decline in mortality during the previous decade were probably responsible in part for this change, in that they must have done much to convince the immigrant that the journey to Sri Lanka was no longer the gamble it once had been. The increase in arrivals between 1870 and 1873 may be fairly regarded as a response to the rise in demand created by the extension of the acreage under coffee and as a manifestation of growing confidence on the part of the immigrant. After that time the abundance of labour had more to do with circumstances prevailing on the mainland. The heavy immigration of 1874 was caused by an excessive drought which had fallen heavily on India, and the massive inflow of the years 1876 and 1878, by one of the worst famines in South Indian history. Indeed, in this latter period so many decided to remain in Sri Lanka until conditions bettered at home that the Government was saddled with the problem of "immigrant unemployment" and was obliged to launch a number of new schemes in the Road, Railway and Irrigation Departments, in order to provide work for the surplus.[21]

The falling off in arrivals and the rise in departures after 1879 reflects well the growing crisis in the economy. As the effects of the leaf disease and the Great Depression came to be felt, the closing down of estates and the curtailment of the Government's public works programme so restricted the demand for labour, that the direction of the annual flow was reversed and larger numbers began to leave the Island that entered it. This novel trend continued unchecked until the new products, and tea in particular, had developed sufficiently to require more labour than the resident Indian community could supply. By 1886 the resources of this local market appear to have been exhausted, for a year later the old familiar pattern was restored and an annual excess of arrivals over departures became again the normal characteristic of the immigration returns.

IMMIGRANT RETURNS[22]

Arrivals

Year	Men	Women	Children	Total
1871	70,090	15,471	2,968	88,529
1872	64,018	12,216	3,887	80,121
1873	70,687	14,166	4,159	89,012
1874	95,659	21,400	8,097	125,156
1875	66,659	14,358	5,695	86,712
1876	121,743	28,670	14,384	164,797
1877	106,796	41,786	18,614	167,196

1878	70,247	21,584	9,262	101,093
1879	49,423	14,110	13,364	76,897
1880	36,092	6,286	3,222	45,600
1881	42,679	7,789	3,419	53,887
1882	40,901	7,301	2,705	50,907
1883	31,778	4,759	2,667	39,204
1884	36,381	6,203	3,193	45,777
1885	37,181	6,945	3,670	47,794
1886	31,602	5,525	2,780	39,907
1887	56,582	11,696	4,382	72,660

Departures

Year	Men	Women	Children	Total
1871	55,603	9,660	3,347	68,610
1872	59,005	10,783	4,247	74,035
1873	63,238	12,075	5,316	80,629
1874	73,210	10,699	5,818	89,727
1875	77,074	11,808	6,637	95,519
1876	73,668	11,522	6,770	91,960
1877	72,791	10,458	5,360	88,609
1878	72,148	13,512	5,528	91,188
1879	63,431	12,162	5,157	80,750
1880	54,410	12,524	6,794	73,683
1881	48,686	9,776	4,778	63,240
1882	44,725	8,814	4,281	57,820
1883	41,137	8,148	3,677	52,962
1884	39,365	7,083	3,637	50,085
1885	38,695	6,592	3,576	48,863
1886	36,009	6,190	3,051	45,250
1887	45,226	6,796	3,059	55,121

The Economic and Social Conditions of the Indian Immigrant

Though there is much to suggest that the situation regarding immigrant mortality in the closing years of the coffee era was far from satisfactory,[23] a cursory glance at the annual immigration returns does not convey that impression. In the period 1871-1886, arrivals amounted to 1,302,589 and departures to 1,152,930—leaving 149,659 to be accounted for. Since this deficit of a mere 11.4% must necessarily cover both mortality and settlement, it appears at first sight that neither was of striking importance during the last fifteen years of coffee's history, and that the dispatches, reports and contemporary writings which put the contrary view were flagrantly exaggerated. This seeming contradiction between statistics and first-hand description can be partly resolved by taking into account the consistent excess of emigration over immigration between 1879 and 1886. Until 1881 this efflux would have included labourers whose three-yearly contracts had come to an end, but after that date it is most unlikely that the planting body, plagued by the leaf disease and declining prices, would have entered into very many long term contracts, and it follows that a considerable number of hitherto permanent Indian residents must have left the Colony. Their enumeration under the head of "Departures" effectively masks the true state of affairs by reducing the deficit between total entries and exits over the whole period, and makes it seem that mortality and settlement had greatly diminished. Once allowance has been made for this phenomenon it becomes evident that settlement may well have been high for at least part of the period under consideration and that mortality may also have reached quite considerable levels. Indeed, there is every reason to expect the latter, given that the heavy immigration of 1874, 1876, 1877 and 1878 was largely induced by drought and famine in South India, and that many of those entering the Island were said to be in poor physical condition.[24]

An Island-wide census in 1881 recorded that 204,933 Indian workers of all types, i.e. resident and transcient, were in employment on the estates. Once again, there is said to have been a fair degree of undernumeration, i.e. of 9.59%,[25] but this total even if suitably adjusted, cannot be used as a rough bench-mark in the manner of that of 1871. There, a computation based on likely rates of settlement and natural increase provided a second, related total, which could be used as some sort of a cross-check. That same device cannot be employed for the 1870s since so little is known about those who "settled" temporarily in the Colony to avoid drought and famine at home. Projections based on the 1881 census to cover the remaining years of the coffee era are equally of little value. In every one of those years, emigrants outnumbered immigrants and the ranks of the former must certainly have included both permanent and temporary settlers, and to complicate matters further, children born to the latter during their stay in Sri Lanka. In a quantitative sense there is nothing one can say about the probable size of the permanent work force, or about those who neither settled nor returned to India, i.e. about probable mortality.

On the qualitative side, on the other hand, there is considerable discussion of the question of immigrant mortality. The tone of much official correspondence implies that the immigrant death-rate was unconscionably high, and that this was so not only in the "famine" years, but also in those which were allegedly normal. But these opinions have to be viewed with some caution. The total of arrivals alone in the period under consideration amounted to 1,302,589 immigrants, hence even a moderate death-rate for those times, say 7.5%, would in absolute terms have been represented by almost 100,000 corpses. Death on that scale could not possibly be ignored and was bound to produce a strong official reaction. Whereas many deaths in earlier years had passed unnoticed, the increase in the number of hospitals, the regular medical returns, the greater knowledge of what was occurring on the Northern Route, the acceptance of the fact that "unrecorded departures" were not likely to be as large as before, etc., must all have made the Administration of the 1870s more aware of mortality. It is hardly surprising that the almost visible proof of so many thousand dead should have created the impact that it did. To many Governors, doctors and officials in the Colonial Office, it must have seemed that more immigrants were dying in the Colony than at any previous time and that the general condition of estate labour had not improved, but had greatly deteriorated.[27]

The evidence available on the social and economic environment in which the immigrant found himself between 1870 and 1886, makes it apparent that in certain directions conditions had bettered considerably, but that in others they had remained virtually unaltered, despite some official attempts at improvement. At the Manaar ferry many advances were effected early in our period. An additional vessel was put into service in 1872, medical attendance on board was sanctioned and "every attention . . . paid to cleanliness and sanitation."[28] An important feature of these times, was the growth of immigrant traffic between South India and Colombo. With the opening of the Tuticorin railway in 1875, an increasing number found it more convenient to use this alternative route and within a year or two almost a quarter of the total annual immigration was being channelled through Colombo. However, since the Passengers' Act of 1865 covered only the ferry service at Manaar, the "native boat" was given a new lease of life, and conditions on the voyage from Tuticorin to Colombo soon resembled those the immigrant of the 1840s had experienced in the north.

"The principal mode of transport is in small native sailing vessels, the majority of which are unfit to carry passengers. The holds of these vessels contain ballast consisting principally of sand on which the coolies, especially the women and children, lie; it becomes polluted by vomit, excreta etc., and is seldom changed at the end of each voyage. These small vessels are also defective in ventilation and in rough weather when the hatches have to be closed, the air between decks becomes most foul."[29]

Official measures to control this new abuse were not long in coming. Immigration Agents were appointed to Tuticorin and Colombo with instructions to exercise a strict check on all boats plying between the two ports and, in 1879, Ordinance 5 of that year extended the provisions of the Passengers' Act to cover the traffic to Colombo.[30] It is unlikely, however, that these measures met with complete success. They had proved successful in Manaar since the low fares charged at the ferry had sufficed to eliminate all competitors, but as no Government-operated system was introduced on the Colombo-Tuticorin run, the small-boat owner was able to stay in business, and it would not have required much ingenuity for him to flout the regulations without ostensibly appearing to do so.

Where the Northern land-route was concerned, the Government seems to have concluded that the further construction of rest-sheds, medical stations and wells was now unncessary. In 1872 there were nineteen "cooly bungalows" between the port of arrival and Matale, and the number remained unchanged through the remaining years of the century.[31] With bungalows never more than fifteen miles apart, the Northern Route was no longer the "sandy jungle" it had been twenty-five years before and no really useful purpose would have been served by any fresh construction. All that was needed was to keep the existing facilities in good repair and this evidently was done. Governor Gregory reported on their "excellent condition" in 1872[32] and no criticisms of any sort were levelled against them in the remaining years of the coffee period.

For rather different reasons no attempt was made to provide any facilities at all on the road beteen Colombo and Kandy. When the immigrant traffic on this route began to assume significant proportions, it was believed that labour gangs would avail themselves of the railway and travel to the coffee districts by train. But before long it was apparent that nothing of the sort was occurring. The Immigration Commission of 1878 discovered that all but 8% had decided to walk! The distance between the two towns was seventy five miles and the cost of the ticket per man, seventy five cents. It was estimated that by walking all the way the immigrant could live on sixty four cents and save eleven, and this slim margin appears to have been considered sufficient compensation for the physical effort required to accomplish the journey on foot.[33] Even when this was brought to light the Government made no move to set up halting stations at convenient points on the line of march. It was held that the walk was relatively short and that the road ran through healthy and settled country where supplies of food and drink were easily obtainable. All this was no doubt perfectly true, but it seems to have been overlooked that the weather was often inclement and that incoming labour had to walk uphill over the greater part of their journey.

Despite the nineteen bungalows on the Northern Route, and the alleged salubrity of the march from Colombo, labour gangs continued to arrive on the plantations in a "weary and emaciated" condition.[34] It hardly needs to be said that the Coast Advance System was the villain of the piece. Its malignant influence was less heavily felt by those who travelled via Colombo,[35] and the facilities available between Manaar and Matale must have done much to relieve the suffering the system always caused and to have reduced the number of actual deaths; but the debilitating effects of the system upon the human constitution were not eradicated and the immigrants' predisposition to disease thus virtually guaranteed a considerable mortality.

That there was a close connection between the Coast Advance System and the immigrant death-rate was common knowledge at Whitehall and throughout the 1870s the Government in Sri Lanka was the recipient of a number of suggestions intended to eliminate the evils arising out of recruitment through the agency of the Kangany. It was suggested that rice should be issued to incoming labourers, that entry to the Colony should be limited to the young and robust, and that Kanganies should be issued with licences which could be withdrawn on evidence of bad behaviour. But for a variety of reasons not one of these proposals was attended with any success.[36]

The only measure which temporarily produced results was a local variant of the Colonial Office proposal that rice should be issued to incoming labour. At the end of 1871, Governor Robinson suggested that this should be done in the case of immigrants discharged from hospitals on the line of march, and his successor in office, Sir William Gregory—having refined the plan somewhat—put it into force in the last quarter of 1872. Thereafter, immigrants leaving a medical station were issued with tickets which entitled them to a supply of gratuitous food at the next station on the road. Here again more tickets were issued and thus did the immigrants pass on until they arrived at their destinations.[37] In the past it had been the practice to turn convalescents loose upon the highways, where deserted by their kanganies and invariably without any means of support, many had died by the roadside. Others had either re-entered hospital in a worse state than when they were first admitted, or else had reached their estates in so attenuated a condition that they were rarely fit enough to undertake any sustained labour.

The new arrangement appears to have worked successfully for a year or two, but the famine in India between 1876 and 1878 seems to have led to its collapse, and no more is heard of it again. That this should have happened was most unfortunate, for the scheme was an imaginative one and had the events of the seventies not occurred, it might, if properly run, have succeeded in countering one of the most callous features of the Coast Advance System.

In terms of hospital accommodation, the immigrant of our period was much better provided for than any of his predecessors. Between 1871 and 1886 nearly £460,000 was expended on the maintenance and construction of hospitals, and over £350,000 on the medical establishment. These totals represent an island-wide expenditure on facilities availed of by both immigrant and indigene and one cannot determine precisely how much was spent on each. Nevertheless, it is abundantly clear that the immigrant must have benefitted from a high proportion of these disbursements since nearly half of the institutions for which funds were appropriated show a heavy incidence of immigrant admissions.[38]

Shortly before he left Sri Lanka, Governor Robinson had stressed the necessity for a more extended medical system in the planting districts,[39] and the implementation of such a project became one of Sir William Gregory's earliest tasks when he assumed the Administration in 1872. While continuing to enlarge and equip the existing General hospitals, Gregory provided for the establishment of new medical institutions through Ordinance 14 of 1872, popularly known as the "Medical Wants Bill." The Ordinance divided up the entire planting area into twenty-two regions and these were permitted to unite according to geographical convenience, for the purpose of setting up—at the expense of the resident planters—a chain of District hospitals with qualified doctors in charge.[40] The increase in medical facilities which this measure brought seems to take much out of the criticism that the growth in the acreage under coffee was not accompanied by an expansion of the hospital system, for within three years District hospitals had been constructed in at least sixteen of the twenty-two regions created by the Ordinance.[41]

The extent of this advance, however, should not be overstated While the Medical Wants Bill produced a marked augmentation in the number of hospitals available to the estate labourer, conditions within certain of the new institutions were far from satisfactory. The Medical

Inspector of the Coffee District, Dr. J.D.M. Coghill, in a report issued in 1878, observed that "several of the District Hospitals, noteably Lindulla, Dimbula, Matale East, Rangala, Morowak Korale and Rakwana, are quite unsuited for the reception of patients." Their construction was so flimsy that "from the cheap and frail nature of the material several are falling to pieces," and their location was often in inaccessible and elevated places "difficult for sick coolies to be sent to, and entailing much unncessary suffering, by keeping them in an atmosphere of cold and wet." The equipment, moreover, was "most deficient," there being "no stoves or good blankets" available to the sick, and in rainy weather the Inspector had "frequently found the doors and windows closed and the wretched patients huddled together in the dark for warmth, often even without a cumblie*, and blue-black from cold." Considering what he had seen at first-hand, one is hardly surprised by the conclusion to which Coghill finally came, "To force a sick man to enter one of the so-called hospitals I have indicated, is, I unhesitatingly affirm, downright cruelty."[42]

If the remaining District hospitals were in a better state than those condemned by Coghill, they were nevertheless so imperfect that a Commission of Inquiry was appointed in 1878 to review the working of the Medical Wants Scheme.[43] The Commission's conclusion that the scheme had failed and the planting community's subsequent admission that they were unable to operate it satisfactorily, led the Administration to assume responsibility for the project in 1883.[44] When this was done, six strategically situated hospitals only were taken over, i.e. those at Haputale, Dick-oya, Lindulla, Uda Pussellawa, Kelebokka and Madulsima, and made part of the Government's general medical system.[45] The establishment of hospitals worthy of the name in the newer planting districts thus did not take place until the coffee period was almost at an end, and even when they did appear they were just six in number and not the twenty-two that had been originally envisaged.

Though it failed in its general purpose, the Medical Wants Bill was not without so e successes. One of its clauses required the setting up on every estate of sick-rooms in which could be housed those not ill enough to be dispatched to hospital, and another established the principle that women were to receive wages for one month after confinement, unless earlier reported fit by the Medical Officer.[46] These advances were by no means unimportant ones, for the ailing labourer had a smaller chance of recovery if obliged to remain in an overcrowded line-room, and economic considerations no longer jeopardized the lives of mother and new-born infant by forcing the former to report for work before she had fully regained her strength. Some life-saving and no doubt a great reduction in human suffering must have followed upon the introduction of these two measures, and they can both be reckoned amongst the distinct gains of this period.

In the General hospitals maintained by the Government, conditions continued to show a gradual improvement. Largely, this was due to the prodding of the Colonial Office which carefully scrutinised the annual medical reports and unfailingly brought to the Governor's notice any shortcomings which were apparent. In 1874, for instance, the attention of the local Administratior was drawn to the poor sanitation in some hospitals, to the lack of baths in others, and to the general failure in all to provide patients with filtered water;[47] while in 1877, the question of overcrowding was taken up and the shortage of baths pointed to again.[48]

Neither Whitehall's vigilance nor the efforts of the Colonial Government made any immediate impression upon immigrant mortality in the hospitals. For a time it seemed that the case-rate was lower, but this was a statistical illusion, created by the failure to distinguish between "immigrant" deaths and those of the local inhabitants. When this distinction was made—as it was in 1877 and thereafter, it was discovered that immigrant mortality in the hospitals was still excessive and that there were no grounds for any official complacency.

General Case-Rate[49]

General Hospital	1871	1872	1873	1874	1875	1876
Ratnapura	10.48%	16.55%	11.67%	15.43%	17.41%	12.95%
Kurunegalla	6.13%	10.97%	5.81%	5.91%	7.76%	5.47%
Puttlam	11.82%	13.79%	7.20%	6.81%	4.77%	3.62%
Kandy	12.30%	12.88%	12.65%	14.33%	12.71%	11.99%
Gampola	14.37%	15.93%	16.10%	12.81%	17.55%	12.39%
Badulla	16.61%	14.72%	13.27%	14.41%	14.27%	16.60%
Matale	26.40%	32.71%	25.82%	20.69%	16.16%	28.03%
Nuwara Eliya	——	——	——	16.23%	14.63%	25.97%

Immigrant Case-Rate[50]

General Hospital	1877	1878	1879	1880
Ratnapura	23.03%	30.84%	27.64%	14.38%
Kurunegalla	16.17	11.03	16.38	17.96
Puttlam	——	16.13	11.94	19.20
Kandy	31.75	37.25	31.46	21.70
Gampola	31.68	42.91	39.41	28.01
Badulla	28.98	28.50	29.48	25.72

Matale	41.37	37.63	31.40	26.82
Nuware Eliya	34.32	32.04	29.46	22.09
Colombo	23.35	31.58	23.98	20.18
Kegalle	14.62	9.29	7.80	6.42
	1881	**1882**	**1883**	**1884**
Ratnapura	9.37%	11.84	13.26%	19.35%
Kurunegalla	14.28	12.00	17.10	18.84
Puttlam	15.83	10.87	13.18	13.59
Kandy	16.66	18.76	16.52	19.07
Gampola	25.41	18.13	23.91	27.10
Badulla	24.03	19.77	27.88	25.77
Matale	28.10	30.93	19.95	25.20
Nuware Eliya	15.45	9.77	22.30	12.80
Colombo	19.92	11.80	11.83	13.93
Kegalle	4.46	7.08	10.84	27.86

The returns of the District hospitals, first drawn up for the year 1877, were not issued again until the Medical Wants Scheme passed under the control of the Government in 1883. After that date regular statistics were kept, and they make scarcely less dismal reading than those relating to the General hospitals.

Immigrant Case-Rate[51]

District Hospital	1877	1883	1884	1885	1886
Lindulla	43.20%	18.73%	19.27%	18.23%	17.52%
Raputale	58.82%	25.88%	23.62%	19.12%	16.11%
Dickoya	44.19%	23.51%	25.13%	22.90%	20.30%
Uda Pussellawa	47.94%	15.17%	13.15%	10.75%	11.95%
Kelebokka	—	13.48%	22.22%	17.85%	18.57%
Madulsima	62.48%	25.00%	14.28%	19.13%	11.25%
Rakwana	57.11%	—	—	—	18.18%
Balangoda	—	—	—	—	19.56%
Badulla	50.11%	—	—	—	—
Pussellawa	47.10%	—	—	—	—
Rangalla	44.11%	—	—	—	—
Katmale	14.20%	—	—	—	—
Maskeliya	39.90%	—	—	—	11.11%
Maturata	54.83%	—	—	—	—
Matale West	41.11%	—	—	—	—

In both sets of returns it will be noticed that generally speaking, mortality was at a peak in the closing years of the 1870s. This was a result of the great Indian famine which brought an unprecedented number of immigrants into Sri Lanka between 1876 and the end of 1878. So emaciated were a high proportion of the arrivals, that they either failed to reach the hill-country altogether, or else having arrived there, found themselves too weak to undertake any sustained labour. One way or another, they succumbed easily to the merest afflictions and crowding into the hospitals served to push up a rate of mortality which was already high.[52]

The dramatic fall in the case-rate in most General hospitals over the years 1881 to 1883 while partly due to a decline in the influx from India, was as much the outcome of a Government ruling in 1880 which laid down that all estate labour had henceforth to be treated in the District hospitals, and that entry to the General hospitals should be limited only to immigrants found by the wayside or in the towns i.e. to masterless men.[53] An immediate effect of this measure was that the number of serious cases entering medical institutions far removed from the line of march e.g. Ratnapura, Nuwara Eliya, Kegalle etc. were greatly reduced, thereby causing a marked lessening in the rate of mortality. Hospitals situated along the route, e.g. Matale, Kandy and Gampola, continued to get their quota off the roads and the case-rates at these centres consequently did not fall off by quite as much. Unfortunately, no District hospital returns are available for these years, but with the sick from the estates being sent exclusively to them, it seems likely that their death-rates must have been higher than those recorded at any of the General hospitals.

In 1883, with the inauguration of the new Government scheme, estate labour was once again permitted to enter certain of the General hospitals, and this led to a rise in case-rates in most of those institutions. A decline in mortality in a majority of the District hospitals was simultaneously recorded, but this could not have been due solely to the syphoning off of a proportion of the serious cases which would otherwise have entered them. Government control brought with it a general improvement in equipment, hygienic facilities etc., and this must also be reckoned as part of the explanation why in all but one of these institutions, the case-rate was lower in 1886 than it had been in 1883. Moreover, it must not be forgotten that the annual immigration from India was of a most restricted nature in the last years of the coffee era. With fewer undergoing the trials of the overland journey, that section of the estate population which was most vulnerable to disease was considerably reduced, and this could not but be reflected in the medical returns of the Colony. In 1886, for example, when only 39,907 arrivals were recorded, even the General hospitals—particularly those in Matale and Kurunegalla—showed a fall in mortality. When large-scale immigration was resumed in 1887, the case-rates in all medical institutions, District and General alike, went up above the 1886 level.[54]

All things considered, therefore, it would seem that the provision of additional hospitals, and the stricter attention paid to hygiene and sanitation did not produce the results the Administration had hoped for. But, if immigrant mortality in the hospitals remained high, it is nevertheless true that relatively speaking some gains were achieved. After 1883, the immigrant case-rates at all medical institutions compared favourably with the "mixed" rates of the late 1860s, and this indicates that immigrant mortality in the hospitals had declined since that time. Again, the number admitted for hospital treatment during our period was almost three times as great as it had been in 1868-69. Thus, if in absolute terms the total dying in hospital was somewhat larger, it also follows that more were being cured and that as many as before could not have perished on the estates.[55]

The constant interest of the Colonial Office in the problem of immigrant mortality produced the usual crop of explanations as to why deaths were excessive both in the hospitals and out. The familiar argument that caste prejudice and an antipathy towards Western medicine kept some away from the medical institutions and led others to seek entry when they were past relief, was put up regularly by Administration and doctors alike, but with the difference that whereas every Governor of Sri Lanka from 1871 to 1886 considered it the major reason for the high death-rate,[56] the medical men merely regarded it as one of many. As we have pointed out before, there can be no doubt that caste considerations and a distrust of Western treatment were factors to be reckoned with, but judging by the increasing number who sought admission to the hospitals, it is obvious that the prejudice had broken down considerably, and that other forces must have been just as important.

That the immigrants' tardiness in entering hospital was often a result of circumstances beyond their control was readily admitted by the doctors. Early in the 1870s the Principal Medical Officer, Dr W.P. Charsley, drew attention to what he described as the "false economy" of the planting community. Estate superintendents, he said, had for financial reasons taken to doctoring the labourers themselves, and it was only when a case was far beyond their skill, and when it was usually too late, that a patient was sent to hospital.[57] This practice could not have lasted long, for the extension of the medical system some years later was paid for by the planting community through an export tax, in return for which their labour was treated without charge in the hospitals. Yet, at the time Charsley's accusation was made, there were sound economic grounds for the planters' behaviour and as we have already shown,[58] there is ample reason to believe that the employers' desire to curtail expenses was for many years partly responsible for the moribund condition in which so many reached the hospitals.

The distance between hospital and estate was yet another consideration which medical men came increasingly to emphasize.[59] Before the Medical Wants Scheme was implemented, the sick had often to travel up to thirty miles to reach the nearest hospital, and even after the District hospitals were set up, the problem was not altogether eliminated. The planting area was a large one and the number of hospitals still relatively restricted; so much so, in fact, that as late as June 1885 the Principal Medical Officer was led to remark that there was no doubt that "the distance of the hospital from many of the estates makes the Malabar reluctant to seek admission until it is often too late."[60] On the other hand, from the patient's point of view, there was soon little purpose in his undertaking the journey to hospital until he had fallen gravely ill.

By the 1880s the District hospitals had grown too small to cater to all those who wished to enter them, and it had become official policy to admit "only the serious cases, . . . there being no room for trifling ailments."[61] It would seem therefore that distance and the lack of accommodation often combined to keep the immigrant *out* of hospital until he was practically moribund. Yet, pointing to his extreme condition upon entry and ignoring the reasons why he had reached that state, many still chose to regard it as further proof of their argument that mortality was excessive because of the antipathy to Western medicine and a reluctance to accept treatment until it was too late.[62]

Finally, one must also consider the competency of the doctors in whose charge the hospitals were placed. The District institutions were staffed by men specially brought out from England who, though well-qualified, had little experience of tropical diseases. Moreover their ignorance of the language and customs of the patients they were called on to treat, prevented them from understanding the immigrants' patterns of thought and this made diagnosis uncommonly difficult. These shortcomings appear to have had tragic results, for in 1878 and again in 1882, they were specifically listed amongst the underlying causes of the high mortality in the hospitals.[63] Inadequacies of this sort must, of course, have exacted a toll throughout the coffee era, but the official notice now paid to the subject suggests that deaths from "misadventure" had increased sufficiently to attract attention.[64]

On the causes of general immigrant mortality as distinct from the death-rate in the hospitals, numerous observations were made in the course of our period. The question of diet, intermittently raised throughout the entire coffee era, came now to be regarded from a new standpoint. Before 1870 interest had been centred on the consumption of unwholesome foods and the ailments to which this practice had led. The new approach emphasized the nutritive value of what was eaten under normal circumstances and established a relationship between diet and the ability to resist disease. "To form a right estimate of the success attending their treatment when sick, it is necessary to enquire into their condition previous to admission. Their staple food is rice which they consume in large quantities to compensate for the small percentage of nutriment to be derived from it. To this is added salt, chillies, a piece of dried fish, or a vegetable curry, by way of relish. They seldom eat animal food owing to their penurious habits. Possessing little stamina they rapidly succumb to sickness."[65] This acceptance of a connection between diet, disease and income, makes it evident that the medical men were beginning to adopt a more realistic attitude towards one of the most serious of the immigrants' problems. True, it was not actually said that low wages were responsible for malnutrition, but after the mid-1870s it is notable that no further references were made to the consequences of "perverted" appetites. There seems to have been an awakening to the fact that the immigrant ate what he did largely because he had to, and that there was little justification for criticizing him on that score.

Another question towards which a change in attitude became discernible concerned the influence of climate upon health. In earlier times it was commonly argued that the sudden transference from the hot, dry plains of India to the cool, wet hills of Sri Lanka was injurious to the immigrant's physical well-being. Just why this was so was never explained, but it was implied that this was a phenomenon about which little could be done.[66] Now, however, the "want of adequate clothing" came increasingly to be emphasized as a reason for the immigrant's inability to adapt to the changes in climate,[67] and though it was not suggested that this in turn reflected the low wages and general poverty of the estate labourer, it is obvious that the analysis did not need to be pushed much further before that conclusion was reached.

Besides the desire to find more meaningful answers to the questions surrounding the health of the adult immigrant population, the Medical department came also to interest itself in infant mortality on the estates. The first survey conducted in 1884, yielded the incredible rate of 237 deaths per 1,000 born, and in all probability this figure was something of an understatement. The comments which the Chief Medical Officer, Dr W.R. Kinsey had to offer on these findings were in keeping with the "new" attitude of those times. The colossal number of deaths, he wrote, were the result of "the habits, customs and poverty of the immigrant female labourers which compels them to work, leaving their infants at home without proper attendance or food, or taking them to work, placing them on the ground rolled up in a blanket, exposed to the sun and the rain."[68] A generation earlier these self-same women may well have been charged with heartlessness, or at best with indifference to their offspring. Now the accent was thrown on the economic and social conditions which made them behave as they did, and no attempt was made to tax them with any lack of human feeling. Nothing in the way of a solution to the problem was suggested. Indeed, Kinsey went on to remark that "the causes were beyond control or remedy,"[69] but his manner of presenting the facts was such that the Colonial Office was prompted to act immediately in the interests of the newly-delivered mother. As the law then stood, a woman after confinement had to be provided with food and lodging for fourteen days and was not required to work for a period of one month. In December 1885, the Secretary of State suggested that these terms be made more liberal—"the infant mortality rate, so far as it is due to the mother returning to work too soon, to the neglect of her child, could be checked by requiring the Superintendent of the estate to supply any female labourer employed on the estate with sufficient food and lodging for the period after childbirth not exceeding one month during which the medical officer may require her to be kept from work."[70]

The growing tendency to look for the origins of immigrant ill health in their socio-economic environment, led inevitably to a closer scrutiny of their living conditions. In 1879 the Principal Medical Officer held that one of the main reasons for the generally unhealthy state of the immigrant population was "the defective sanitary arrangements on estates; badly built lines, defective sites, impure water-supply and over-crowding."[71] Prior to this time there had been occasional references to the deficiencies of line accommodation and their power to induce specific ailments, i.e. rheumatism, but no general criticisms of the sort made by Kinsey had ever been given official airing. The effect was immediate, for in that very year a Medical Inspector of Coffee Districts was appointed, "with power to enter plantations and inspect labourers' cottages."[72] This measure does not appear to have had much immediate success since "the sanitary defects on the estates" were again castigated in 1882,[73] but the medical men had succeeded once more in demonstrating that responsibility for the immigrant death-rate had a wider spread than was often supposed, and their tenacity led ultimately to more adequate legislation on the housing of the estate population.[74]

One matter on which no direct comments were made was the Coast Advance System. The "long land journey to the estates" was mentioned as a cause of mortality in 1882, yet, no attempt was made to show that the method of recruitment and not merely the march to the hills was the fundamental cause of the "physically unfit" state in which so many arrived on the plantations. The doctors must certainly have been aware of the methods used by the Kangany, and they must also have known that the Northern Route was well supplied with water, resting-places and hospital sheds. Under ordinary circumstances there was now no reason why the overland journey should have had many injurious effects, unless of course, the immigrant was without sufficient food—and this we have seen was an important feature of the Coast Advance System. Why the form of recruitment then employed was not directly impugned it is difficult to understand. It had been strongly criticized at various times by both Colonial Office and local Administration and had been allowed to continue only because no acceptable alternative could be found. It may well be that the broad reference quoted above was intended to cover all aspects of the journey, the system of recruitment included, and that no particular mention of the Kangany's methods were made since the details were too well known to require repetition. But if this was so, if becomes apparent that the doctors had quite failed to see that of the many factors which determined the immigrant death-rate, the Coast Advance System was still one of the most potent.[75]

Of the diseases mainly responsible for immigrant mortality, little need be said. For the most part there was no change in the old familiar pattern. Bowel complaints, specifically diarrhoea, accounted for the largest number of deaths, with dysentery, anasarca and asthenia ranking next in importance. In 1877 the two latter infirmities were dropped from the list of classified diseases and their victims re-apportioned under the new categories of dropsy and general debility, both of which continued to exact a high annual toll. As we have already shown, the first of these titles was no less a general category than that which it replaced, and the same can be said of general debility where the very name sufficiently indicates the inexact nature of the diagnosis.

In the last years of our period, pneumonia and anaemia were introduced into the list of common ailments, and a quite considerable number of deaths were annually recorded under these heads. The former appears to have risen sharply in its incidence with the coming of tea, a crop which flourished in the high, wet regions not considered suitable for the cultivation of coffee, and so provides us with a further pointer to how ill-clad the estate population usually were. Though pneumonia often accompanies the last stages of a variety of diseases, it is clear that the hospital records referred to a virus affliction, for in seeking to explain why it was on the increase, the Chief Medical Officer once remarked that "the Malabar is more exposed to the weather than the Sinhalese or other races; he has to work in a cold climate with very little clothing, and consequently is liable to such grave diseases . . . as inflammation of the lungs."[76]

Though anaemia is a condition frequently to be found in association with a number of other ailments, e.g. hookworm, malaria etc., it seems likely that the complaint referred to in the hospital records was of the sort brought on by a lack of iron in the diet. This form is normally due to nutritional deficiencies,[77] and the growing interest displayed in the immigrants' diet was probably responsible for anaemia's inclusion under a separate head. As it can sometimes be difficult to draw a line between anaemia brought on by malaria and hookworm etc., and those of purely nutritional origin, a fair degree of error may well have entered into the annual returns, but there can be little doubt that the disease was widespread and that the average immigrant's diet in Sri Lanka only made worse a condition he had suffered from all his life.

Throughout the years 1871-1886 wages tended to remain at the traditional 18s. per month.[78] A rise in rates was prevented by the supply of labour being so large that the perennial shortage on the estates ceased for the first time to be a feature of the planting industry. In the circumstances one might have expected wages to fall, but this did not happen, partly because the continuous expansion of the railway network which was taking place in the Island provided a steady alternative source of employment to those unable to find work on the plantations,[79] and partly because railway construction was also going on in South India and it was feared that a lowering of rates would persuade the immigrant that the tiresome journey to Sri Lanka was hardly worth the effort.[80]

After 1880, the falling off in supply and the outward movement of some who were part of the residential Indian community greatly reduced the size of the annually available work-force. Yet, the employer suffered no shortages, for these were the years when the coffee fungus and financial difficulties were rapidly reducing the area under cultivation. It would not have been surprising if wage-rates had declined somewhat during this period, but there is no evidence to suggest that this did in fact occur. Apparently, those who had managed to remain in business either as coffee planters or as cultivators of the new crops decided that tampering with wage levels could prove dangerous in the long-run, for there was always the likelihood that labour supplies would not be readily forthcoming when better times returned.

Policy and Legislation

Believing that immigrant mortality was still of "scandalous" proportions despite the many improvements effected on the Northern road, the Colonial Office in the early 1870s decided that the time had come for a serious re-evaluation of policy.[81] As a result, perhaps, of the constant references to "coarse" and "perverted" feeding, and of the large number of deaths from bowel disorders annually recorded in the hospitals, the first experiments in the formulation of a new policy sought to reduce the death-rate through a forced improvement in the immigrant's diet. In 1871, on the suggestion of the Immigration Commission, Sir Hercules Robinson was asked to consider whether it would not be feasible to introduce in Sri Lanka "the system then operative in Mauritius of making rations a part of the wages of the coolies."[82]

Whitehall's proposal was by no means sympathetically received in the Colony. The Planters' Association, the Government Agents, and the Assistant Government Agents, all of whom had been asked for an opinion, unanimously opposed the idea on the grounds that "any extension of the ration system in Ceylon, beyond what already existed was unnecessary and would be very strongly objected to by the coolies themselves," and the Governor declared that the local Administration "entirely agreed with this view."[83] This stand was essentially the correct one to take. After the 1850s it had become standard procedure on the estates for the labourers to be issued with a weekly ration of rice, and the benefits expected of this practice had already been derived. Robinson was not content merely to pass this information on to the Colonial Office. Seeming to regard the proposal as an act of censure on the approach he had hitherto adopted, he went on to contend that the Home authorities had quite misunderstood the situation in Sri Lanka. Their suggestion he said, was obviously "made upon the assumption that the mortality amongst the Tamil coolies in Ceylon is excessive and that it is produced by unwholesome food," but it could be conclusively demonstrated "that both suppositions are incorrect."[84]

The arguments put up by the Governor can by no stretch of the imagination be regarded as "conclusive." On mortality in the hospitals he had nothing to offer beyond the now orthodox argument that the patients admitted were normally in a moribund condition, while on the death-rate in general he attempted with a peculiar use of statistics, to prove that it was not in fact excessive, though superficially it appeared to be so.[85] In his opinion, all that remained to be done consisted of (a) the purchase of an additional vessel for the ferry, (b) the building of two additional halting stations between Mankulam and Madawachchi and between Madawachchi and Mihintale, "the distances of eleven and thirteen miles between these stations being too great"; (c) the provision of rope-bridges over three streams, and (d) the construction of a hospital between Manaar and Anuradhapura. When this programme was completed, implied the Governor, the immigrant would have nothing to complain of and such deaths as continued to occur would be altogether unavoidable.[86]

The Secretary of State, Lord Kimberley, although prepared to withdraw the suggestion that rations should be issued as part of the immigrants' wages was clearly unimpressed by Robinson's other arguments. Despite protests to the contrary, he continued to hold that deaths were excessive, and now that it had been shown that this was so despite the issuing of rice on the estates, concluded that matters could only be improved if something positive was done to eliminate the evils emanating from the Coast Advance System. In a letter which could not have left Robinson in any doubt as to the lack of confidence felt by the Colonial Office in the policies being applied in Sri Lanka, Kimberley approved the further improvements suggested for the Northern Route, but went on to observe that "as long as the coolies continue as now to perform the journey unsupplied with sufficient food, the provision of wells and bungalows however useful, cannot prevent the sickness and mortality from which they suffer."[87] Here, he claimed, lay the crux of the problem, and since he could see "no difference in principle between the gratuitous supply of rice and the gratuitous provision of wells and bungalows," he advised that in future every immigrant on the march should be supplied by Government with food sufficient to keep him in health until his destination was reached. Moreover, in anticipation perhaps of another attempt on Robinson's part to contest the views of the Colonial Office, the Secretary of State ended with a threat over which not even the thinnest of veils was drawn. "I trust," he wrote, "that your Government will take early measures to remedy as far as possible the evils which are still suffered by the coolies, as it might otherwise be necessary (though I should much regret the necessity) that I should consider whether the arrangements which have been found requisite in other Colonies for the reception of immigrants by the Government on their first landing, and their supervision and maintenance until employed should not be introduced into Ceylon."[88]

Neither threats nor arguments, however, could move Sir Hercules Robinson. Sarcastically referring to the "impression" Whitehall seemed to have "derived from other sources," he held that nothing short of disaster would follow upon the implementation of a plan which the situation in Sri Lanka rendered unnecessary and impracticable. The Northern road passed through country which was well supplied with cheap rice and other food, and bazaars had sprung up in the vicinity of every halting station.[89] Immigrants returning to India were invariably possessed of money and therefore quite able to purchase all they needed, while those coming into the colony marched under the supervision of a Kangany whose employer had provided a cash advance sufficient to feed the gang on their journey to the hills. It therefore seemed quite clear that there was "no reason for supplying food at the public expense either to those going to, or coming from, India."[90] When one considers that Robinson had been in Sri Lanka for six years prior to expressing this point of view, it seems incredible that he should still be unaware of the Kangany's practice of skimping on food, and of the subsequent harmful results. But as we have already shown, the Governor's understanding of the immigrant problem was never deep, and it is too much to expect that he should have seen through the dishonest refinements perfected by the Kangany.[91]

Robinson was prepared to admit that there were certain individual immigrants who required aid similar to that proposed by Kimberley. These were the sick, abandoned on the road by the Kangany and left without any means of support. "In these cases the coolie is taken to hospital and attended to and fed at Government expense, till he is able to proceed. The only defect in the present system appears to be that when a coolie is convalescent he is almost always without money and has to beg his way from bazaar to bazaar or obtain some employment to enable him to reach his destination.[92] To overcome this problem the provision of food sufficient to take the convalescent to the coffee districts would prove useful—even though he had no doubt that the scheme would be abused and that the immigrant would sell part of the rice issued to him. Once this was done "all that was really necessary on the road in the shape of gratuitous rationing would have been accomplished."[93]

On the difficulty of implementing the Colonial Office proposal on the free issue of rations, Robinson built up a much stronger case. He pointed out that to begin with, it would be scarcely practicable to maintain any distinction between out-going and in-coming immigrants, i.e. between those who had funds of their own and those who had not.

Moreover, it would be impossible, without expensive supervision all along the road, to exercise any efficient check upon either the issuers or the recipients of relief. The result would be that the supply of immigrant labour would no longer be regulated with any reference to the demand in the coffee districts. Some would come over without any intention of labouring at all, and others would plant their fields in India and then repair to Sri Lanka to live on the road until their crops were ready to be harvested. The Colony in short would become "a pauper asylum for the south of India." Notwithstanding the views of the Secretary of State, there seemed therefore to be this important difference in principle between the gratuitous supply of rice and the gratuitous provision of wells and bungalows—that while the latter could hardly be abused, the former was almost certain to be so. It could be said with certainty that no one would travel from India to Sri Lanka for the sole purpose of taking advantage of the bungalows and wells, but if food was to be supplied free, the results would be very different. The Tamils themselves had a significant proverb, "if you scatter rice on the ground will not the crows of the air gather to it."[94]

The truth or otherwise of Robinson's arguments depended essentially on whether the existing pattern of immigration was to be allowed to function unaltered. As things then stood the dire consequences which the Governor foresaw would undoubtedly have followed upon the introduction of a rationing scheme, but with adequate control and new restrictions, many of these evils might have been quite simply avoided. When making his suggestions the Secretary of State had probably believed that the Colonial Administration with its better understanding of local conditions would propose ways and means of efficiently applying the Colonial Office plan. But Robinson, too assured perhaps in his conviction that immigrant mortality was not of serious proportions, seems not to have envisaged any innovations in the current method of recruitment. The Secretary of State had consequently to draw up these arrangements himself. It was made clear to the Governor that Whitehall did not share his opinions on the efficacy of the Coast Advance System, and it was particularly emphasized that the proposal to issue rations had been devised as a form of insurance against the avarice of the Kanganies. The latter were not under Government control and so long as they were the creditors of the incoming labourers for food supplies on the road, then so long would they be exposed to the temptation "to abandon to certain hardships and possible starvation, those of their debtors who were unlikely to live or work long enough to repay them."[95]

Adverting to the Governor's fears that the Colonial Office scheme would be abused and that Sri Lanka would be converted into a "pauper asylum for southern India," Kimberley pointed out that such problems would not be overly difficult to avoid. A strict control at the ports would enable the Government to prohibit the entry of paupers, and if immigrants still continued to come in merely for the sake of free food, arrangements could be made as in other labour-importing countries for planters to furnish the Administration with an annual estimate of their requirements, and the total immigration for the year could then be limited to that number. Similarly, it would not be difficult to prevent the immigrant—convalescent or otherwise—from selling part of his rations, if instead of his receiving on arrival a quantity of food sufficient for the entire journey, a series of depots set up along the road were to issue only as much rice as would suffice for the day's march. This measure on its own would not curb the avarice of the Kanganies and there was always the likelihood that they would evolve some method of putting the new scheme to their advantage, but this could be countered by requiring them to take out licenses. These could be granted after an inquiry into the character of the applicant and made subject to forfeiture on proof of misconduct. The fear of revocation would in all probability ensure good behaviour, and with the Government's influence over water transport preventing unlicensed immigration, there was no reason why an effective control could not be set up.[96]

These proposals, comprehensive and detailed though they were, were not forced upon the Colonial Government. Robinson, his term of office at an end had been followed by Sir William Gregory, and with the opportunity of securing another opinion now at hand, and also no doubt out of courtesy to the new Governor, Kimberley indicated that his mind was not quite made up and invited Gregory to submit his own views on the question.[97]

Though he claimed to have "visited considerable portions of the Coffee district," and to have "collected information from all quarters,"[98] it is evident that Gregory's understanding of the Coast Advance System was at first no better than his predecessor's. In a description of its mechanics, he showed an awareness of how the Kangany was supposed to function, but no knowledge at all of the corruption that existed in practice. "Advances are given to the Kangany by the planters to bring over the number of coolies they require; and each cooly receives a small sum which is sufficient . . . to provide him with sustenance to his journey's end."[99] One can hardly be surprised, therefore, that the Governor should have expressed agreement with all that Robinson said earlier and that he should have condemned the Colonial Office scheme as one that was unnecessary and only likely to lead to the growth of a "loafing population."[100]

The proposal that Kanganies should be licensed, Gregory accepted in principle and agreed to try, but he had little hope that the arrangement would prove successful. No one, other than the planter who employed him, was acquainted with the Kangany, hence references to his good character would be hard to secure. Again, there were nearly two thousand Kanganies moving between India and Sri Lanka and it would be impossible for an Immigration Officer to identify the person described in a license which might well have passed from hand to hand.

It was for the suggested limitation of labour supplies that the strongest protests were reserved. On the one hand it was held to be impracticable, "no regulation could keep the cooly out, since he would land on an unfrequented part of the coast, using native craft instead of the transport vessels."[101] If, on the other hand, limitation was taken to mean the rejection of people unfit for work, then it was superfluous, for this was already being done by the Immigration Officer. Again, there were dangers inherent in interfering with the free flow of immigrants at that particular time. Railway construction had begun in Tuticorin, and there was every reason to believe that the availability of employment on the mainland would curtail the annual rate of supply. The great object of the Government should be "to facilitate the flow of Indian labourers to the Colony," not impede it by imposing restrictions which could be "attended with the most disastrous consequences."[102] The Secretary of State, the Governor implied, did not seem to be aware of the many advantages which the "free immigration of Ceylon" had over "the indentured immigration of other Colonies," and by tampering with the one would only reduce it to the level of the other. "The Ceylon cooly," he wrote, "is free to come and go; he can select the District and the Estate which he prefers; he can leave at a month's notice. In other Colonies with an indentured immigration, the cooly enlisted in India is bound to serve for a term of years on a certain estate, and under a certain master, of whom he knows nothing. From the time he enters into this agreement up to the end of his hiring he is bound to serve according to its terms; he cannot change his master, who may treat him with great harshness, provided only that he keeps within the law; and between the cooly and his home, there is an impassable sea."[103]

Once again Gregory's own words make it apparent how totally unaware he then was of the more questionable side of the methods of recruitment used in Sri Lanka. This being the very problem over which the Colonial Office was growing increasingly anxious, it is hardly surprising that Governor and Secretary of State should have held such widely divergent points of view. There was no doubt much truth in Gregory's claim that illicit landings along the coast would lead to the growth of a "loafing population" if the ration scheme was introduced, and there was some point also in his argument that interference with the supply of labour was a dangerous expedient. In fact, Whitehall appear to have accepted his reasoning on both these issues, for no further attempt was made to press their acceptance. But what continued to irritate the Home authorities was the Governor's insistence that the immigrant had nothing to complain of on his journey to the hills. In a series of medical reports, sent in the month before by Gregory himself, the doctor at Matale hospital had reported that "Malabars were being brought in off the roadside in the last stages of prostration," and his counterpart at Badulla had described a class of "vagrant Malabars" who, too ill to find employment, begged "from door to door, eating stale food—the leavings and the wastage of the bazaars till they end in hospital in the last stages of sickness and starvation."[104] A fair number of these patients were in all probability, victims of the overland route. True, the dead no longer littered the highway from Manaar, but half-starved, and subject to forced marches by the Kangany, a proportion of every gang was usually in a state of collapse by the time Matale was reached. Some, unable to continue, entered hospital in that town, while others fell out as the trek progressed through Kandy, Gampola and Badulla.

Gregory's inability to see the connection between immigrant mortality and the conditions under which the march was performed, led to an increasing scepticism on the part of the Colonial Office. Kimberley, for instance, pencilled into the margin of the Governor's dispatch the uncomplimentary comment, "I have no faith in them," and in his official reply to Sri Lanka, observed that "viewed as a whole, the picture of the coolies' condition presented by the administrative officers of the Ceylon Government was difficult to reconcile with the accounts constantly given by the medical officers."[105]

In the meantime, Gregory had come to recognise some of the shortcomings of the Coast Advance System, and had introduced the arrangement whereby immigrants leaving hospitals on the line of march were provided with sufficient food to get them to the coffee districts.[106] One of the main reasons for the Coast Advance System being productive of so much suffering was thus removed at a stroke. Ignoring Kimberley's sarcasm, the Governor was therefore able to reply that he had made a personal inspection of the Northern road and had found that "the excellent wells and rest-houses . . . constructed all along the road, the bazaars which have quite recently sprung up at intervals, the precautions taken by the appointment of wardens to convey to the hospitals any persons who may from sickness have fallen back from the gang, and the gratuitous assistance given to these persons to enable them after recovery to pursue their journey—all these precautions seem effectively to have overcome the mortality which, it is alleged, formerly marked the passage of immigrants from India to the plantations."[107] This fresh expression of opinion was left unanswered by the Secretary of State, but the internal correspondence between his subordinates gives a clear indication of the general uneasiness at Whitehall on the question of immigrant morality, and of the rising disbelief with which Gregory's views were treated. "How," asked one Under-Secretary, "does this capital condition of the coolies from first to last bear on the explanation given of the excessive mortality in some of the hospitals, which was attributed to the exhausted and moribund condition of the coolies who reached them," and another, in more caustic vein remarked, "The two things are not consistent, the one with the other. But they are said by different sets of officials, though both alike are transmitted and apparently endorsed by the one Governor."[108] This was by no means fair comment, for the officials concerned were referring to medical reports which were descriptive of conditions in the previous year, and were ignoring Gregory's information that food was now being gratuitously provided to convalescents. Had the time-lag been allowed for, it would have been evident that the medical and administrative officers were not necessarily contradicting one another. Gregory should perhaps have given greater prominence in his report to the new steps he had taken, but to have done so would have been tantamount to admitting that his earlier impressions were incorrect, and this the Governor may well have been unwilling to do.

The final result of these exchanges was that the Home authorities decided to drop both the rationing scheme and the proposal for a restricted immigration. No reasons for this decision were offered, but considering Whitehall's threat to enforce welfare measures in Robinson's time, there is every reason to assume that similar steps would have been taken against Gregory if Kimberley had still believed strongly in rationing and restriction. Obviously he did not, and we can only conclude that the Secretary of State had come to realize that the objections to his proposals raised by Robinson and Gregory were reasonable enough. Clearly, Kimberley was unconvinced by Gregory's argument that the rigours of the Northern Route had been overcome, but he seems at the same time to have come to accept that the measures he had suggested would create more problems than they solved.

With the withdrawal of two of the three proposals which had comprised the original Colonial Office draft, the licensing of the Kangany became the sole instrument through which London hoped to counter the deficiencies of the Coast Advance System. Gregory's prediction that the difficulty of identification would allow licenses to be passed from hand to hand, was evidently not considered a serious threat to the efficacy of the measure. And rightly so perhaps, for no one who had "borrowed" a license would be foolish enough to jeopardise his chances of borrowing it again by committing some misdemeanour.

To overcome the problem of finding persons willing to testify to the good character of the Kangany, a further regulation was introduced which in effect made every Kangany his own sponsor. It was ordered that on arrival in Sri Lanka each Kangany should be provided with a printed form on which the number in his gang and the name of every member had to be entered. This was to be checked by a special government officer when Dambulla was reached, and any Kangany whose list fell short of the original number had to issue a certificate stating where and in whose hands the missing persons had been left. Those unable to meet this condition were to have their licenses revoked, presumably after they had been suitably warned.[109]

Though carefully drawn up, the details of the new arrangement were not without their defects. It would, for example, have been more useful to locate the checking post at Matale, as Dambulla was not a great distance away from Manaar, and the results of short rations and forced marches were more likely to be in evidence further down the road. Again, the expansion of the coffee districts had been so extensive that to many an immigrant, Dambulla did not represent even the mid-point of his journey. Another check at Pussellawa or thereabouts was needed if an effective surveillance of the Kangany was to be established, for it would not have taken the latter long to realise that he could still clear a sizeable profit if he were to keep his gang on full rations until Dambulla was reached and starved them thereafter. On the other hand, there can be no doubt that part of the annual immigrant force was bound to derive some benefits from the scheme, and that at least, was better than nothing.

Though Gregory had earlier declared in favour of licensing, it soon became apparent that he was not wholehearted in his support. As far as we know, only twenty-six Kanganies out of an estimated total of two thousand were issued licenses, and the practice seems soon to have fallen into disuse. Moreover, from the very outset, defaulters were threatened not with revocation of their licenses but with fines, and even this lesser penalty was never strictly applied, as it was feared that it "might frighten the Kanganies and lead to a decline in the number of immigrants."[110] In this abdication of humanitarianism before expediency we see the influence of a consideration which had figured before in the history of Indian Immigration, i.e. that the local Administration could not but view the question of labour supply with more concern than it did the welfare of the labourer. Gregory had now been in Sri Lanka long enough to recognize the relationship between the health of the general revenue, the state of the coffee industry and an undisturbed immigration, and in establishing the priorities he did, he was merely following a well-beaten path. What all this ultimately meant was that the plans of the Colonial Office were reduced to nought. For Whitehall could hardly jeopardise the interests of British investment by insisting that the Kanganies should be controlled even if the supply of labour was likely to decline. Some alternative scheme, intended to serve both immigrant and planter should perhaps have been put up, but clearly the Home authorities could think of none, for Kimberley remarked to a subordinate that he "did not think it necessary to pursue this matter further at present."[111] The phrasing of that comment suggests that the Secretary of State was not disposed to let the matter rest for long, but eventually nothing was done and for the remaining years of the coffee era the Coast Advance System continued to function unchanged.

So long as the arrangements for issuing rations to convalescents were in force, the consequences which followed upon the continued use of an uncontrolled Coast Advance System were less severe than in earlier times. Labour arriving in the planting districts was still semi-starved and prone to disease, but deaths on the road of those abandoned because of illness, were no longer common. When the rationing system broke down in the second half of the 1870s, reports of immigrants being brought into the hospitals off the line of march began to come in again and continued to do so even after the famine was over,[112] but the Government by then was in financial straits, and evidently not disposed to expend funds on the reintroduction of a modified rationing scheme.

Though Gregory was "thoroughly satisfied with the condition of the cooly when well," he was "not equally so with his condition when sick." The Central hospitals he believed, had proved a great success, but they were too few in number and it was "very difficult and inconvenient to carry a sick labourer some fifteen to twenty miles to the Central Establishment, and the result is that too often cases are not brought in until medical aid can no longer avail."[113] Gregory was not the first to notice or comment upon this shortcoming. Shortly before he left Sri Lanka, Sir Hercules Robinson had expressed the opinion that besides the large Central hospitals, some provision for the medical relief of each district was required,[114] and not long after, the doctor in charge of the Badulla hospital had partly attributed the immigrant's tardiness in seeking Western treatment to the fact that "many estates were thirty or more miles distant."[115] The Colonial Offices were therefore aware of the problem and the Secretary of State in one of his first dispatches to Gregory held that there was a strong case for setting up hospitals and dispensaries on the estates, remarking that "if estates were thirty miles away, and a sick man had to walk that distance, he may well be helpless and on the verge of the grave when he arrived, and many would be deterred from making the journey."[116]

Taking up Kimberley's suggestion, Gregory in July 1872 drew up what came to be known as the Medical Wants Scheme. The Governor proposed that the entire planting area should be divided into a number of medical zones "for the supply of medical advice and of medicine to the cooly population,"[117] and that within these there should be set up on each estate, or on contiguous estates, a small hut to which the sick could be removed, "where their diet could be controlled and where they could enjoy some of the appliances of the hospital, however simple, especially as regards cleanliness and ventilation."[118] As it was the Governor's intention to finance the Medical Wants Scheme by an assessment on the coffee industry, a circular was sent out to certain of the better known planters asking for their opinion of the project. Of the two-hundred and seventy-nine replies received, one hundred and three opposed the scheme on the grounds that the death-rate on the estates was low, that the existing medical arrangements were in any case quite satisfactory, and that they did not, therefore, wish to be saddled with an unnecessary expense. The remaining one hundred and seventy-six supported in varying degree the principle that medical aid should be extended to the estates and showed no objection to an assessment being levied to meet the costs of the scheme. All shades of opinion were united in the view that medical relief should not be brought under governmental control, an attitude which Gregory attributed to their fear that they would have to expend large sums on accommodation and other line facilities, "since some of the medical officers may endeavour to acquire a character for zeal and efficiency by exaggerating reports as to the sanitary conditions of the coolies."[119]

What the planters who favoured the scheme wished to have was a system of medical relief managed by a purely voluntary agency, but with an assessment for the purpose made legal by Ordinance. With this Gregory was not at first inclined to agree. The Governor believed that there was no alternative to official control since the migratory nature of the labourer and the constant change of owners and managers of property made for a feeble link between employer and employee which prevented planters from developing a permanent interest in their labour. In these circumstances "it was hopeless to expect a uniform, continuous and well-sustained system of medical relief by voluntary agency."[120]

When the nature of the replies to the government circular became public knowledge, a flood of letters poured into the offices of the Planters' Association. The great majority of these strenously opposed the suggested innovations, using the familiar argument that mortality on the plantations was not high and that the scheme was therefore unnecessary. Some of those who declared in favour of the scheme, however, described conditions on their own estates—which could not have been very different to the others—and it is plain that the death-rate on the plantations was not to be lightly dismissed. One such letter, from Mr J. Taylor of Lalkandura estate, portrayed so well what must have been the normal state of affairs on many a plantation, and in the process so effectively bared the economic considerations involved that it is edifying to quote extensively from it. Having first emphasized that managers often did not hear of a labourer's death, and that the hospitals were so far away that "in bad weather it was criminal to send a cooly all that distance," Taylor went on to write, "if I were to send all the coolies whose cases of illness may, for ought I know, be serious enough to the hospital, the expense and coolies required for the transport would be considerable. . . . One way or the other, I have treated coolies, evidently seriously ill, myself, rather than send to the hospital or incur the expense of getting a doctor from Kandy to see them, who have died, and I have understood and felt sure after, that they would have been cured in all probability by a doctor. I am very certain that deaths occur, and that a great deal of suffering would be prevented, were a proper doctor's attendance readily available."[121]

Of the incidence of mortality the writer had this to say. "I have doubts of the correctness of returns of deaths I used to send in. On this place a considerable number of the deaths take place without my knowing or being told. The coolies may or may not have got physic from me some time before. But with the multitudinous things of such various sorts that a Superintendent has to attend to, I likely never once recollect of the case again; or I suppose the cooly is better if he does not send or come back again for further treatment. For me to go regularly to find them and treat them in their lines, except in particular cases brought to my notice, is impossible, and attend to other things I must do. A dozen sets of lines scattered over a mile in direct line are not soon got over. The check roll is no help in the matter. The name may not be there, the cooly not having worked the month before he dies; and so many names are continually dropped in the roll, of coolies run away, gone for a time to contract work, to see their friends, or to be idle, or lent to other estates."[122]

With the majority of the Planters and hence the Planters' Association itself, hostile to the medical aid system, Gregory appears to have thought it politic to revise his earlier stand. The broad outlines of his plan remained unchanged, but the Governor now gave way on the important matter of official control. In its place he agreed that the proposed scheme should be voluntarily worked, and that each district should be allowed to make its own medical arrangements, i.e. appoint its own medical officers and make its own assessment.[123] This was a significant concession in that it established the principle that medical care should be recognised as the duty of the employers, and be carried into effect by local committee, the action of the Government being restricted to the enforcement of the performance of that duty.

Though Gregory had conceded much, in fact he had given those who had originally favoured the scheme all that they had asked for, hence the majority of the planting body remained hostile[124] and it was in the face of their opposition that the new arrangements were voted into the Statute Book in December 1872 as Ordinance 14 of that year.[125]

The Ordinance, which came to be known as the Medical Wants Bill, divided up the estates into twenty-one districts.[126] In each district the planters were authorised to elect for a period of three years, a local committee known as the District Medical Council, to which was delegated the power of providing for the medical wants of their area and of assessing the estates to pay for it. This assessment was to be based on the size of the several plantations, with a maximum limit set at Rs 1/-per acre.[127] In the case of those who failed in their payments, property to the value of the assessment due could be seized and put up for sale. In each district or in unions of districts, the funds collected by assessment were to be utilized to set up and run a Central hospital and to provide for the appointment of a qualified medical officer and his staff. The management of those affairs was to be left to the individual councils, but if for some reason the functioning of a local committee was thought to be unsatisfactory, the Government could step in and make such arrangements as it thought suitable. To ensure the smooth operation of the system, the Ordinance imposed a variety of obligations on the managers of the estates. They had at all hours to allow access to their lines to the appointed Medical Officers of the district; they had to set apart, on being required to do so by the Government, one or more rooms on each estate for the use of the sick, in such places and of such size and description as the Government prescribed; they had, on the requisition to that effect of the Medical Officer of the district, to remove patients at the expense of the proprietors of the estates to the nearest Central hospital; they had in future to report within twenty-four hours every birth and death on the estate; and they had to provide female labourers with wages for one month after confinement unless the latter were reported fit before that time by the Medical Officer.[128]

In the meantime, the annual hospital returns had been drawn up and it was found that mortality had risen in practically every hospital serving the planting area. With the Colonial Office already uneasy about the state of the immigrants in the Island, it became necessary for Gregory to tender some explanation accounting for the increase. The Governor seems to have accepted the planters' views on the subject of immigrant deaths, for making no reference to the reasons he had himself earlier put forward, he fell back on the well-worn argument that mortality was high because of the estate labourers' prejudice against Western medicine. This interpretation was received with an understandable impatience by the Colonial Office. The Governor's reply was described as quite "unsatisfactory" and one Under-Secretary remarked in a note to Kimberley that "the Governor should not believe too readily what the Planters tell him of the reluctance of the coolies to make use of hospitals, their preference for their own huts etc., . . . and . . . he should give due weight to the other obstructions to which he had himself averted,—the disinclination of the superintendents of estates to send a sick cooly away till they had exhausted their medical resources, the distances to which they would often have to be sent; to which he should add the cost to the estates of sending them, and the payment per head per day to which the estate is subject whilst they are there."[129] The Secretary of State, however, was not inclined to pursue the matter at that time, presumably because the Medical Wants Scheme which had just been formulated, was expected to counter many of the shortcomings referred to.[130]

The Medical Wants Scheme took time to implement. The several planting districts had first to be demarcated, then district councils had to be elected and their rules drawn up, hospitals had to be built, and arrangements had to be made to secure doctors from abroad. Consequently, it was not until early 1874 that the Ordinance actually went into force.[131]

An early result of the new Bill was that in a relatively short time it greatly increased the accommodation available for the care of the sick, but beyond this, much success did not attend it. Complaints against the Ordinance, in fact, began to come in before the end of 1875 and with every passing year to grow both in severity and number. Yet, since the scheme was of recent introduction and still on trial, no decided steps were taken in regard to it until July 1877, when two resolutions were passed at a meeting of the Planters' Association; the one "that Government be requested to remodel the Medical Ordinance, which having been fully and fairly tried, this Association considers costly and vexatious to tax-payers, and a source of increased disease and death among Indian labourers, for whose special benefit it was framed"; the other, "that Government be requested to form a mixed commission of Planters and civilians to take evidence on the operation of the Ordinance with a view to its revision."[132]

Gregory's first reaction to these demands was to propose that the entire working of the Medical Wants Scheme should be handed over to the Government. But the Planters' Association would not agree and continued to press for a Commission of Inquiry.[133] It may appear strange that the planters should so adamantly have adhered to their request as there was nothing to prevent them from openly stating their views, but it seems that the Association was a house divided on the issue and with some in favour of continuing with the voluntary system and others disposed to hand the operation of the scheme over to the Government, it was probably thought that an inquiry would enable the membership to reach a unanimous decision.

By now Gregory's term of office had come to an end and it was left to his successor, Sir James Longden, to take the next step. If the new Governor had any doubts as to whether such a Commission was necessary, they must have been quickly dissipated by the publication of the annual hospital returns. The statistics for 1877 which differentiated for the first time between immigrant and non-immigrant deaths, showed an incredible mortality, particularly in the District hospitals and this alone was sufficient grounds for acceding to the planters' request. The Governor therefore agreed to the holding of an inquiry and in 1878 appointed a Commission of four, comprising two planters, Messrs. W.D. Gibbon and A.T. Karslake, and two members of the Public Service, Mr. F.B. Templar, Government Agent of the Central Province, and Mr. F.R. Saunders, Acting Government Agent of the Western Province.[134]

After one of the most exhaustive inquiries yet held in Sri Lanka, the

Commission came out in March 1879 with a report which adduced five reasons for the failure of the Medical Wants Bill. It was held firstly that the Ordinance had been introduced too soon. "The medical assistants and dispensers required to carry it out had not been obtained, nor the requisite machinery provided." Moreover, the surgeons specially imported from England were "new to their work, unused to the climate and the conditions of health incidental to it, unused to the coolie, unacquainted with his language and therefore unable to sympathise freely with him, unversed in his habits and unfamiliar with the nature of the diseases to which from race, climate and food he was especially liable."[135] Secondly, the influx of immigrants during the famine of 1876-78, when many who arrived on the estates were too feeble to work because of the privations they had undergone, had put "a strain on the Ordinance. . . . While the machinery was still imperfect." Thirdly, the impression had been created that the Superintendents were relieved by the Ordinance of the personal responsibility which they had previously felt for the welfare of their labour. This, said the Commissioners, was one of the principal reasons for the failure of the scheme. The Ordinance had been introduced to supplement and aid the system then in force and not to replace it. Unfortunately, those entrusted with the care of plantation labour were from the first imbued with the notion that they were to be relieved of responsibility by the bill, provided they complied with its requirements. "The consequence has been that they have not given that attention to their coolies in the early stage of disease which they bestowed before, and the coolies have necessarily suffered."[136] Fourthly, the immigrant population had shown a reluctance to enter hospital, and fifthly, the medical districts had been so faultily demarcated that "for want of a bridge or a road, an estate could be more accessible from a more distant than from a nearer district."[137]

In the light of the evidence put before the Commission, one cannot help but feel that their final report was not an altogether satisfactory one. Of the five reasons advanced for the failure of the Ordinance, four were acceptably explained, but the fifth, i.e. that which held that the immigrant population was reluctant to enter hospital, was so inadequately accounted for, that in the final analysis it can be described as absolutely misleading. According to the Commissioners the estate population showed an unwillingness to enter medical institutions because "they dislike the separation from their friends; they think death more probable, and look upon it with greater dread in the hospital than in their own lines, and to a limited extent they are actuated by caste prejudices."[138] There is no doubt some truth in this statement, but it throws the responsibility for the high case-rate very heavily upon the immigrant and in so doing suppresses information of great relevance to the question at issue. The Medical Inspector of the Coffee districts, Dr J.M. Coghill, when presenting his views before the Commission had strongly criticised the location of a number of hospitals set up under the Medical Wants Bill, had condemned the state in which many of them were, and had drawn attention to their general deficiency in equipment.[139] No report on the fortunes of the Medical Ordinance could have been conclusive without an examination of these institutions, but despite the urging of the Inspectors, this was not done. As a result, no allowance was made by the Commissioner for a "reluctance to enter hospital" which might have been induced by the poor condition of the hospitals themselves, and this omission tended to weigh unfairly the charge against the immigrant labourer.

Again, apart from the state of the hospitals, the terrible mortality within them was sufficient to create a prejudice amongst would-be patients. Yet, this was not amplified in the Report, even though the Surgeon at Pussellawa hospital made it clear that there was a general tendency amongst immigrant labourers to regard admission to hospital as synonymous with death.[140] The Chief Medical Officer, Dr W.R. Kinsey, on reading the findings of the Commissioners was moved to address a letter to the Governor in the course of which he remarked, "It is stated that he [the immigrant] has the greatest objection to go to hospital, unless hopelessly ill, but this is not the experience in the Civil hospitals of the Colony, where every available bed is filled and many apply for admission who have to be refused. But in view of the large [District] hospital mortality it is not to be wondered at if coolies object."[141]

Finally, the Commissioners omitted altogether an abuse to which the Medical Wants Bill had been put. The Medical Inspector and a number of the doctors made it a point to emphasize that those who derived the greatest advantage from the Ordinance were the planters themselves.[142] As the law then stood, doctors appointed under the scheme were required to attend upon the Superintendent and his assistants and this is said to have led in many instances to a neglect of the very estate-workers in whose interests the bill had been passed. "The coolies have been grossly neglected in their illnesses, and the legitimate object of the Ordinance—viz. the medical care and treatment of the Indian immigrant labourer, has been diverted into a totally illegitimate channel— the medical care and treatment of the European residents, or as the late Lieutenant Governor tersely put it, "two for the planter and one for the cooly."[143] No one objected to the European residents having the benefit of European medical skill, "but for this," said Coghill, "they must be prepared to pay, and not saddle the assessment as a means of providing themselves with free medical attendance, and then cry out that the whole scheme is a farce. It was never for a moment contemplated that the maximum assessment would provide this and cover the cost as well of hospitals etc. for the immigrants. The result is that there are no funds available for native medical assistants in sufficient numbers to relieve the European officers of part of their duty."[144] The influence of the two planting members and a general desire to avoid offending the planting community were probably responsible for the omission of these strictures from the final report. But if this was so, the Commissioners need not have been too sensitive about the planters' feelings, for the Chairman of the Planters' Association, Mr H.W. Saunders, in his opening address to that body in 1879, himself commented that "the assessment under the Medical Wants Ordinance was expended in offering a premium to the medical men to settle in private practice in the coffee districts."[145]

To overcome the many defects of the Ordinance of 1872, the Commission of Inquiry made four major recommendations. They proposed that the existing medical districts should be re-arranged; that each district should have the option of being brought under the voluntary scheme or of one conducted by the Government, in the latter case the Government would fix the maximum rate of assessment; that if after a district had been brought under the voluntary system it was found that satisfactory arrangements were not made, or in the event of any exceptional mortality, the Government was to have the power of making such arrangements as they deemed necessary for the medical wants either of the district or of any individual estate or estates, and to assess accordingly to meet the expenses of such arrangements; and that Medical Inspectors and Visitors should be appointed by the Government.[146]

The nature of these recommendations makes it evident that the Commission was attempting to tighten up on the working of the Medical Wants Scheme without unduly antagonising the planting community in the process. On the one hand the planters were not forced to accept a Government-run scheme, but were permitted to make their own arrangements if they so wished. On the other, the appointment of Medical Inspectors and Visitors would make certain that the lines were kept in a sanitary condition and that the sick were sent off to hospital in good time; while the provision allowing the Government to take over in case of "exceptional mortality" or "unsatisfactory arrangements" would ensure that the hospitals were well built and fully-equipped and give employers an incentive to get their patients to hospital before they were passed saving.

Surprisingly, the Colonial Office had no comments of any importance to offer on the Commission's report. Lord Kimberley was no longer Secretary of State for the Colonies and it appears that his successors[147] were not as interested as he in the general problem of immigrant welfare. In Sri Lanka, too, no firm expression of opinion was to be had from the Government. Longden personally favoured the continuation of the system then in force, which he believed could be vastly improved at a very small expense, but he was not prepared to take a determined stand on the issue, and ultimately went along with the Commission's findings.[148] As a result, in December 1879 an amended Medical Aid Bill based on the recommendations of the Commission of Inquiry was brought before the Legislative Council. In all, there were six important differences between the new Ordinance and its predecessor. Government control was offered as an alternative to the voluntary system, the Government was empowered to assume the medical charge of a district if dissatisfied with the manner in which it was being run by a voluntary committee,[149] hospitals and medical officers had to be maintained in every individual district and not in unions of districts as hitherto, voluntary committees could call on the Government for a loan of up to Rs. 100,000 to meet their primary expenses in setting up a hospital,[150] a Medical Inspector with the right to enter plantations, inspect labourers' cottages and visit district hospitals, was to be appointed by the Government,[151] and confined women were to receive food and lodging for a period of one month.[152]

When the new Ordinance was read for the first time in the Legislative Council, the Planters' Association, still hopelessly divided on the question, requested a postponement of all further discussion until they had come to an understanding amongst themselves. A large and influential section of the planters were by now in favour of handing the entire scheme over to the Government. The retention of the voluntary system was acceptable to them in theory, but experience had shown that it had practical disadvantages of a very serious nature. Attendance at meetings of the district committee, for example, was a heavy drain on the planter's time and had been found particularly onerous when coffee was in crop. Considerable internal dissension had also arisen over the method used to raise the funds needed to finance medical relief. A portion of the membership had begun to tout the idea that a duty on coffee actually exported should be substituted for the existing system of equal assessment upon the acreage of each estate. The latter method, in their opinion, was unjust since it pressed unfairly on the less productive estates, which besides yielding a smaller margin of profit out of which the assessment had to be paid, actually required fewer hands to cultivate than the more fertile plantations.[153]

In order that these differences should be resolved, Longden agreed to withdraw the Ordinance of 1879 and to wait for some months before presenting it again to the Legislative Council. A full year was allowed to pass before any further moves were made, but in that time the Governor came round to the view that the voluntary scheme should be done away with altogether. In the circumstances this was much the best course to adopt, for the planters could scarcely be forced to serve on district committees and attend to the other details of running the medical relief system. Ordinance 17 of 1880 therefore dropped the voluntary principle and brought the medical care of immigrant labour completely under the control of the Government. Like its predecessor the new bill made arrangements to divide up the estates into a number of districts and to appoint a Medical Officer to each with an assistant where necessary.[154] In every district a hospital was to be built, and to these Superintendents of estates could, and in certain cases had to, send their labour.[155] The medical officers were to visit the hospitals every day and call on the sick who were not in hospital as often as required. It was made the duty of Superintendents—under penalty in case of default—to maintain their lines in a fair sanitary condition, to keep registers of their employees, and to report all cases of sickness. In order the better to carry out the last duty, it was required, again under penalty, that every Kangany should inform the Superintendent of all cases of sickness in his gang. Finally, the operation of the entire scheme was brought under the general supervision and direction of the Principal Civil Medical Officer to whom the District Medical Officers were expressly subordinate.

To meet the cost of the medical aid proposed by the Ordinance, a tax of 20 cents per hundredweight was to be charged on the actual produce of the estates. This change from the acreage tax was, as we have seen, earlier suggested by a faction in the Planters' Association and obviously Longden had been persuaded of the justice of their case.[156]

When the new Ordinance was put before the Legislative Council, it encountered the violent opposition of the planting community. In the year allowed them to settle their differences, the planters had experienced a complete change of attitude towards the Medical Wants Scheme. In terms of their own self-interest there were ample grounds for this relatively sudden reversal in opinion. On the one hand, the ravages of the leaf-disease had in the past few years led to a catastrophic fall in output and though transport economies and higher prices had kept the industry a remunerative one, quotations on the London market had begun to decline and it seemed that profit margins were to be greatly reduced.[157] On the other hand, labour was no longer difficult to get; in fact, there was now an unprecedented excess of it. With a large resident Indian population and a still sizeable annual immigration to draw upon, the planter found no difficulty in maintaining the strength of his workforce. Most estate owners had always regarded as unnecessary any improvements which raised labour costs but brought little advantage to the employer, and their willingness to pay for welfare had in the main been based upon the purely utilitarian consideration that it helped sustain supply. Now that supply presented no problems, the incentive to support the Medical Wants Scheme was removed and not unsurprisingly the planting community soon came to adopt a new line on the question.

In their opposition to the new Ordinance, the representatives of the planting body went beyond mere detail and attacked the first principle on which the bill was founded, i.e. "the liability of the planters to find medical aid at all for their immigrant labourers." No objections to the scheme being implemented were voiced, but it was suggested that it should be paid for by an import duty on rice, "the food of the people" as the Governor put it. What the planters wanted was a duty of 3 cents per bushel on rice imported through the ports of Galle, Colombo and Batticaloa, the centres from which the plantations obtained their stores. Since the ruling price was then 29 cents per bushel, the duty represented a 10% increase which the population of the maritime provinces would also have to bear, since they were partly dependent on imported rice. Moreover, there was always the danger that the planters would raise the price of rice on the estates and so transfer their share of the burden on to the hapless immigrant labourer. With these considerations in mind, Longden rejected the proposal outright, observing to the Secretary of State that "enormously as the Colony as a whole has benefitted by the coffee industry, it may be said that it has scarcely affected the native population, their occupations, or their mode of living. . . . To throw the cost of the Immigrant Medical Service of Ceylon upon the General Treasury . . . would shift a burden which rightly viewed is a part of the cost of production, from the growers of coffee to the native population, the vast majority of whom do not derive their living in any way through the coffee industry."[158]

As an additional argument against the Planters' Association Longden claimed that their stand amounted to a repudiation of obligations already imposed upon them by law. He reminded the Colonial Office that

Ordinance 11 of 1865, which defined Master and Servant relationships, specifically stated that "any servant who shall be incapacitated by sickness from labour, whilst in the service of any employer, shall be entitled to lodging, food, as well as medical care *at the expense of such employer* during such incapacity."[159] The obligation to provide medical care for their labourers at their own expense, was imposed upon the planters by the very law under which they could enforce their labour contracts.[160] One is disposed, however, to hold the validity of this reasoning in question. The Labour Ordinance did not specify the *manner* in which medical aid was to be dispensed and if the issue was taken to a court of law the planters could reasonably claim that the term "medical care" could not be stretched to cover a Government-sponsored Medical Wants Scheme.

With Lord Kimberley again in office as Secretary of State for the Colonies, the new Medical Aid Bill was assured of immediate sanction and went on to the statute book as Ordinance 17 of 1880. But while the Colonial Office agreed in principle with the Governor that the planting community and not the general public should bear the cost of immigrant medical relief, the methods suggested for raising the necessary funds were not approved of. It was thought that the new and rising tea, cinchona, and cocoa industries would be adversely affected by a duty on exports, so in its place was recommended a tax based on the number of Indian workers employed on each estate.[161] That such a proposal should have been put up does not reflect well on Kimberley's advisers. The growers of tea, cinechona and cocoa would, under the former scheme, have commenced payments when the estate produced its first crop, whereas under the new arrangements they would have to bear the assessment from the very opening up of the estate. Far from being protected, the new enterprises would be penalised if the Secretary of State's plan was implemented.

When Kimberley's dispatch was received in Sri Lanka, the Administration immediately assumed that tea, cinchona and cocoa estates were to be exempted from the labour tax as this was the only rational interpretation they could give to instructions which claimed the encouragement of the new industries as their objective. Acting Governor John Douglas wrote back to inquire whether the new levy would not unfairly force the coffee industry to carry the burden of the entire planting sector.[162] The Secretary of State thereupon reversed his earlier argument and dropping all talk of stimulating the new industries recommended that they be brought under the Ordinance. Moreover, he also went on to claim that he had earlier opposed the export duty because it would fall unequally on the planting interest by allowing labour from the new estates to use the facilities provided by the Medical Wants Scheme, though the proprietors paid nothing towards its upkeep owing to the output of their plantations being negligible![163]

While this strange episode was taking place, the planting community, plagued now by both falling prices and declining output, put up a completely new plan which they said would do away with the need for a tax on the plantations. In a petition to the Queen they proposed (1) that all Government Civil Hospitals in the Central Province should be opened to estate labour, the maintenance of the patients being borne by the estates that sent them in, at the usual rate of thirty cents per day; (2) that six of the District hospitals then owned by the District Medical Committees should be given over free of charge to the Government, and that the patients admitted to them should be paid for by their employers; (3) that the salaries of medical officers appointed for service in the coffee districts in addition to the existing staff of the Civil Medical Department should be paid out of the general revenue.[164]

Though this new scheme did not eliminate subsidization altogether, Longden was inclined to give it his support. In the preceding year the troubles of the coffee industry had intensified and with prices and output greatly reduced, the value of the exported crop had fallen by almost 36%. It was obvious that the industry was in no condition to bear a heavy fiscal burden, and the Governor having emphasized this to the Secretary of State urged him to accept the Association's plan.[165] But Kimberley could not be persuaded to accept the proposals in their entirety. With the taking over of the hospitals he agreed, as this would relieve the planters from any special taxation for the maintenance of medical institutions, but he refused to sanction the payment out of the general revenue of the salaries of the doctors to be appointed under the Ordinance, since in his opinion "the depression in coffee cultivation did not . . . afford a sufficient ground for relieving the planters at the expense of the general community of the medical care of the labourers whom they employ."[166]

The finances of the Government were too dependent on plantation agriculture for this decision to stand for long. It was soon evident that the coffee industry was on its death-bed, and though tea, cinchona and cocoa were fast replacing it, some form of assistance had to be extended to the new industries during the period of transition. Moreover, Longden was convinced that the method of assessment proposed by Kimberley was far from suited to a country like Sri Lanka. In colonies where indentured labour was present, the Government could always exercise a check on the number employed, but in Sri Lanka agreements were often verbal and contracts sometimes for as short a period as one month. The precise number of workers employed was thus difficult to verify and the proper collection of a labour tax would be virtually impossible.[167]

So effectively did the Governor argue his case that the Secretary of State finally decided to give way, and in May 1882 indicated his willingness to permit the Government to bear half the cost of maintaining the staff required by the Medical Wants Scheme.[168] By the time the dispatch conveying this concession arrived in Sri Lanka the state of the coffee industry had deteriorated still further and Longden was convinced that the time had come to waive taxation altogether. He suggested now that the Colonial Office instructions should not be implemented, and that immigrant labour should henceforth be treated in the same manner as the indigenous population with the entire expense of their medical relief being borne by the Government.[169] For one who had long held that the planting community should meet the costs of the medical aid received by their work-force this was a complete reversal of opinion, but the significance of the change appears to have made no impression on Kimberley. In a reply which made no direct reference to the Governor's plea for greater relief, he complained that the capitation tax might well have worked if the planters had been prepared to co-operate, but since they would not, he had no objections to the tax being withdrawn—provided an export duty on plantation products was substituted in its place.[170]

Since it was obvious that the Secretary of State was determined to make no further concessions, Longden laid before the Council an amended Medical Wants Ordinance in which provision was made for the imposition of an export tax of 20 cents per hundredweight on cinchona and of 10 cents per hundredweight on coffee, tea and cocoa. The planters were loud in their opposition and now not only contended that the costs of the entire scheme should be borne by the general revenue, but also that the Government should pay for the District hospitals it proposed to take over.[171] Neither of the demands were granted, but the Governor, appreciative of the problems which faced the plantation sector, decided to experiment with a lower scale of duties than those laid down by Ordinance and accordingly set the schedule at 10 cents per hundredweight on cinchona and 5 cents per hundredweight on tea, coffee and cocoa.[172]

While the reduction in the new tax no doubt provided the planters with a modicum of relief, its ultimate result was a financial disaster for the Government. It had been hoped that even with the lower duties the

Medical Wants Scheme would largely pay for itself. Some subsidization was anticipated but this was regarded as permissible since a proportion of those treated in the District hospitals were likely to be indigenous inhabitants and so the financial responsibility of the Colonial Government. When the accounts for 1883 were drawn up, it was found that while the total expenditure under the Ordinance had amounted to Rs. 134,032, the duties and income from medicine sold to the plantations had brought in only Rs. 30,021. As four-fifths of the patients treated had come from the estates the Government should only have contributed Rs. 26,806, instead of which it had paid out Rs. 104,011, i.e. it had subsidized the planters to the tune of Rs. 77,205.[173]

With the general revenue of the Colony some 25% lower than it had been a mere five years earlier, subsidization on this scale was something the Government could ill afford. Moreover, in the course of 1883 the acreage under tea, cinchona and cocoa had rapidly increased, and since the new crops were in the main grown on what had once been coffee land by those who had once been "pure" coffee planters, it seemed that the plantation sector was now in a position to bear a higher levy. In 1884 the export duties were therefore raised to the maximum limit permitted by law.[174] The added income that this step brought in was not sufficient to eliminate subsidization altogether, but immediate further increases in taxation were out of the question, and Government decided to charge the loss to the general revenue until the plantation sector was economically sound enough to carry a higher schedule of export duties.

	Income from Medical Aid Bill[175] —export duties and income from medicines sold Rs.	**Expenditure on working Medical Wants Ordinance Rs.**
1883	30,021	134,032
1884	93,985	118,614
1885	118,521	126,816
1886	97,770	149,172

From the stand point of numbers treated and of hospital case rates, the reconstructed Medical Wants System was more successful than its predecessor of 1872. Yet, there was ample reason for the Administration to feel a sense of dissatisfaction. In the six District and eight Civil hospitals appointed for the reception of estate labour, mortality was in an absolute sense still distressingly high. No Commissions of Inquiry were set up to look into the question but the Government was concerned enough to call the problem to the attention of the Principal Medical Officer, Dr W.R. Kinsey, in 1885.[176] After an investigation into the working of the Ordinance, Kinsey concluded that much could be done to improve its efficacy. Governor Sir Arthur Gordon, who had followed Longden in December 1883, and Major-General Sir John McLeod, who administered the Government for four months when Gordon was away on leave in mid-1885, were both inclined to fall back on the argument that deaths were numerous because the immigrant was hostile to Western medical treatment,[177] but the Principal Medical Officer thought differently. Indeed, in direct contradiction of his superiors he made it a point to emphasize that the existing hospitals were too small to cater to the large numbers seeking admission and recommended that they be enlarged.

In his report, Kinsey proposed a number of measures which he believed would bring down mortality rates in the hospitals and on the plantations. He suggested first, that the sick should be sent to hospital in an early and curable stage, and stressed that this would necessitate the Superintendent taking a greater personal interest in the health of his labour. Second, that all cases, whether serious or trifling, should receive prompt treatment and free food upon the estate, unless sent at once to hospital. Third, that every case of sickness occurring on an estate should be seen by the Superintendent or some other person. Fourth, that a sick list should be kept in which the names of all patients should be entered, with the date of admission, the date the illness was first reported by the Kangany, the condition of the patient, the treatment given etc. and that this should be produced when medical officers visited the estate. Fifth, that Superintendents should enforce the "Kangany" clause of the Ordinance more vigorously. Sixth, that the hospitals should be enlarged and their number increased. And seventh that in extensive districts such as Dickoya, Haputale, Lindulla, Badulla and Nawalapitiya, additional medical assistants should be appointed.[178]

Kinsey's proposals were particularly significant in that apart from his last two suggestions, the tone of the others implied that the deficiencies of the Medical Wants Ordinance were due in part to a lack of interest and co-operation by the planting community, and in part to the failure of the Ordinance itself to frame an adequate set of rules for the Superintendents of the estates. To overcome these shortcomings, Kinsey recommended that the additional duties required of the planters should not merely be made the subject of an appeal to their goodwill, but be given legal standing by a change in the existing law.[179] This recommendation was not immediately acted upon as the Governor had yet to be convinced of the truth of his Principal Medical Officer's arguments, and so it was that an improved but still far from perfect Medical Wants Scheme was in force when the coffee era came to an end in the following year.[180]

One question to which much attention had been devoted in earlier years, but which now was apparently thought to be undeserving of special mention was the subsidization of the immigratory process. This change in attitude was no doubt connected with the falling off in acceptance of the laissez-faire credo and, as pointed out earlier, was already evident by the end of the 1860s. In the 1870s and 1880s the burden imposed upon the general revenue tended to grow steadily in magnitude and that this was not remarked upon shows how completely the principle had come to be accepted by both Colonial Office and local Administration.

Year	Expenditure on Immigration	Income from Passage Money	Year	Expenditure on Immigration	Income from Passage Money
1871	6,250	n.a.	1879	10,880	2,086
1872	8,396	2,418	1880	11,081	1,277
1873	8,746	n.a.	1881	10,425	1,276
1874	9,467	n.a.	1882	9,320	1,170
1875	9,576	2,720	1883	8,018	873
1876	9,721	3,243	1884	7,545	949
1877	13,633	3,417	1885	8,029	1,055
1878	12,814	2,705	1886	7,735	882

With regard to Policy, these last years of the coffee era had a character all their own. The dominating feature of the times was the Medical Wants Ordinance and the vast extension of medical aid it inaugurated. The measures adopted had their shortcomings, nonetheless they constituted a considerable advance in the field of labour welfare. Once the scheme had been mooted, it received Whitehall's enthusiastic support. Indeed, during Kimberley's tenure of office as Secretary of State, the initiative in developing the scheme passed from Colombo to London. All the same, the Medical Wants Ordinance merely represented the best welfare arrangements the Home authorities were able to obtain in Sri Lanka during this period, and not the best they would have liked to have had. Their dispatches make it clear that they were quite perturbed about the situation in the Colony and that they wished above all to exert a strict control over the Coast Advance System. In the entire history of Indian immigration to Sri Lanka, there is no parallel to the suspicion and cynicism with which Robinson's and Gregory's views on mortality and conditions on the Northern Route were viewed. The private notes and internal correspondence of officials in England make it patent that they felt they were being out-smarted on these issues, and the frustration with which they finally accepted Colombo's stand is exemplified in the cryptic private comment made by one of Kimberley's assistants, "we get beaten along the whole line, but I do not see what more is to be done beyond what has been done."[182]

Though it was the question of welfare that most dominated official thinking in this period, there is ample evidence that both Colonial Office and local Administration were not unmindful of the matter of labour supply. In the past, the perennial shortage of estate labour had led policy makers to concern themselves with measures intended to increase the flow of immigration. In the last years of coffee's reign, the sufficiency of labour pushed this aspect of policy into a somewhat lesser role, and both Colombo and London came to concentrate on merely maintaining supply at existing levels. It was with this objective in mind, for instance, that Gregory decided not to persist with the proposal that Kanganies should be obliged to hold "passes," and it was doubtless for the same reason that the Secretary of State did not insist that he should. This continuing, if somewhat circumscribed, interest in the question of labour supply reflected the attention which had always been extended to the coffee industry because of its connection with the state of the Island's finances.

In these last years, a further consideration to which local Administrators had to give due weight was the evolution of the planting body into a political pressure group which by the last decade or two of the coffee era had come to possess sufficient influence to make things unpleasant for a Governor who was overly unsympathetic to their interests. That the Colonial Government had grown aware of this political fact is not difficult to demonstrate. It is reflected in the manner in which Gregory sought planting opinion on how the Medical Wants Scheme should be funded, it is evident in his support of the "voluntary" principle when he himself believed in official control, and it is to be seen in Longden's willingness to accommodate the planters by delaying the second reading of the amended Medical Wants Bill.

Despite this growing sensitivity to planting opinion, a feature of the Medical Wants Scheme was that both local Administration and Colonial Office wished it to be financially self-sufficient; through planters' subscriptions during its voluntary phase, and through special taxation after it had passed under Government control. Given the direction policy had taken over the nineteenth century this stance shows an inconsistency which is difficult of explanation By the 1870s it had been accepted in both London and Colombo that the costs of immigrant welfare should be met out of the general revenue, and that the immigratory process itself should be heavily subsidized. As we have seen, Kimberley was prepared to go so far as to provide free food on the line of march on the grounds that this was not different in principle to the "gratuitous provision of wells and bungalows."[183] Yet, the extension of medical facilities in the planting districts, which was just as much a part of welfare, had to be the financial responsibility of the employers of estate labour.[184] That ultimately this objective was not met, and that a considerable degree of subsidization was permitted does not counter the point at issue. When the concession was made, it was not due to any reversal of policy, but to the exigencies of a deteriorating economic situation which had put the future of British investment in Sri Lanka in jeopardy.

NOTES

1. C.O.54. 488. 13th October 1873—Gregory to Kimberley; C.O.54. 493. 10th June 1874—Birch to Carnarvon; Ferguson, *The Ceylon Directory 1873*, p. 211; Administration Report on the Central Province, 1871.
2. C.O.54. 493. 11th August 1874—Birch to Carnarvon; Ferguson, *Ceylon in the Jubilee Year*, p. 64.
3. Prices for the years 1870-1872 have been calculated on the basis described in Chapter IV. After that date official returns have been used, since the practice of fixing the value of exported plantation coffee at 54s. per cwt. was discontinued by the Customs Department in 1873.
4. C.O.54. 467. 14th September 1871—Robinson to Kimberley; Ferguson, *op, cit.*, p. 64.
5. C.O.54. 493. 10th June 1874—Birch to Carnarvon; C.O.54. 494. 6th October 1874—Gregory to Carnarvon; C.O.54. 494. 12th October 1874—Gregory to Carnarvon; C.O.54. 534. 22nd November 1881—Longden to Kimberley.
6. Ferguson, *Ceylon in 1884*, p. 60.
7. Ferguson, *Ceylon Directory 1883*.
8. C.O.54. 508. 20th August 1877—Birch to Carnarvon; C.O.54. 512. 10th February 1878—Longden to Carnarvon; B.P.P. of 1882. Vol. XLIV. Report of 12th August 1882.
9. Ceylon Blue Book.
10. In some areas Liberian coffee was introduced in the hope that its greater size, strong habit and ability to grow at low elevations would enable it to resist the leaf fungus, but without success. Trials were also made with

Nakanaad Mysore coffee seed, but as in the case of the Liberian variety, the disease seemed to find a more congenial host in the newcomers than in the ordinary Arabian species. *The Coffee Manual*, p. 262; Ferguson, *Ceylon in the Jubilee Year*, p. 82; Shand, *Journal of the Royal Society of Arts*, Vol. 38, p. 182.

11. C.O.54. 542. 21st December 1882—Longden to Derby; B.P.P. or 1881, Vol. LXIV, Report of 30th October 1880; The Statist of 12th April 1884; Shand, *op. cit.*
12. Blue Book.
13. C.O.54. 522. 20th November 1879—Longden to Hicks-Beach; C.O.54. 528. 30th November 1880—Longden to Kimberley; The Statist of 28th June 1879 and 24th July 1886.
14. C.O.54. 527. 10th August 1880—Longden to Kimberley; C.O.54. 533. 14th July 1881—Douglas to Kimberley; C.O.54. 536—Miscellaneous Correspondence—letter of W.T. Thiselton— Dyer to the Colonial Office; C.O.54. 542. 21st December 1882—Longden to Derby; C.O.54. 548. 4th July 1883—Longden to Derby; C.O.54. 548. 15th August 1883—Longden to Derby; Ferguson, *Ceylon in 1903*, pp. 64 and 65.
15. Ferguson, *Ceylon Directory 1891*.
16. Blue Book.
17. Lewis, Sixty-four years in Ceylon, pp. 126-28. Of the 1,700 European planters in Ceylon in 1880 Lewis estimates that 400 had left by 1886.
18. C.O.54. 531. 18th January 1881—Longden to Kimberley; Ferguson, *Ceylon in 1893*, p. 73. Cinchona did not prove profitable for long, but cocoa after some initial setbacks spread slowly in the mid-country and reached an acreage of 23,696 at the turn of the century—Ferguson. *Ceylon Handbook and Directory 1906-1908*.
19. Blue Book.
20. Governor Gregory's address to the Legislative Council of 14th October 1874. Governor's addresses, Vol. II, p. 339.
21. C.O.54. 507. 15th March 1877—Birch to Carnarvon; C.O.54. 507. 18th May 1877—Gregory to Carnarvon; C.O.54. 509. 8th November 1877—Longden to Carnarvon. *The Madura Gazetteer* referring to "the great famine of 1876-78 which affected disastrously so many other districts in this Presidency" offers the following description of events. "The South West and North East Monsoons of 1876 both failed . . . and by the end of the year not only were all agricultural operations at a standstill, but in many places the water available was insufficient even for domestic purposes. . . . The ryots began to sell their cattle and other property and to emigrate in thousands to Ceylon and elsewhere. So great was the crowd at Paumben waiting to get away, that the food supplies there ran out, and Government authorized the collectors to buy grain and sell it at cost price to the emigrants." Madras District Gazeteers, Madura, p. 163.
22. Blue Book.
23. C.O.54. 476. 9th July 1872—Gregory to Kimberley; C.O.54. 478. 9th

October 1872—Gregory to Kimberley (Encl.); C.O.54. 497. 31st May 1875—Gregory to Carnarvon; C.O.54. 507. 15th March 1877—Birch to Carnarvon; C.O.54. 507. 4th May 1877—Gregory to Carnarvon; C.O.54. 509. 8th November 1877—Longden to Carnarvon; C.O.54. 513. 27th April 1878—Longden to HicksBeach; C.O.54. 541. 15th September 1882—Longden to Kimberley; C.O.54. 544. 9th July 1884—Gordon to Derby; C.O.54. 559. 19th June 1885—Gordon to Derby; C.O.54. 560. 4th September 1885—MacLeod to Stanley. Ferguson, *The Ceylon Directory 1874*, pp. 247 and 248 and 310; see also the annual hospital returns in the Ceylon Blue Book.

24. C.O.54. 509. 8th November 1877—Longden to Carnarvon; C.O.54. 513. 27th April 1878—Longden to Hicks-Beach; C.O.54. 521. 10th September 1879—Longden to Hicks-Beach.
25. Sarkar, *op. cit*., p. 59.
26. Another difficulty regarding computations of the permanent Indian workforce is that in the 1870s an increasing number of immigrants sought employment in areas unconnected with direct estate work, i.e. as grooms, domestics, grass cutters etc. Some also set up as traders and others as small-scale growers of coffee. The census of 1881 gives returns for all these categories but does not tell us how many were of Indian origin.
27. C.O.54. 541. 15th September 1882—Longden to Kimberley; C.O.54. 554. 9th July 1884—Gordon to Derby; C.O.54. 559. 19th June 1885—Gordon to Derby; C.O.54. 560. 4th September 1885—MacLeod to Stanley.
28. C.O.54. 476. 9th July 1872—Gregory to Kimberley; B.P.P. of 1873. Vol. 48. Papers relating to Ceylon, pp. 20-21.
29. Report of the Coolie Immigration Commission (1878). C.O.57. 72, p. 575. The voyage from Tuticorin could also be accomplished on the steamers of the British India Company, but the cost of a passage on this service was so high that the bulk of the annual immigration usually came in by native boat. The average charge per head on a British India steamer was Rs. 3.04, against Rs. 1.25 on the native boat.
30. C.O.57. 72, p. 575; Legislative Enactments of Ceylon—Ordinance 5 of 1879.
31. The bungalows were situated at Matale, Dambulla, Elagamuwa, Maradankadawala, Tivapane, Mihintale, Rambawa, Madawachchi, Mankulam, Chettikulam, Periyakattu, Puliyadiuirakkam, Combansandekulam, Oikilankulam, Taladi, Manaar, Pesalai and Oyodappanni.
32. B.P.P. of 1873. Vol. 48, p. 21.
33. C.O.57. 72, p. 575. This was a false economy though, for by walking the immigrant lost time, and therefore wages.
34. *Ibid.*
35. *Ibid.* The evidence laid before the Commission of Inquiry emphasized that those using the Colombo route were generally in better shape than

those arriving via Manaar. But it was also stressed that they too were emaciated and worn out.

36. For a discussion of these proposals see "Policy and Legislation," infra p. 127.
37. C.O.54. 468. 26th November 1871—Robinson to Kimberley; C.O.54. 476. 19th June 1872—Gregory to Kimberley; C.O.54. 479. 14th November 1872—Gregory to Kimberley.
38. Ceylon Blue Book.
39. C.O.54. 468. 26th November 1871—Robinson to Kimberley.
40. C.O.54. 476. 9th July 1872—Gregory to Kimberley; C.O.54. 478. 9th October 1872—Gregory to Kimberley.
41. In 1877 a return of mortality in the District Hospitals listed thirteen institutions, i.e. Lindulla, Rakwana, Madulsima, Badulla, Pussellawa, Dickoya, Rangalla, Kotmale, Haputale, Maskeliya, Matale West, Maturata and Uda Pussellawa. However, there is reason to believe that more hospitals had been built, for the same document mentions that "some" had failed to submit returns. Three others, i.e. at Matale East, Dimbulla and Morawak Korale were referred to in a Medical Inspector's report in 1878, and there is thus every likelihood that hospitals had been built in a few of the remaining districts, i.e. in Ramboda, Punduloya, Kalebokke, Knuckles and Hunasgiriya. C.O.54. 521. 10th September 1879—Longden to Hicks-Beach (Encl.); Ceylon Sessional Papers of 1879—Report of the Medical Inspector of the Coffee Districts.
42. Ceylon Sessional Papers—1879. Report of the Medical Inspector, p. 1.
43. C.O.54. 521. 10th September 1879—Longden to Hicks-Beach; Ceylon Sessional papers—1879, Report of the Commission on the Medical Wants of Coffee Districts, pp. XI and XII.
44. C.O.54. 521. 10th September 1879—Longden to Hicks-Beach; C.O.54. 522. 20th December 1879—Longden to Hicks-Beach; C.O.54. 537. 20th February 1882—Longden to Kimberley.
45. C.O.54. 559. 19th June 1885—Gordon to Derby; three more District hospitals were opened at Maskeliya, Balangoda and Rakwana in 1886—Ceylon Blue Book.
46. C.O.54. 478. 9th October 1872—Gregory to Kimberley; C.0.54. 521. 10th September 1879—Longden to Hicks-Beach.
47. C.O.54. 507. 4th May 1877—Gregorv to Carnarvon.
48. C.O.54. 493. 15th July 1874—Birch to Carnarvon; C.O.54. 507. 4th May 1877—Gregory to Carnarvon.
49. Ceylon Blue Book.
50. *Ibid.* By 1877 the flow of immigrants through Colombo had assumed fair proportions and Indians of many descriptions, i.e. estate labour, domestic help, grooms etc. had begun to find their way into the Colombo General Hospital.
51. For 1877 returns see C.O.54. 521. 10th September 1879—Longden to Hicks-Beach. For others see Blue Book.
52. C.O.54. 507. 15th March 1877—Birch to Carnarvon; C.O.54. 509. 8th

November 1877—Longden to Carnarvon; C.0.54. 513. 27th April 1878—Longden to Hicks-Beach; C.O 54. 521. 10th September 1879—Longden to Hicks-Beach.

53. C.0.54. 522. 20th December 1879—Longden to Hicks-Beach; C.O.54. 599. 19th June 1885—Gordon to Derby (Encl.).
54. Ceylon Blue Book.
55. *Ibid.*
56. Governors Robinson, Gregory, Longden and Gordon all expressed this point of view. C.O.54. 463. 28th February 1871—Robinson to Kimberley; C.O.54. 479. 14th November 1872—Gregory to Kimberley; C.O.54. 497. 31st May 1875—Gregory to Carnarvon; C.O.54. 541. 15th September 1882—Longden to Kimberley; C.O.54. 554. 9th July 1884—Gordon to Derby. Gregory at first considered the question of distance important i.e. whether the remoteness of many estates from the hospitals was not the cause, but later changed his opinion in favour of the "orthodox" stand— C.O.54. 476. 9th July 1872—Gregory to Kimberley.
57. C.O.54. 468. 26th November 1871—Robinson to Kimberley (Encl.).
58. See Chapter 4, p. 184.
59. C.O.54. 476. 4th May 1872—Gregory to Kimberley; C.O.54.559. 19th June 1885—Gordon to Derby.
60. C.O.54. 539. 19th June 1885—Gordon to Derby. In the 1870s the number of District hospitals was, of course, larger, but as we have shown many were in such a shocking state that it was wise to avoid them.
61. C.O.54. 559. 19th June 1885—Gordon to Derby.
62. Even after it had been pointed out that the hospitals were overcrowded Acting Governor Major-General J.C. McLeod reported that the death-rate "would not improve until the coolies were less disinclined to become indoor patients." C.O.54. 560. 4th September 1885—McLeod to Stanley.
63. C.O.54.521. 10th September 1879—Longden to Hicks-Beach; C.O.54. 541. 15th September 1882—Longden to Kimberley.
64. Doctors in the ordinary General hospitals were sometimes also lacking in understanding. The Officer-in-Charge of Badulla Hospital once said of the immigrants that "when sick their natural apathy and indifference to life prevents their seeking early advice." Obviously the doctor did not realise that the Indian's very presence in Sri Lanka was a manifestation of his desire to remain in the land of the living. C.O.54. 476. 4th May 1872— Gregory to Kimberley.
65. C.O.54. 476. 4th May 1872—Gregory to Kimberley (Encl.). Similar sentiments were expressed a few years later in a report on immigrant mortality. C.O.54. 541. 15th September 1882—Longden to Kimberley.
66. See Chapter 2, p. 23.
67. Ceylon Sessional Paper—1879. Report of the Commission on the Medical Wants of the Coffee Estates—pp. xi and xii; C.O.54. 559. 19th June 1885—Gordon to Derby (Encl.).
68. C.O.54. 560. 4th September 1885—McLeod to Stanley (Encl.).
69. *Ibid.*

70. C.O.54. 560. 4th September 1885—McLeod to Stanley (Encl.).
71. Ceylon Sessional Papers—1879. Report of the Commission on the Medical Wants of the Coffee Estates, p. 181.
72. C.O.54. 522. 20th December 1879—Longden to Hicks-Beach. A Medical Inspector had been appointed in 1872, but had no legal power to enter estates. The bill rectifying this omission was confirmed in 1880.
73. C.O.54. 541. 15th September 1882—Longden to Kimberley (Encl.).
74. A stricter control on sanitary conditions in the lines was imposed by Ordinance 5 of 1905.
75. The alternative argument i.e. that the doctors did not mention the Coast Advance System because they believed that its influence was not injurious cannot seriously be held owing to a great deal of evidence to the contrary. See section on Policy and Legislation.
76. C.O.54. 559. 19th June 1885—Gordon to Derby (Encl.).
77. Manson-Bahr, *op. cit.*, pp. 19-30.
78. There were slight differences between the several coffee districts, but 18s. per month remained the average wage. The large number of immigrant women and children employed on the plantations in this period brought a hardening of wage-rates for these two categories. The former received between 12s. and 14s. per month and the latter between 8s. and 10s. per month. C.O.54. 485. 24th March 1873—Gregory to Kimberley.
79. Railway construction in Sri Lanka went on with hardly a break throughout the period 1871-1885. The main Kandy line was extended through Gampola and Nawalapitiya to Nanu-Oya between 1872 and 1885. The Matale line was constructed between 1879 and 1880, and the Coastal railroad from Colombo to Kalutara, between 1878 and 1880.
80. C.O.54. 476. 9th July 1872—Gregory to Kimberley.
81. C.O.55. 117. 26th June 1869—Granville to Hodgson.
82. C.O.54. 463. 28th February 1871—Robinson to Kimberley (Encl.).
83. *Ibid.*
84. C.O.54. 463. 28th February 1871—Robinson to Kimberley.
85. *Ibid.* See chapter 4, pp. 101-2 for a full description of the calculations sent in by Robinson.
86. C.O.54. 463. 28th February 1871—Robinson to Kimberley.
87. C.O.55. 120. 17th June 1871—Kimberley to Robinson.
88. C.O.55. 120. 17th June 1871—Kimberley to Robinson. Short of removing a Governor from office on grounds of inefficiency, the Colonial Office could hardly have subjected him to greater humiliation than by legislating over his head.
89. Since the shops erected at the several halting-places stood usually on Government land, the Government Agents "took care that in places where there was but little competition extortion was not permitted." C.O.54. 468. 26th November 1871—Robinson to Kimberley.
90. C.O.54. 468. 26th November 1871—Robinson to Kimberley.
91. Robinson's Executive Council may, of course, have been aware of the

shortcomings of the Coast Advance System, but the Governor may well have been so firmly convinced that immigrant labour had little to complain of that he refused to give due weight to their advice.

92. C.O.54. 468. 26th November 1871—Robinson to Kimberley.
93. *Ibid.*
94. C.O.54. 468. 26th November 1871—Robinson to Kimberley.
95. C.O.55. 120. 18th February 1872—Kimberley to Gregory.
96. C.O.55. 120. 15th February 1872—Kimberley to Gregory.
97. *Ibid.*
98. C.O.54. 476. 9th July 1872—Gregory to Kimberley.
99. C.O.54. 476. 9th July 1872—Gregory to Kimberley.
100. *Ibid.*
101. *Ibid.*
102. C.O.54. 476. 9th July 1872—Gregory to Kimberley.
103. *Ibid.*
104. C.O.54. 476. 4th May 1872—Gregory to Kimberley (Encl.).
105. C.O.54. 476. 9th May 1872—Gregory to Kimberley (Encl.).
106. Supra, p. 118.
107. C.O.54. 477. 3rd August 1872—Gregory to Kimberley.
108. *Ibid* (encl.).
109. C.O.54. 478. 30th September 1872—Gregory to Kimberley (Encl.).
110. C.O.54. 479. 14th November 1872—Gregory to Kimberley.
111. C.O.54. 479. 14th November 1872—Gregory to Kimberley (Encl.).
112. C.O.54. 507. 4th May 1877—Gregory to Carnarvon; C.O.54. 509. 8th November 187—Longden to Carnarvon; C.O.54. 513. 27th April 1878—Longden to Hicks-Beach; C.O.54. 541. 15th September 1882—Longden to Kimberley; C.O.54. 541. 23rd November 1882—Longden to Kimberley; C.O.54. 554. 9th July 1884—Gordon to Derby.
113. C.O.54. 476. 9th July 1872—Gregory to Kimberley.
114. C.O.54. 468. 26th November 1871—Robinson to Kimberley.
115. C.O.54. 476. 4th May 1872—Gregory to Kimberley (Encl.).
116. *Ibid.*
117. C.O.54. 476. 9th July 1872—Gregory to Kimberley.
118. *Ibid.* (Encl.)
119. *Ibid.*
120. C.O.54. 476. 9th July 1872—Gregory to Kimberley.
121. C.O.54. 478. 9th October 1872—Gregory to Kimberley (Encl.)
122. C.O.54. 478. 9th October 1872—Gregory to Kimberley (Encl.)
123. *Ibid.*
124. *Ibid.*
125. The Planters' Association representatives voted against the bill in the Legislative Council. C.O.54. 521. 10th September 1879— Longden to Hicks-Beach.
126. The Twenty-one districts were later increased by sub-division to twenty-two. C.O.54. 521. 10th September 1879—Longden to

Hicks-Beach.

127. Rs. 1 in local currency then exchanged for ls. 10d.
128. C.O.54. 478. 9th October 1872—Gregory to Kimberley.
129. C.O.54. 479. 14th November 1872—Gregory to Kimberley.
130. *Ibid.*
131. C.O.54. 521. 10th September 1879—Longden to Hicks-Beach.
132. Ceylon Sessional Papers 1879. Report of the Medical Aid Commission, p. VI.
133. *Ibid*; C.O.54. 521. 10th September 1879—Longden to Hicks-Beach.
134. Ceylon Sessional Paper 5 of 1879; C.O.54. 529. 30th December 1880—Longden to Kimberley.
135. C.O.54. 521. 10th September 1879;—Longden to Hicks-Beach; Ceylon Sessional Paper 5 of 1879, p. XI.
136. The replies given by the planters appearing before the Commission show how firmly they had come to believe that they no longer were responsible for the medical welfare of their labour. Said one, "We pay for medical attention for the coolies and there is therefore no reason why we should give that attention to them ourselves." Another observed that since "they paid for the doctor now, they did not see why they should do the doctor's work." Ceylon Sessional Paper 5 of 1879, p. 25, replies to Question 9.
137. *Ibid*. p. XI; C.O.54. 521. 10th September 1879—Longden to Hicks-Beach.
138. Ceylon Sessional Paper 5 of 1879.
139. *Ibid*. Report of the Medical Inspector of the Coffee Districts.
140. *Ibid*, p. 8. Evidence of G.F. Fowler, M.D. Answer to question 12. The Doctor observed that "they say they die as well in the lines among friends, and that there is no use in going to the hospital."
141. Ceylon Sessional Paper 5 of 1879, p. 181.
142. *Ibid*. See the evidence of Doctors Coghill, Duke, Allardyce, Tothill and Kinsey, replies to question 19.
143. Mr. A.N. Birch is the Lieutenant-Governor referred to.
144. Ceylon Sessional Paper 5 of 1871. Report of the Medical Inspector of the Coffee Districts, p. 2.
145. *Ibid.*
146. Ceylon Sessional Paper 5 of 1879, pp. 11-12.
147. Kimberley was followed by the Earl of Carnarvon on 21st February 1874 and Carnarvon in turn by Sir Michael Hicks-Beach on 4th February 1878.
148. C.O.54. 521. 10th September 1879—Longden to Hicks-Beach.
149. In the Ordinance of 1872, the Government possessed a similar right to intervene, but could only draw up and impose such rules as it thought "suitable"—not take over the running of the scheme.
150. A very sensible provision, since the lack of funds had hampered many a medical committee in the past.
151. A Medical Inspector had been earlier appointed by the Government, but strangely enough the post had not been legally recognised by the Ordinance of 1872. Stranger still, this anomaly had not been rectified

throughout the life of the Ordinance, and the Inspector, Dr J. Coghill, had suffered considerable indignities at the hands of hostile planters who had at times denied him entry to the District hospitals and estates. C.O.54. 522. 20th December 1879—Longden to Hicks-Beach.

152. *Ibid.*
153. C.O.54. 522. 20th December 1879—Longden to Hicks-Beach.
154. The medical districts were to be the same as those decided upon in 1879.
155. The Civil hospitals in the Central Province, i.e. Kandy, Gampola etc., were closed to estate labour. Superintendents in those districts had henceforth to send their sick to the District hospitals. The six District hospitals were sited at Lindulla, Haputale, Dickoya, Uda Pussellawa, Kelebokka and Madulsima. In 1886 three more were opened at Rakwana, Balangoda and Maskeliya.
156. C.O.54. 529. 30th December 1880—Longden to Kimberley.
157. See section I of this chapter on "The Economic Background."
158. C.O.54. 529. 30th December 1880—Longden to Kimberley.
159. See clause 27 of Ordinance 11 of 1865.
160. C.O.54. 529. 30th December 1880—Longden to Kimberley.
161. *Ibid.* (Encl.)
162. C.O.54. 533. 8th July 1881—Douglas to Kimberley. The Acting Governor did not believe that a tax on the number of labourers employed would be easy to collect, for employers could always submit incorrect returns. The point, however, was not pressed and in any case Kimberley was not prepared to countenance a change.
163. *Ibid.* (Encl.)
164. C.O.54. 537. 20th February 1882—Longden to Kimberley (Encl.).
165. *Ibid.*
166. *Ibid.* (Encl.)
167. C.O.54. 3 June 1882—Longden to Kimberley.
168. C.O.54. 539. 25th May 1992—Longden to Kimberley.
169. C.O.54. 539. 3rd June 1882—Longden to Kimberley.
170. *Ibid.* (Encl.)
171. C.O.54. 542. 30th December 1882—Longden to Derby.
172. *Ibid.* The new duties came into force in 1883.
173. C.O.54. 554. 9th July 1884—Gordon to Derby; also see the Ceylon Blue Book.
174. C.O.54. 565. 6th February 1886—Gordon to Stanley.
175. Blue Book.
176. C.O.54. 559. 19th June 1S85—Gordon to Derby.
177. C.O.54. 544. 9th July 1884—Gordon to Derby; C.O.54. 560. 4th September 1885—McLeod to Stanley.
178. C.O.54. 560. 4th September 1885—McLeod to Stanley (Encl.).
179. *Ibid.*
180. The suggestion that the hospital system be extended was, however, acceded to. In 1886 three additional District hospitals were opened at Maskeliya, Balangoda and Rakwana.

181. Blue Book. Though the total flow of incoming and outgoing labour was heavy during these years the income from passage money was relatively low, since it was earned only at the Manaar ferry. On the Colombo route the traffic was in private hands.
182. C.O.54. 477. 3rd August 1872—Gregory to Kimberley (Encl.).
183. C.O.55. 120. 17th June 1871—Kimberley to Robinson.
184. It might seem that the Government was prepared to extend free "welfare" treatment to "masterless" men who were brought in off the road, but that it expected planters to pay the medical costs of labourers who fell ill while in their employ. The argument, however, does not hold since masterless men were also taken into the District hospitals set up under the Medical Wants Scheme.

Chapter 6

Retrospect

Indian immigration to Sri Lanka did not come to an end with the collapse of the coffee industry. The new crops which took coffee's place were no less dependent on Indian labour and the use of the latter remained a prominent feature of the plantation sector. This continuation of immigration beyond the end of the first phase of plantation history imposes some constraints on the nature and validity of the concluding remarks one might make, nonetheless, the duration of the coffee era was long enough for some definite trends and tendencies to appear, and many of these are deserving of comment.

The history of Indian immigration to Sri Lanka in the coffee era is on the whole a cheerless one. It was the poverty of the South Indian village that stoked the movement, and that so many should have migrated so regularly over so long a period, is a potent index to their dire economic straits. Physical suffering was a constant companion of indigence: imposed on the migrants by the rigours of the march, a heartless system of recruitment, demanding employers, a shortage of medical facilities, and by their own sense of false economy. That the intensity of this suffering decreased as the coffee period progressed is beyond question. The improvements at the ferries and on the Northern road, the realisation by employers that it was in their long-term interest to win the goodwill of labour, the gradual extension of medical facilities, the endeavours of the local Administration, and the vigilance of the Colonial Office, all these slowly made easier the lot of the immigrant. But the Coast Advance System of recruitment remained uncontrolled, and though its malefic effects were blunted during the course of the century, it was still productive of much distress at the end of the coffee era.

Mortality trends reflect well the effects of what was done, and of what was not, to ameliorate the socio-economic environment of the immigrant. Admittedly, the uncertainty surrounding the immigration returns prevents the computation of even an approximate death-rate, and throws the burden of proof upon qualitative rather than quantitative evidence; but the latter is plentiful and not difficult to unravel. It emerges that immigrant mortality was of a quite staggering order for about the first fifteen years, and that it declined steadily thereafter, except when temporarily raised as a consequence of famine and drought in South India. The overall decline in deaths, however, did not suffice to equalize immigrant mortality with that of the local population, and was still a matter of official concern at the end of our period.

That the immigrant was prepared to face the risks and rigours associated with employment on the plantations makes it evident that economically speaking the exercise was worthwhile. To those who came only when there was famine or drought in India, migration was merely the price of survival, and to many others the expected benefits of working in Sri Lanka must have been just marginally more attractive than those expected from employment at home, else immigration would not have fallen off in the way it did when railway construction, irrigation works, etc., in their own country provided alternative occupations nearer at hand. But the great body of immigrants were regular commuters, hoping both to earn and to save more than they could in India. How far this objective was accomplished is problematical. There are several estimates of likely savings ratios computed by contemporary journalists and planters for different phases of the coffee period, but these are of little use as there is no information whatever on whether any consequential proportion of the workforce ever succeeded in achieving these targets.[1] From time to time one comes across references to small land owners in different parts of South India who "made their first start with savings earned by a few years in Ceylon."[2] Yet, there is no way of knowing whether the numbers involved were a meaningful proportion of the total migration to the Island. The question of whether immigrants saved significant amounts or not has therefore to be left open, though perhaps it is worth observing that had the aggregate savings annually repatriated been sizeable, it would surely have been noticed and officially commented upon.

Plantation workers who chose to settle in Sri Lanka during the course of the century generally ended, as they had begun, as paid plantation labourers. This is not to say that individual migrants did not progress on the economic scale. The Kanganies with their head money and profits earned through the Coast Advance System had the opportunity to accumulate a considerable capital—and some apparently did. There is evidence to show that in the 1860s and 1870s, Indians were leasing or buying small parcels of land in the planting districts so that they could set up as small-hold growers of coffee, and the records indicate that many of the purchasers were Kanganies. The total involved, however, was inconsequential. In 1875 there were merely forty to fifty small proprietors who had come from the ranks of the estate labour force, and even this small number decreased significantly with the collapse of coffee.[3]

The problems associated with immigration early thrust themselves upon the attention of both local Administration and Colonial Office. By the 1840s plantation coffee had become a major prop of the general revenue, and it had grown apparent that a steady supply of immigrant labour was vital to the industry's continued prosperity. The laissez-faire prejudices of the time precluded any direct official support on the side of supply, but Government could hardly ignore the reports that were coming in of privation and death on the march to the coffee districts, and of cruelty and other abuses on the estates. A liberal interpretation of laissez-faire permitted intervention on behalf of immigrant labour, and it was through a concern for their welfare that Government first came to be involved in the immigrant labour question. Once the process had begun there was literally no end. To wells on the line of march were added rest-sheds and medical stations, legal enactments to safeguard employees, laws to regulate conditions on the ferries, and finally a network of hospitals. These facilities, no doubt, had many imperfections, nevertheless by the end of the coffee era official endeavour had had many successes and had laid the foundations of a quite extensive welfare structure. In all of this, it was not the local Administration that always took the initiative. As the coffee period progressed, the Colonial Office had often to coax and prod Colombo into action, and at times even to threaten. By the 1870s open disagreements had become frequent, and the blunt comments of the Secretary of State and his subordinates—though not always justified—are indicative of how far Whitehall's confidence in the Colonial Government had been eroded.

On the side of labour supply, official participation was more gradual. In keeping with the axioms of laissez-faire there was no intervention with the immigratory process, and no financial assistance of any sort for the first twenty years of the coffee period. This stand was abandoned in 1858—enthusiastically by Colombo and with some hesitation by the Colonial Office—with the recognition that the Island's finances were dependent upon the success of a planting sector to which a reliable flow of labour was a crucial consideration. A return to non-interference and financial self-sufficiency was made in the early 1860s, but the reversal in policy was brief. After 1865 Whitehall showed no reluctance in agreeing to the Colonial Government's requests for a direct subsidization of the immigratory process out of public funds, and by the end of coffee's reign the practice was so generally accepted that it no longer evoked comment. Nor should it have; for by then the drift from laissez-faire was well under way, and "intervention" and "assistance" were no longer a violation of the official credo.

NOTES

1. Roberts, *op. cit.*, part II, pp. 115-21.
2. *Madras District Gazetteer*—South Arcot, p. 144; Moral and Material Progress, p. 71; Hardgrave, *op. cit.*, pp. 52-53; Jeffrey, *op. cit.*, p. 50; Kumar, *op. cit.*, p. 140.
3. Ferguson's *Directory* of 1874 and 1887 describes the location, acreage etc. of these small holdings.

Bibliography

A. Documentary—deposited at the Public Records Office, London.

The most important official sources are the Colonial Office Papers relating to Sri Lanka. These are classified as follows:

C.O.54— The dispatches of the Governors of Ceylon, with enclosures; Colonial Office minutes, comments, drafts and correspondence with other Government departments. There is also a Miscellaneous Volume for each year containing other letters received by the Colonial Office.

C.O.55— The dispatches of the Secretary of State to Ceylon, and out-letters of the Colonial Office.

C.O.56— The Legislative Enactments of the Government of Ceylon.

C.O.57— Sessional Papers and minutes and proceedings of the Executive and Legislative Councils of Ceylon.

C.O.58— Ceylon Government Gazettes.

C.O.59— The Blue Books of the Ceylon Government (Vol. 30 onwards).

C.O.323— Some volumes contain the opinions of the Law officers on Legislative Acts, and some contain letters to the Under Secretaries.

C.O.324— Some volumes contain letters from the Under Secretaries.

C.O.381— Some volumes contain instructions to the Governors of Ceylon.

C.O.416— The Evidence collected by the Commissioners of Eastern Inquiry.

B. Parliamentary—The Parliamentary debates in Hansard contain references to Sri Lanka. There are also several Parliamentary Papers which contain published dispatches and other relevant information.

C. Newspapers—A number of useful editorials, articles, comments and letters are to be found in *The Colombo Observer*, *The Ceylon Times* and *The Examiner*. Many of these are attached as enclosures to the Governor's despatches.

D. Printed Works

Arasaratnam, S. *Indians in Malaysia and Singapore*. Bombay: O.U.P., 1970.

Benedict, B. *Indians in a Plural Society: A Report on Mauritius*. London: H.M.S.O., 1961.

Bhatia, B.M. *Famines in India* 1860-1965. London: Asia, 1963.

Brown, A. *The Coffee Planter's Manual*. Colombo: Ceylon Observer Press, 1872.

Cumpston, I.M. *Indians Overseas in British Territories*, 1834-54. London: Oxford University Press, 1953.

Danson, J.T. *Economic and Statistical Studies* 1840-1890. London: T.F. Unwin, 1906.

Days of Old; *or, the Commencement of the Coffee Enterprise in Ceylon*. By two of the pioneers. Colombo, A.M. and J. Ferguson, 1878.

De Silva, K.M. *Social Policy* and *Missionary Organisations in Ceylon* 1840-1855. London: Longmans (published for the Royal commonwealth Society), 1965.

Doyne, W.T. *The Causes which have retarded the construction of Railways in India, referring to the Ceylon Railway; with remedies suggested*. London, 1860.

Extracts of Letters from Ceylon on Courtship; Marriage etc.; with a peep into jungle life. London: J. and A. Darling, 1848.

Ferguson. *Review of the Planting and Agricultural Industries of Ceylon*.

Ferguson, A.M. *Ceylon-Summary of Useful Information*. Colombo, 1859.

_____. *Ceylon-Summary of Useful Information*. Colombo, 1880.

_____. *Ceylon-Commonplace Book, Directory etc*. Colombo, 1861.

Ferguson, A.M. and J. *Ceylon Directory* 1866-68. Colombo, 1868.

_____. *Ceylon Directory* 1874. Colombo, 1874.

_____. *Ceylon Directory* 1887-88. Colombo, 1888.

Ferguson, J. *Ceylon in 1883*. London: S. Low, Marston, Searle and Rivington, 1883.

_____. *Ceylon in the "Jubilee Year."* London: J. Haddon, 1887.

_____. *Ceylon in 1903*. Colombo, A.M. & J. Ferguson, 1903.

_____. *Pioneers of the planting enterprise in Ceylon: from 1830 onwards*. Colombo: A.M. & J. Ferguson, 1894, 1898, 1900. 3 volumes.

Jeffrey, R. *The Decline of Nayar Dominance*.

Geoghegan, T. *Note on Emigration from India*. Calcutta, 1873.

Gillion, K.L. *Fiji's Indian Migrants: a history to the end of indenture in 1920*. Melbourne: O.U.P., 1962.

Gregory, Lady I.A. *Sir William Gregory—An Autobiography*. London: J. Murray, 1894.

Kondapi, C. *Indians Overseas 1838-1949*. (New Delhi: Indian Council of World Affairs) Bombay: Oxford University Press, 1951.

Kumar, D. *Land and Caste in South India*. Cambridge: C.U.P., 1965.

Lewis, Frederick. *Sixty-four Years in Ceylon: reminiscences of life and adventure*. Colombo: Colombo Apothecaries, 1926.

Manson-Bahr, Sir Philip H., ed. *Manson's Tropical Diseases: a manual of the diseases of warm climates*. London: Cassell, 1921.

Mellor, George R. *British Imperial Trusteeship* 1783-1850. London: Faber and Faber, 1951.

Millie, P.D. *"Thirty Years Ago" or reminiscences of the early days of coffee planting in Ceylon*. Colombo: A.M. & J. Ferguson, 1878.

Mills, L.A. *Ceylon under British Rule 1795-1932*. London: Oxford University Press, 1933.

Morris, M.D. *The emergence of an industrial labour force in India*. Berkeley:

U.S.A., 1965.

_____, et. al. *The Indian Economy in the 19th Century—A Symposium*. Delhi: The Indian Economic and Social History Association, 1969.

Pelzer, K.J. *Die arbeiterwanderungen in Sudostasien*. Hamburg: Friederichsen, de Gruyter, 1935.

Pridham, C. *An historical, political and statistical account of Ceylon and its dependencies*. London: T. & W. Boone, 1849. 2 Vols.

Sabonadiere, W. *The Coffee Planter of Ceylon*. (2nd edition and revised) London: E. & F.N. Spon, 1890.

Sandhu, Kernial Singh. *Indians in Malaya*. Cambridge: C.U.P., 1969.

Sarkar, N.K. *The Demography of Ceylon*. Colombo: Ceylon Government Press Printers, 1957.

Sirr, H.C. *Ceylon and the Cingalese*. London: William Shoberl, 1850. 2 Vols.

Skinner, T. *Fifty Years in Ceylon*. Ed. Annie Skinner. London: W.H. Allen, 1891.

Speculum. *Ceylon: Her present condition: revenues, taxes and expenditure*. (Described in a series of letters addressed to *The Ceylon Observer*.) Colombo, 1868.

Steuart, J. *Notes on Ceylon audits affairs during a period of thirty-eight years, ending in 1855*. London, 1862.

Suckling, H.J. *Ceylon. A general description of the island, historical, physical, statistical, containing the most recent information*. London: Chapman & Hall, 1876. 2 Vols.

Tennent, Sir James Emerson. *Ceylon, and account of the Island, Physical, historical and topographical*. London: Longman, Green, Longman and Roberts, 1860. 2 vols.

Tinker, H. *A New System of Slavery. The Export of Indian Labour Overseas 1830-1920*. London: O.U.P., 1974.

Villiers, Sir Thomas L. *Mercantile Lore*. Colombo: The Ceylon Observer Press, 1940.

E. *Articles*

Boyd, Wm. "Ceylon and its Pioneers," *The Ceylon Literary Register*. Vol. II, no. 32, February 24th, 1888; and no. 36, March 23rd, 1888.

De Silva, K.M. "Indian Immigration to Ceylon—the first phase c. 1840-1855," *The Ceylon Journal of Historical and Social Studies*. Vol. 4, July-December 1961, and Vol. 9 January to June 1966.

Dickman, H. "An Account of Malabar Coolies in Ceylon," *The Ceylon Miscellany*, December 1853.

Morris, M.D., "Towards a re-interpretation of 19th century Indian economic history," *The Journal of Economic History* (New York), vol. XXXIII (IV), 606-18.

_____. "Economic change and agriculture in 19th century India," *The Indian Economic and Social History Review* (New Delhi), III (II), 185-209.

Naguleswaran, P. "History of the Working Class Movement in Ceylon," *Ceylon Historical Journal*, Vol. 1, no. 3, 1952.

Pieris, Ralph. "Society and Ideology in Ceylon during a 'Time of Troubles 1795-1850,'" *University of Ceylon Review*. v/0 (3) July 1951, 1710185; v.9 (4) October 1951, 266-79; v. 10 (1) January 1952, 79-102.

Roberts M. "Observations of the Mortality Rate among Immigrant Indian Labourers in Ceylon in the Coffee Period," *Ceylon Journal of Historical and Social Studies*. Vol. 9, no. 3, 1966.

_____. "The Master and Servant Laws of 1841 and the 1860s and Immigrant Labour," *The Ceylon Journal of Historical and Social Studies*. Vol. 8, no. 1, 1966.

_____. "Indian Estate Labour in Ceylon during the Coffee Period (1830-1880)," *The Indian Economic and Social History Review*. Vol. II, no. 1, March 1966 and Vol. III, no. 2, June 1966.

vanden Driesen, I.H. "Indian Immigration to Ceylon; the first phase, c. 1840-1855—a Comment," *The Ceylon Journal of Historical and Social Studies*. Vol. 7, July-December 1964.

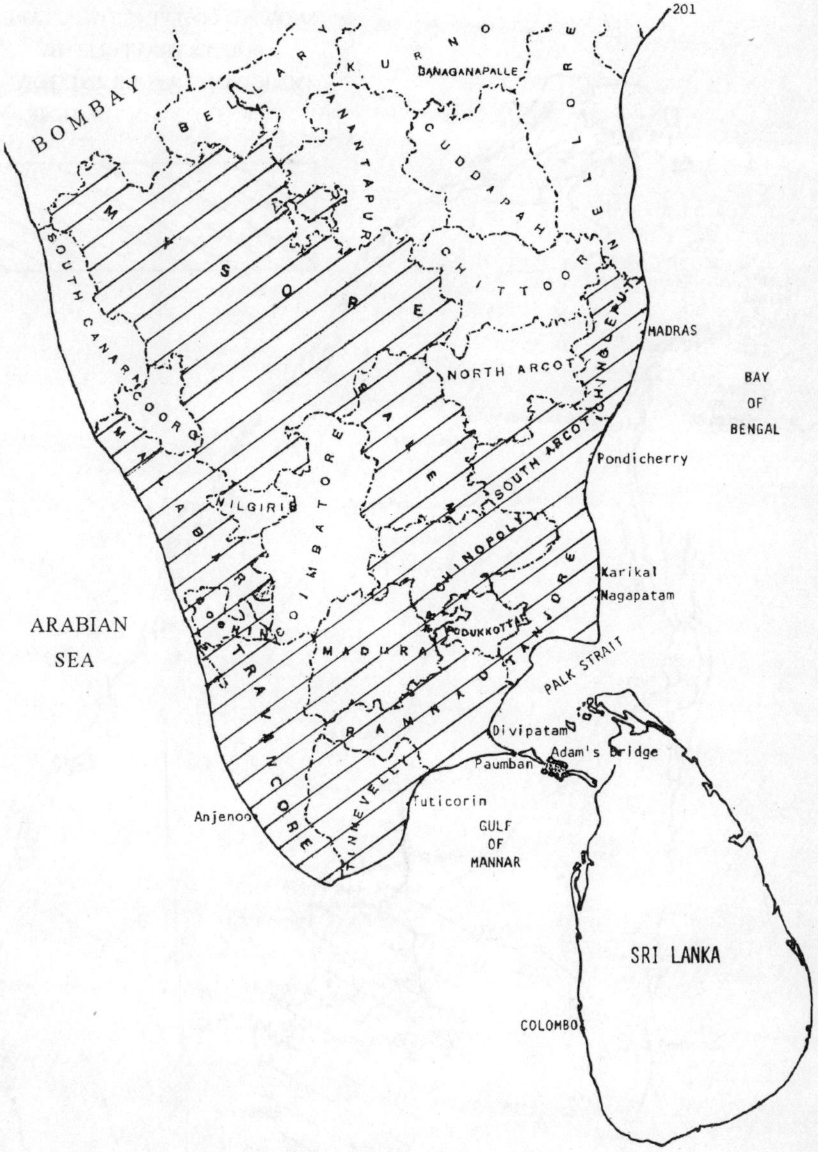

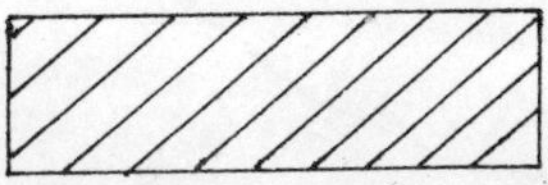

CHIEF SOUTH INDIAN DISTRICTS
FROM WHICH PLANTATION
LABOUR WAS RECRUITED

SRI LANKA

SHOWING COFFEE GROWING AREA, ROUTES TRAVELLED BY IMMIGRANT LABOUR AND TOWNS MENTIONED IN THE TEXT

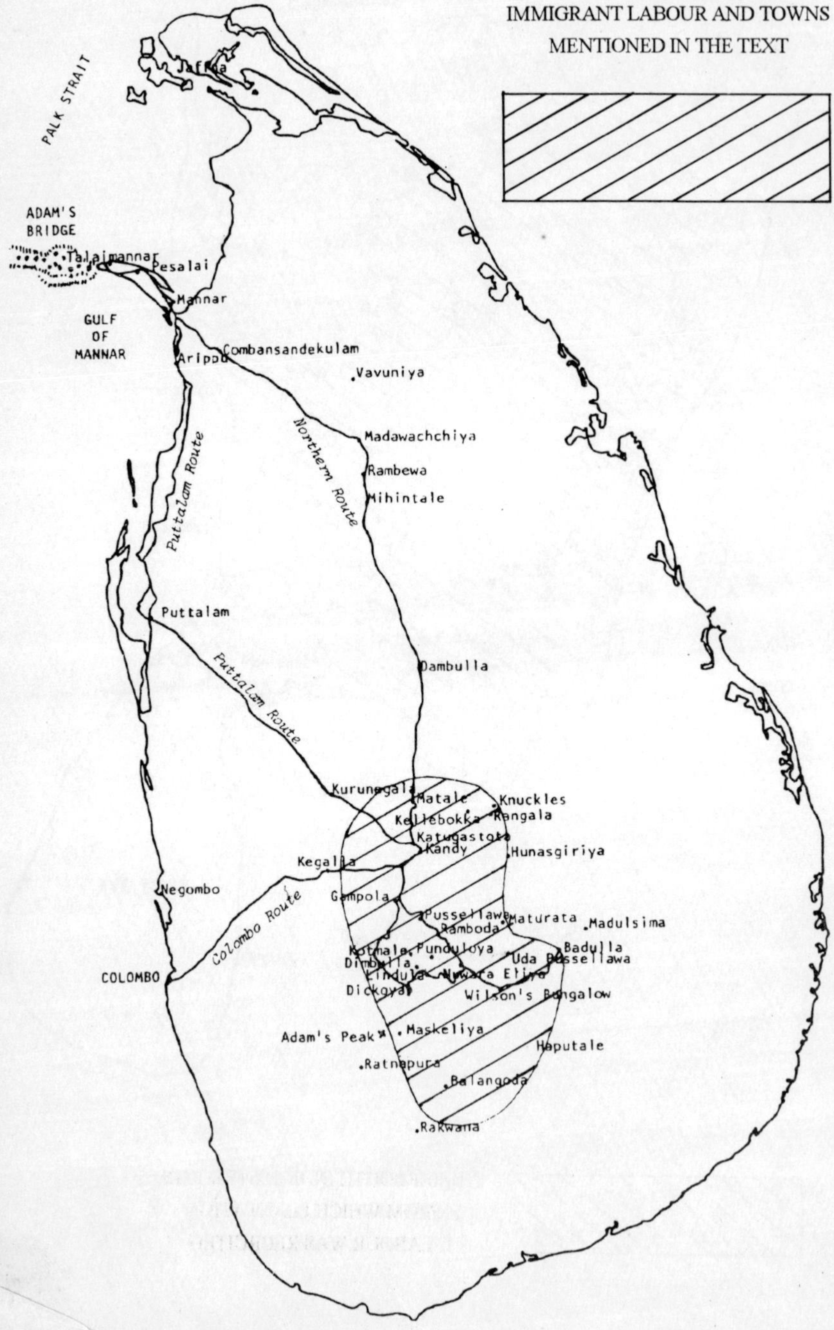